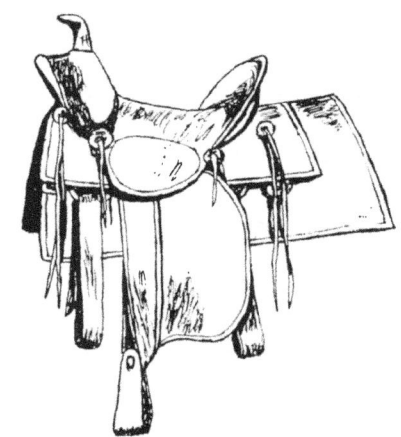

Bygone Days of The Old West

FRED LAMBERT OF THE CIMARRON

Bygone Days of The Old West
Revisited

BYGONE DAYS
OF
THE OLD WEST
Revisited
BY

Fred Lambert

Illustrated by The Author

SANTA FE

© 2012 by Frederick Neil Lambert. All Rights Reserved.
Printed on acid-free paper
∞
Library of Congress Cataloging-in-Publication Data

Lambert, Fred, 1887-1971.
  Bygone days of the Old West : revisited / by Fred Lambert [and] illustrated by the author.
    p. cm.
  Poems.
  ISBN 978-0-86534-904-9 (softcover : alk. paper)
  I. Title.
  PS3523.A428B8 2012
  811'.54--dc23
                                                2012030966

WWW.SUNSTONEPRESS.COM
SUNSTONE PRESS/PO 2321/SANTA FE, NM 87504-2321
(505) 988-4418/FAX (505) 988-1025

Dobie Sam came a ridin'
　　From the range one summer day,
Whoopin' an' shootin'
　　Down the streets of Santa Fe;
Thirty minutes later
　　He was as silent as the rocks!
Ridin' calm and peaceful
　　In a little wooden box.

FOREWORD

There's no doubt about Fred Lambert's having heard the elephant and seen the owl in all sorts of places. It's a mighty good thing his hide is tough and thick, owing considerably to the alkali dust that's drifted into it all these years and the Cimarron water that's more to set the dust than to wash it off. He's got so much genuine humanity packed inside that hide that if it wasn't tough, it would bust open as wide as a drouth crock, and the people would see the man's human nature running down a canyon for two miles like the fat out of that big bear Nat Straw killed on the dry gorge cutting into Black River.

I don't know why Fred Lambert took to writing in verse instead of talking prose. Just the same his rhythm is as natural and regular as a hound dog's elbow thumping on a ranch galley floor after dark when the fleas get into action. This foreman Wild Hoss Charley that tells so many bunkhouse tales in the book is really one of the creations of the West. He deserves to stand up beside Pecos Bill and Paul Bunyan. He's a liar, of course, but he's authentic as the Encyclopedia Britannica. His talk is better tonic than a whole case of Peruna, with a dozen bottles of Cod Liver Oil thrown in.

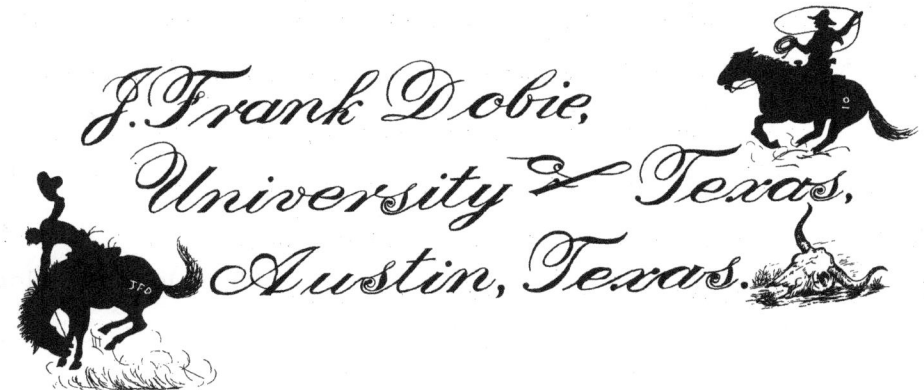

J. Frank Dobie,
University of Texas,
Austin, Texas.

INTRODUCTION

One of the richest assets to our Country's history is the early pioneer days of the West.

Seldom do we realize the meaning of the day in which we are living. No, most of us live on the memories of the past and the hopes of the future. In the early days of the West there were a great many heroes and heroines that played leading roles in the hand of fate, some for, others against the law.

Not many years ago it took a pioneer with his prairie schooner and ox-team a long, lonesome half year's journey to cross this mighty country of ours. Then a new land, wild, rent and broken up, with a rough track called the Santa Fe trail ever leading on to the West - To the Land of the Setting Sun, a land so strange and new, seemingly but half finished by the hand of God.

It was more than a dream of riches and pleasure that took the Old Timers to the far West - Some tremendous power there was that inured men to hardship and scant living, severe winters with but little protection and shelter. Dreams of homes and democracy, inspirations of a greater nation to be. Knowing no such words as fear, defeat or failure - It was a dream no more cherished by them than the freedom we now enjoy.

Look Back! See those long and winding lines of old prairie schooners, the bleaching bones and grass-covered mounds by the wayside; everywhere the parched alkali plains with cactus and mesquite. Prairie-dog towns, and herds of buffalo and antelope scattered here and there- This old trail should have been called the "Trail of Tears".

The pioneers and scouts ever on the watch for the Eagle-feathered head-dresses and Pinto ponies lurking in the shadows of the malpi ridges and high mesa points beyond. Ever on the lookout for a daily supply of grass and water, and a campsite having natural protection. Camp fires by night with the wagon-train drawn in a great circle, brawny men busy with the ox-teams, women and children huddled around the campfire cooking their evening meal - While the faithful scouts kept silent watch in the nearby shadows.

A rugged and unbroken story it is, with long deserts of shifting sand and mirages and dark scum-covered water holes. The hot copper sun blazing down on the dry sage-brush, cactus, gilas and rattle-snakes.

These rugged pioneer souls blazed a new country for YOU and for ME, gathering laurels to those that rode and braved the Indians, drouth and blizzards. Leaving along the old trail here and there, brave hearts to build log-cabins, small settlements and trading posts.

Land of the Setting Sun - Wonders of a vast solitude where nature sleeps in all her naked majesty, there the infinite expanses weigh in from all sides and from above, mighty land of future and promise.

Glowing fund of legend and romance, its glorious sunshine, its vivid life and matchless sweep, its mystery of antiquity.

Pioneering days in the West are over, only the plains and mountains standing sentinel. Many of the historical stories of the Old West will go down unwritten, as many of the Old Timers one by one are taking the Long, Long Trail and crossing the Big Divide to the Happy Hunting Ground beyond.

The Author was born January 23rd, 1887 in Cimarron, New Mexico, the son of Mary and Henry Lambert. His birth took place in the old St. James hotel which his father had built in 1870.

In the adjoining bar-room were many noted characters enjoying their liquor, playing poker and buckin' the Monte games. Among these guests were Clay Allison, young Davy Crockett and Buffalo Bill, who offered a toast to Mr. and Mrs. Lambert and their son, suggesting that they christen him "Cyclone Dick" because of a severe windstorm raging outside. However, his mother did not approve but named him Fredrick in honor of this old family friend, William Fredrick Cody (Buffalo Bill). Nevertheless, the name of "Cyclone Dick" stayed with him through his younger days and the Old Timers tsill call him by that name.

The Senior Lambert owned a cow ranch which was located in the Ute Creek country, some twelve miles west of Cimarron on the Ute Reservation where the son spent much of his early life. With the environment of Mexicans, Indians and Men of the Range, his childhood was filled with excitement and pleasures that only the Western boy could know.

The Author's formal education was limited but through the school of experience he has gained a very broad education of the out-doors, human beings and the range- all and much more of which he so ably portrays in verse and pen-pictures. Under the tutorship of the old waddies on his father's ranch he learned all they knew about horses, cattle, riding, shooting, roping and reading brands and trail signs.

Then of an evening they would gather in the bunk-house and show him how to work up rawhide, horse-hair and buckskin into many useful things used by the cowboys in their daily work; For it was indeed a poor puncher that could not plait a rope, quirt or make his own hackamore and cinches, as well as to repair his chaps and saddle. Many old punchers know how to make up a fancy pair of spurs or a good riding bit, and of course they all knew how to shoe their own horses.

During the busy summer seasons the author was compelled to leave the ranch and work in his father's saloon. In those days there were still a lot of tough hombres in the country and often in Lambert's saloon things would tighten, there would be a sudden call, plenty of cussin', fire and brimstone - and when the smoke cleared away it was always the same old story - Just another puncher or two gone to where the Whang-a-doodle mourneth and you don't pay any rent. After one of these thriller's, an old puncher who was leaning on the end of the bar quietly remarked to the author, "Helluva-country, some people come here for their health, others because it wasn't healthy where they were living and not much healthier after they arrived here."

This book is a work of love to our pioneer Mothers and Fathers. A tribute from the heart to a region incomparable for beauty and fascination - such is this offering of verses and pen-scratches, wrought in idle moments of the gleanings from the contacts and experiences of a busy out-of-door life as a New Mexico Mounted Police, U.S. Deputy, Sheriff, and for a number of years as manager of a large, old Spanish Land Grant.

The Santa Fe Trail

Trail of a continent, tell us your story,
    Full and complete through the vista of years.
Tell of the yearning, the hope, and the glory
    Sown in adventure and watered in tears,
How, creeping on, ever on toward the gloaming,
    Rutted and scarred in an unbroken span,
Adding your lure to the romance of roaming,
    Weaver of destiny — speak if you can.

Tell of the fight when the campfire was dying;
    Tell of the night when the dusky foe crept.
Tell of the hell, the water hole drying;
    Tell how the straggler passed out as he slept.
Tell of the men, of the women who sought you,
    Long passed away on the unchartered trail.
Tell of the valor, the price that they brought you,
    Down through the ages where now you prevail.

Bygone Days Of The Old West

Oh, what a halo of splendor hangs o'er you,
    'Round and about your illustrious name,
Oh, what a mission the fates placed before you.
    Well did you carry, and just is your fame,
Grown from a path that led on to the morrow,
    Into the pride of a nation, your tale
Could not be equalled no need to borrow
    Fiction or fantasy -- sturdy Old Trail.

Somehow your name brings a tear and a choking;
    Somehow the thought of your far reaching way
Brings to our minds creaking of wagons and yoking
    Of slow plodding oxen that drag through the day.
Then come the shadows, deep drawn, with dangers;
    Weird is the sound of the vagrant night's call,
Ships of the desert, marooned among strangers,
    Tensed by the vastness, the silence, and all.

Trail of a continent tell us your story,
    Full and complete through the vista of years.
Tell of the victory, tell of the story,
    Shout of the laughter and whisper of tears.
Graven in stone is your name, and forever
    Downward through time shall your praises
        live on,
Serving the clan that may follow, but never
    Forgetting the tread of a people now gone.

The Legend of Angelo.

Down where the sage and cactus grow,

From the Rio Grande to the Angelo,

A legend hangs - a tragic tale

Of Western ways and a haunted trail.

The Butte of Angelo commands

A broken view of brush and sand,

Far reaching on to the mist of hills

That fringe the plains in fantastic frills.

Assembled thus it would seem to hide

The dreary waste of world inside,

Where the buzzard, wolf and rattle-snake

Combined with the bandit band to make

The only life the desert knew,

Or cared to know, or dared to woo,

A loveless, silent, hopeless spot

That heaven shunned or else forgot.

And there a man and a woman came
Builded a shack and staked a claim
And seemed content to bid good-bye
To all behind - though God knows why
A human soul would choose to dwell
On a sun baked plain with the heat of hell.
But thus they lived and loved and lost
Where a gruesome trail met theirs - and crossed.

Four horsemen loped through a deep defile
Onto the plain, in bandit style,
Out from the hills; and the one who led
Had a heart as black as the hair was red;
And his eye discovered the ray of light
That shone from the shack through the silent night,
Where the woman prayed to the one above
For the safe return of her sheltered love
For the man that rode at the break of day
For food to the outpost miles away.
And she heard no sound of the horsemen four
As they slipped from their steeds and approached the door.

Oh the man returned as a daybreak came,
And the sun arose like a lurid flame,
Returned - and found his love was dead,
And her fingers clutched a lock of red.
And he dug a grave and laid her low
In the sand by the Butte of Angelo,
And vowed a vow that had to do
With the God above and the horsemen too;

And he marked the grave in a plainsman's way-
Cried to the desert and tried to pray-
And he prayed for naught but sufficient strength
To follow the trail to its bitter length;
Then he turned to the West and the fringe of hills
That skirted the plain in fantastic frills.

The shack still stands as it did of yore,
But a tale is told on its crumbling door-
A tale of hate and a ceaseless foe,
By the ghastly objects - in a row-
Each one the thatch from a human head,
And the topmost one of the row is red;
And the bandit band of horsemen four
Trouble the hills and the plains no more.

They tell with awe of a madman's wail
That echoes along the haunted trail-

(But it may be only the ebb and flow
Of the winds on the Butte of Angelo.)

BRANDING IRONS

"Oh, heat me hot in the ember's glow
    For I am both deed and chattel;
I burn my trace and the red lines show
    My stamp on the dull-sensed cattle."

The song of the iron sung for years
    In a land where the mist-mirage appears,
Land of distance, romance, steers,
    Cactus bloom and sages.
On flinching flank in quaint design
    Its theme has shown in cryptic sign,
Circle, quadrant, angle, line,
    Down through the long drawn ages.

Bygone Days Of The Old West

"Oh, Heat me hot in the embers, bright,
    And guide my point in the turning
Of symboled form as the made brutes fight
    The sting of my dreaded burning."

A story thrilling, it might be said,
    Could be written, might be read
Of frontier days when cattle fed
    On the wide free range unhampered,
The law was unto the man self-made,
    A draw, a flash and a ready spade
When the rustlers plied a thrifty trade
    And brands were changed or tampered.

"Oh, Heat me hot in the ember's glow
    For I am both deed and chattel;
I burn my trace and the red lines show
    My stamp on the dull-sensed cattle."

"I fashion my mark at swift command
    The skillful touch of a master hand,
Singing I sink the searing brand
    In quivering flesh, for-ever.
No man may question my witnessed trace
    For the records hold it, form and place,
The deep seared lines will not erase
    From the hide of the brute, No, Never."

"Oh, Heat me hot in the ember's gleam
For mine is the work of glory;
And deep in my history pages teem
The wealth of an untold story."

"Oh glad I am as I burn my way
　　Through a "Diamond C" or a "Tumbling K"
A "Turkey track", an "X-bar-J"
　　Or the "Flying U" formations;
A "Swastika", "Lazy V"
　　The "Walking stick", the "Anchored Z",
Then a thousand more creations."

"Oh, Heat me hot in the embers, bright
With a clank and a ring and rattle;
And touch my point that is searing white
To the flanks of a million cattle."

Sunshine Nell

Oh, a Mother cradled her babe to sleep-
With a slumber song unto dreamland deep--
And the lilt of the song was soft and low
Like a summer breeze in twilight's glow,
And the dream of the babe was of happy hours,
Of fairy elves and fragrant flowers,
And the Mother looked into her face and smiled,
And kissed the brow of her dreamland child
And laughed and called her Sunshine Nell.
And the name applied, for truth to tell
Her hair was the gold of an evening sun
In a Western sky when a day is done.

Down in a stretch of broken hills,
Where the Pecos winds o'er sandy rills,
A 'dobe town with crude array
Of huts and hovels, and its day--
A western child with western ways,
And the simple code of the early days-
Where justice slept and the only law
Was delt by the hand and a lightning draw,
And a fame and prestige held and won
By the notches nicked on a trusty gun.

Its deeds were bad and its morals worse,
Its womanhood a blight and curse.
No tale of fiction ever told
Of dangerous men or women bold
Surpassed in its fancied train--
This 'dobe vulture of the plain.
And the lonely graves of cross of wood
Are all that's left where the village stood--
Except the hovels, tumbled down.
A tearless death for a shameless town.

But where is a spot beneath the sun
Where the trail of men and women run--
A sure retreat or a hidden way--
That love won't find, somehow, someday,
And force its eager subtle plaint
On heart of sinner or of saint?

Why, then she knew that love's estate
Had entered the gates of her life - too late!
So two men loved -- a woman's wiles
And a woman's eyes and a woman's smiles
Were given each an equal share,
(For she little thought she would ever care)
Oh, she used the game in a brazen way
And laughed at her work and called it play!
She moved her pawns with a weird delight,
As the mind of a master chessman might.

Bygone Days Of The Old West

She never knew she loved at all
'Till the rivals met in the 'dobe hall
And face to face with shortened breath,
They stood -- a rendezvous with death-
For a moment tense -- and the very feel
Of their eyes were cold as hardened steel.
She also knew (as woman must)
One loved her soul -- the other lust;
And her heart cried out (as a woman's should)
For the life of the man she knew was good--
Cried strong and deep, as a tigress might-
For a whelp that strayed in a jungle night.

She sensed the flash of quick hands sprung
To belts where deadly pistols hung;
And -- leaping between -- her body claimed
The shots the hated rival aimed,
Then sinking low to the floor she smiled
In her lover's face like a weary child.
Oh! a lover cradled his babe to sleep
In a 'dobe hut where the shadows creep,
And he called her Sunshine Nell, and wept
As he kissed her brow where the death damp crept;
And he fondled her hair, as a lover would,
And believed in his soul she was pure and good.

And the mother, wrinkled and old and gray,
Waited her lonely life away--
Waited and wondered, watched and prayed,
And dreamed she trundled a fairy maid,
With hair the gold of an evening sun
In a Western sky when the day is done.

FRIJOLE PAL

I'm cinchin' up my saddle
    And preparin' for a battle
With a rearin', buckin' broncho
    And an onery bunch of cattle,
For there's thunder in the flashes
    And the wind is comin' strong,
So I cinches up my saddle
    And I sings my little song --

Pal, pal, my old frijole pal,
    I'm always hopin' honey
That again you'll be my gal;
    You left me sad an' lonely
When you up and ran away
    From the dobe in the valley
Where the gila monsters play.

Bygone Days Of The Old West 26

Oh, the Lobo's in the canyon,
    And the boss is fast asleep,
And the greaser down the valley
    Is a dozin' with his sheep,
But the thunder is gettin' closer
    And I won't be idle long,
So I cinches up my saddle
    And I sings my little song --

Pal, pal, my old frijole pal,
    You done me mighty shabby
When you up and left me, gal;
    I'm hungry for frijoles
Since you ambled clear away
    From the dobe in the valley
Where the gila monsters play.

Oh, the bronk has gone to buckin'
    And the rain is fallin' fast,
And the cattle are stampedin'
    Like a lot of fools at last;
But I ain't a-pullin' leather,
    And I'm ridin' right along
Roundin' up the cussed cattle
    As I sings my little song --

Pal, pal, my old frijole pal,
    I'd rather trust an Injun
Than a female woman gal;
    If you couldn't cook frijoles
I'd be glad to have you stay
    Any place but in the dobe
Where the gila monsters play.

Oh, I've got 'em all a-millin'
    And a-headin' back up the draw,
The bronc has quit his buckin'
    Calves are lookin' for their maw,
The sun has gone to shinin'
    And the clouds are driftin' along,
I rolls me an onery cigarette
    As I sings my little song.

Pal, pal, my old frijole pal,
    It's many years since you left me
Still in my memory you're my gal;
    I just ramble along in sadness
And let my old pony stray
    Up to the little brown 'dobe
Where the gila monsters play.

THE PASSING OF BRIMSTONE.
+—B

We were sitting in the bunk house
    At the Cross-Bar-Lazy-B,
When Foreman, Wild Hoss Charley
    Told this simple tale to me:

"Yeh, I've rode the range from Reno
    To the Gulf of Mexico;
An' 'twas in the month of August,
    Twenty-seven years ago,
That I happened into Brimstone,
    Jest an ornery 'dobe spot,
With my cayuse lank and sweatin',
    Fer the desert sun was hot."

"An' of all the cussed places
    From the Gulf to Santa Fe,
Or from Dodge out to the cactus,
    Where the gila monsters play,
There was not another like it
    In the mountains or the sage,
With a cem-e-tree a bulgin'
    Like a town ten times its age."

"It was mean, no use in talkin',
    It was mean and dev'lish rough.
Even water there was harder
    An' the beefsteak acted tough;
An' I'll venture there was never
    Such a bunch of forty-fives
In a town before; and, pardner,
    They didn't limit lives."

"There was no hombre* workin',
    But the game run night and day.
Where they got their coin to gamble
    Didn't int'r'st me, someway,
Fer I've seen too many fellers
    That was curious, be sent
Where the whang-a-doodle mourneth
    An' you don't pay any rent."

"There may've been places, pardner,
    That was just as bad or worse,
But I'm tellin' you the piutes
    Hired a feller with a hearse,
An' they run him on a schedule
    Makin' six round trips a day;
An' he never traveled empty
    To the cem-e-tree, they say."

"There's no tellin' what the endin'
   Would of been, y' understand,
If it hadn't been for Nature
   Steppin' in to take a hand;
Fer it sudden started snowin',
   Yes, sir! Snowin' one hot summer night;
An' the flakes was big as dollars
   An' it all was dynamite."

"An' it kep right on a-snowin',
   Till a foot or more had fell;
Then lightnin' struck it, pardner,
   An' it blowed the town to hell."

It was silent in the bunk house
   At Cross-Bar-Lazy-B,
When Foreman, Wild Hoss Charley
   Told this simple tale to me.

The Return of Padre Juan de la Padilla.

You've likely read of the Padre old -
   He whom they say no grave may hold
For the story often written, told,
   Is known as legend purely;
And the facts, distorted, makes it seem
   The colored web of a madman's dream
But the truth I e'en more weird deem
   And worthy the telling, surely.

The facts, unquestioned, came to hand
   From an honored chief, you understand;
An honored chief who, in his land,
   Is known for truth unfailing;
I pass the story on to you,
   And vow the tale as told is true;
For truth is old, and stranger, too,
   Than fiction's fancy trailing.

The Chief, mature, but scarcely old,
   Is not the savage you've been told,
But has the grace to rule and hold
   The confidence that's due him;
A classic face with teeth pearl white,
   Keen eyes that flash as dark as night,
And hair coal black except where light
   Gray strands add lustre to him.

In blanket of the Navajo,
   Turquoise and beads that dull-red glow,
Lace ruffled shirt and chonga bow
   (A Spanish touch that graces),

His moccasins, oak tanned, made fast
   By silver buttons, that add a caste
Of nobles from the ages past
   Brought back from distant places.
'Twas from his lips the story fell,
   In tones clear ringing as a bell,
How Juan de la Padilla fell
   By Gran Quiviras' people,
And how the body found its way
   To old Isleta, where today,
The Padre sleeps beneath the grey,
   Drawn shades of church and steeple.

THE STORY OF CHIEF PABLO ABEITA.

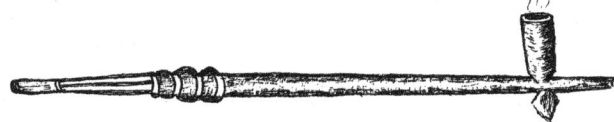

Juan de la Padilla
    Came from Spain long years ago
And wandered from the Gulf-coast
    Into Old New Mexico;
A Padre most beloved,
    Who would yield a helping hand
To the sick, the poor and needy,
    Ever ready at command.
He was known throughout the country,
    Going hither, to and fro,

'Till at last he chose a home-site
    In a small, Indian pueblo
Known as Gran Quivira, teaching,
    Working, preaching, as he prayed,
Growing stronger in the councils
    Through the friendships that he made.
Even to the inner circle -
    The Estufa holds - went he
Learning all the tribal secrets
    That its people held in fee.

Bygone Days Of The Old West

Then came runners bearing rumors -
   Of conquistadores they told
Coronado, marching onward,
   Sought the wealth of hidden gold
That the Gran Quivira country
   Kept in secret, and the word
Roused the council and the warriors
   When the runners had been heard.
Then came mention of the Padre,
   Tribal secrets knew he all
Coming were his blood and people -
   Would he heed the racial call?
Would he cast aside tradition,
   Keep the faith he'd always shown,
Or would lips unloose and babble
   Once they spoke unto their own?

And the council meet decided
   When the call of blood and kin
Met the test of bonded friendship
   That love of race would win.

Killed they then the honored Padre,
   And in fear of Spanish wrath
Bore in secret to Isleta
   In the night by mountain path,
The remains of Juan de la Padilla
   (Foisting thus upon their head
Of the innocent pueblo
   Stigma of the deed instead).

And the people of Isleta,
    Who loved the Padre well,
Called on Manitou to witness
    Called on Thunder Bird to tell
Of their innocence and horror
    At a deed that set aside
All their sacred rites and customs
    Of the ages, true and tried.

So they fashioned him a coffin
    Hewn from log of cottonwood,
And within the church a grave dug,
    Close to where the altar stood.
In the church devoid of flooring,
    By the altar, dug it deep;
And the log, with top close fitted,
    Bound the Padre in his sleep.

The Return

Many moons and many seasons
    Lay the Padre as he should -
Many moons and many seasons
    In the log of cottonwood -

Then the earth began a swelling
    And the startled Chieftians found
Day by day a crevice showing
    In the fast-grown bulging mound.
Though they tamped the dirt within it,
    It was vain; the fissure grew;
Widened now 'till near the surface
    Came the coffin lid to view;

Came a morning when the council
    Entered by the vestry door
And the cottonwood lay resting
    On the hard-beat earthen floor
With the lid removed beside it,
    While within, the Padre's face
Showed in perfect preservation
    Shone with virtue, peace and grace

Cold decay no way had blighted
    Form of feature, garb or gown.
E'en the cottonwood as sturdy
    As when axemen hewed it down.

Then was called a hurried Junta,
    And the grave again was made
In the selfsame spot, and in it
    Once again the body laid,
And the earth tamped hard above it;
    But the passing of the days
Brought again the earth-mound bulging
    To the half expectant gaze;
And upon a tribal feast day
    Came a worshipper who found
Once again the opened coffin
    In repose atop the ground.

And again the grave was deepened,
    Even as 'twas done before;
And within the church, its people
    Laid a strong, substantial floor.
But a force unseen and mighty
    Slowly raised the boards that laid
O'er the troubled earth exactly
    Where the Padre's grave was made;
Large and larger grew the warping,
    Longer could not be ignored.
So the chiefs removed the cov'ring
    That was lifting, board by board,
And from out the ground, protruding,
    Was the coffin; then the tribe
Called to council mighty chieftains,
    Priest, Archbishop, dean and scribe,

That the thing might be of witness
    Which they did, each man with care
Thoroughly paid close attention
    To the weird and strange affair;
Found they then that preservation
    Still remained to flesh and wood;
Mumified, 'tis true, but perfect,

E'en to fibre, gown and hood;
    E'en to feature and expression;
E'en to trace of vein and pore;
    E'en to tasseled fringe adornment
On the skull cap that he wore;
    E'en the knife wound plainly showing
Where there fell the fatal blow
    Of steel on yielding neck-flesh
In the many moons ago.

Wrapped in husks of corn, and with it
    Placed the scroll of Sabine then;
Placed they fluid ink, dark coloured;
    Placed they also there a pen,
That the Padre (should he wish it)
    Might enscribe some longed request
To the people of Isleta -
    Or explain his strange unrest.

Then prepared they affidavits
    Scrolled on bark of the Sabine,
Each attesting, as a record,
    To the matters he had seen;
Made in duplicated writing,
    Stating month, and day, and year;
One retained within the council,
    One consigned within the bier.

Sealed they then the simple coffin;
   Seven feet the grave was made;
Buried they again the Padre,
   Tamped the earth with staub and spade.
And above Juan de la Padilla
   Laid again a second floor;
Placed the altar full upon it,
   Staunch and sturdy as before.

And the people of Isleta
   Wonder as the seasons go
If it be imagination;
   If their eyes deceive, or no
Some declare again the warping
   May be seen along the floor
And the Padre is returning
   To the life he loved once more.

L'ENVOI

Will there be a message written
   To the ancient Pueblo
On the scroll there for the purpose?
   I'll confess I'd like to know.

THAT DOD-GASTED SAXOPHONE

We were playing penny ante
    At the Cross-Bar-Lazy-B
When the foreman, Wild Hoss Charley,
    Dealt a pair of kings to me.

I was ridin' after dogies
    When I noticed, down the trail,
There was something comin' toward me
    With the swiftness of a snail;
An' a funny combination
    Was this antiquated bloke,
Lookin' like a human bein'
    With a pipe too big to smoke.

Well, I axes him some questions,
    An' he tells a lot of stuff
In a mess of broken English
    I opine is plumb enough;
It seems he's sort of loco
    An' a-rangin' all alone --
Heinie Weidel from Hoboken,
    And his trusty saxophone.

So I brings him to the bunk house,
    An' the punchers straight away
Messes up the whole contraption
    When they axes him to play;
For I'm free to state presumpshus,
    Never in the temp'rate zone
Has there been a noise to equal
    That dod-gasted saxophone.

I have seen the steers by thousands
    Bawlin' like their hearts'd break,
I have heard the coyotes chorus
    An' the lobo at a wake;
I have heard a dogie sighin',
    An' its mother's lonesome tone --
They is nothin' as comparin'
    To that cussed saxophone.

So -- we hung him in the canyon,
    Jest as gentle as we could,
An' we hewed him out a coffin
    From a log of cottonwood;
An' we buried him at midnight
    An' we painted on a stone --
"Heine Weidel, from Hoboken,
    An' his trusty saxophone."

An' there's certain nights, I'm statin',
    When the stars grow kinda dim,
That a mist commences hangin'
    Jest above the canyon rim;
An' the steers commence stampedin',
    An' the horses mill about,
An' the coyotes an' the lobos
    Come a hell-rip-rarin' out --

An' the sounds come up the canyon
    Like the fiends are on a tear,
Till they fill th' range an' mesa
    An' the coulees everywhere;
An' I'm knowin' it for certain --
    Though I kinda hates to own
It's the ghost of Heinie Weidel
    An' his derned ol' saxophone.

It was silent in the bunk house;
    Not a muscle moved a speck,
As the foreman, Wild Hoss Charley,
    Stole three aces from the deck.

LIQUID GOLD

Th' ol' miner sniffs th' mornin' air,
    Fer there's Apache injuns nigh.
Afraid of a trap in th' desert lap,
    He scans th' sand dunes high,
Leadin' out on th' sandy trail
    West of th' ol' water hole,
He and th' burro plod silently along
    With his keg of LIQUID GOLD.

Th' errie whir of a rattler's tail,
    As a bald eagle cuts the blue.
A rain of painted arrow shafts,
    Th' burro shot through and through.
Apaches sulkin' in th' gray mesquite,
    Hoping their shots had told.
A broken stave in th' water keg,
    As th' sands lap up th' LIQUID GOLD.

In a shallow 'dip' th' ol' miner lay
    In th' heat of the copper sun.
With a thinnin' belt - a hot carbine,
    Countin' his shots ONE by ONE.
Th' doleful clank of a dry canteen,
    With a deadly thirst untold
Only for a few precious drops
    Of th' desert's LIQUID GOLD.

A thread of shade th' yucca made,
    From th' rays of th' settin' sun.
An eagle head-dress on th' rocky point,
    Th' crack of a distant gun.
Racin' down in th' coulee bed
    Headin' for th' water hole,
Spotted ponies with droopin' heads,
    Drinkin' th' nectar of LIQUID GOLD.

A bugle call and a ringin' cheer
    On th' sandy trail in a runnin' fight,
With th' ball-bats dippin' near,
    As the desert fades to the sheen of night,
Th' soldiers camp-fires brightly gleam
    As a breeze ripples th' ol' water hole,
Kneelin' in th' shadows of th' gray mesquite,
    Th' ol' miner hugs his canteen of LIQUID GOLD.

Sun of the West Good-night

Sun of the West, good-night, good-night!
    Orb of a splendid day!
Slowly you sink from my eager sight
    Into the far away.
And the night comes down and the shadows dare
To creep from the depths of their hidden lair.
Safe 'till the dawn they will linger there --
Sun of the West -- good-night.

Sun of the West, good-night, good-night!
    Ages may come and go,
But you swing on in celestial flight
    'Nor reckon on things below!
But I know naught of my destiny --
    Tomorrow my fragile bark may be
Far adrift on a troubled sea --
    Sun of the West - good-night.

The Old WaterHole.

An eagle sat on a bleak sand dune
    In the after part of a day in June
He knew the sport he would witness soon
    And smiled in appreciation -
For deep in the depths of his eagle's soul
    He loved the fights at the old water hole
And so from the peak of the sand dune's knoll
    He watched in anticipation.

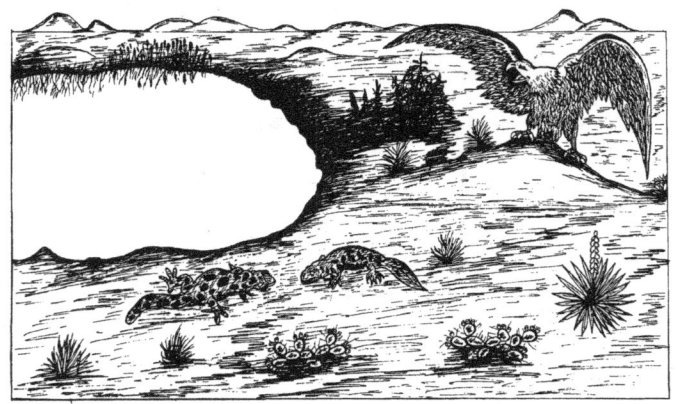

A Juajalota was first to tell
    A water-dog that for quite a spell
He had possession there, and -- well
    He certainly meant to hold it -
The water-dog with heat replied
    His full belief that the other lied
So the fight began -- and the eagle cried
    In delight that his sense foretold it.

A coyote spoke in his long drawn howl
    In bold defy to a warning growl
A she-wolf voiced -- each with a scowl
    Pulled up in quick decision.
A single path was to be tread
    So scissored fang met flashing head
The coyote soon defeated -- fled
    As the eagle screamed derision.

Quick came the sound of a muffled roar
    The fight beginning was quickly o'er
As through the tangle of cactus tore
    A buffalo bull confounding -
His triumph was short for hoof beats told
    Of dark skinned foes and the braggart bold
Dashed on in retreat to a mesa hold
    With the eagle's laugh resounding.

The Injuns' rest had scrace begun
    When spurts of smoke -- from cracking gun
And forms outlined by setting sun
    Told plain the desert story -
The fight was short and sunset found
    The white man master of the ground
The water hole and all around -
    The eagle screamed his glory.

The day was done and from the place
    He winged his way in sweeping grace
To sheltered crag and from the face
    Of some sheer cliff commented
In boastful pride and swaggered sway
    The diary of a perfect day
And gloating o'er the desert way
    He fell asleep contented.

FRED LAMBERT

White spots scattered on the prairie grass,
    Symbol of life from a day that is dead.
Bleached by the summers and winters long gone,
    Lying untouched in the coulee's dry bed.

Trail tracks scratched by travios poles,
    Wallow pits where the old cows lay.
Circles made by the watchful bulls,
    Tell-tale signs of a by-gone day.

White men no longer stalk the herd
 To take only the hump and hide,
Or Indians drive their shafts to kill
 The monarch of the prairie's pride.

Once they meant meat and moccasins
 For both the whites and reds,
War shields and sides for tepees,
 Winter robes for their beds.

The sparrow-hawk sits on the splintered horn.
 Through the eye-sockets the daisies spring.
The rattler lies in the skull's gray shade.
 Within the tarantula weaves ring by ring.

White spots scattered on the prairie grass,

Symbol of life from a day that is dead,

Show ghostly white in the moonlit night,

Lying untouched in the coulee's dry bed.

When The West Calls

There's something keeps pulling, keeps pulling at me --
    And somehow I'm never at ease.
I'm dreaming at night and in visions I see --
    The dust carried on by the breeze.
The great sweep of plains all around and about --
    The road dimming down to a track;
Through the cactus and sage - 'till at last it runs out --
    And -- someway I want to go back.

There's something keeps telling, keeps telling me how
    The stars shed their luster at night
O'er the great silent billows unscathed by the plow,
    Supreme in their vastness and might.
The herd in the offing dreams on 'till the dawn;
    The canyon looms weirdly and black;
The trail to the westward leads on -- ever on --
    And somehow -- I want to go back.

There's something keeps saying, keeps saying again --
    Go back to your place in the west.
To the God-given freedom of coulee and plain;
    Go back to your country and rest;
Where handclasps are strong and come straight from
        the heart,
    Be you ruler of mansion or shack;
And somehow I know I'll be eager to start
    To the land that is calling me back.

There's something keeps pulling, keeps pulling at me,
    As downward I go through the years;
It may be the romance of life that is free --
    It may be the measure of tears;
It may be the pleasure, it may be the pain
    That calls to the unbeaten track;
Or--it may be a mound on a wide sweep of plain --
    That's calling, keeps calling me back.

DOGIES

Huntin' fer dogies* -- trailin' the wake
Of motherless critters in coulee an' brake;
Down in the canyon, out on the range,
Huntin' fer dogies, hell, but it's strange
Trailin' a wanderin', motherless calf
Out in the sage fer a day and a half,
Ridin' the range in the sun and the sand --
Dogies that's lost in a lonesome land.

Huntin' fer dogies; mebbe they be
Longin' fer friends that are lonesome as me;
Somehow I know how the critters must feel,
Weary an' worn an' run-down-at-the-heel;
Thinkin' of home as they wander about,
Lost in the sage an' no way to get out;
Hopin', I guess, as they wallow the sand --
Dogies adrift in a lonesome land.

Huntin' fer dogies; trailin' the wake,
Down in the canyon an' down in the brake;
Out on the mesa, over the range,
Huntin' fer dogies; hell, but it's strange,
Me to be trailin' fer motherless things,
Dreamin' along while my memory brings
Pictures that fade like the tints of the sand --
Dogies adrift in a lonesome land.

SAGE TANG.

There's somethin' when y're sniffin',
    A-smellin' of the sage,
That makes a feller lively,
    Forgettin' of his age.
It's got a tang about it
    When a-batin' of y're eye
An' you feel right fittin'--
    Sorta youthful-like, an' spry.

Yuh whiff it up y're nostrils
    An' commence t' a-feelin' fine;
It tingles in y're bosom
    Like the rarest sort o' wine.
Yuh wanta shout and holler,
    An' y're bustin' full of fun,
An' hittin' down the mesa
    With y're cayuse on th' run.

It's better than a tonic
    Er a swig o' likker, pard;
It hits you nice and gentle,
    But it gits you good an' hard.
An' onct yuh felt its tingle,
    An' onct yuh smelt its whang,
Y're swearin' by its fragrance
    An' dreamin' of its tang.

There's somethin', pard, about it
    That gits yuh, as I say;
Jest whiff it onct -- I'm bettin'
    That yuh'll wanta light and stay.
There's nothin' pard, no nothin'
    In this er any age
Compares t' breezes sweetened
    By th' mesa purpled sage.

THE DESERT

A limitless waste of sage and sand
Which reaches afar the sky;
The waterless home of the lone coyote
That startles the night with it's eerie note;
As it sulks away to some spring remote
Howling to find it dry.

The pitiless heat-waves glance upon
A miser'ble pile of whitening bone
Half buried by the sand and time
Perhaps there's a girl whom he wrote a line,
(She's waiting until he finds a mine)
Back in her Eastern home.

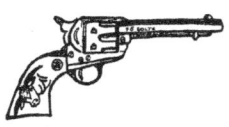

And rising afar above the plain,

As grim as a ghastly wart

A pile of lava rears it's head

That is jagged and scarred, the color of lead,

A headstone fit for the countless dead:

Goal that dreamers sought.

With sibilant hiss a rattler seeks

Shelter beneath the stones.

For even he is forced to retreat

Before the withering noonday heat

That quivers and plays in a shimmering sheet

Over the bleaching bones.

A city arises athwart the sky;

The waters blue of a crystal stream

O'er shadowed by waving palm

Reflecting the shafts of sunlight gleam.

The emigrant hurries his weary team,

Then looks again. 'Tis gone!

There's poisonous spider and centepede,

Big cactus covered with thorn

The land of sagebrush and mesquite,

'Tis little you find to drink or eat,

Such is the Indian's last retreat,

Such is his desert home.

What flowers there are lack of perfume,
Tho' colored beyond compare;
The very birds are a grisly thing,
Like wandering imps, or ghouls a-wing,
So carrion-gorged, they cannot sing
But circle in the air.

Silent but sure as the hand of fate
Is the grip of the desert land;
And woe unto those who shall face the death
That lurks unseen in it's hazy depth,
To be borne on the wings of it's white-hot breath
Over the burning sand.

But over the reach of the desert bare,
'Tis given to some to roam:
Men of the East who have lost their taste
For civilization's code and caste,
Who'd rather dwell in the endless waste,
Scorning a sumptuous home;

Men of the West who've defied the law,

Just seeking a place to hide;

Men of the South who shot to kill,

When cornered at running a "wild-cat still"

Are lurking beneath the long, low hill;

Many of such have died.

For the desert calls them one by one,

And takes them to her breast.

The boy who once was a rich man's pride

And the outlaw chief lie side by side

With trusted men who falsified,

All in silence, all at rest.

In Th' Long Ago

Th' cold winds of ol' December
    Are sweepin' o'er the grassy sea,
Th' pines in th' mountains
    Are swayin' in th' breeze;
My thoughts are on a rampage
    As I sit by th' firelight's dyin' glow
Dreamin', jest a-dreamin'
    Of Christmas Day--
        In th' long ago.

I kin see th' sandy desert
    With th' campfire an' th' sheep,
Th' Eastern Star a-shinin'
    And th' sheperds all asleep;
Mary an' th' Christ Child--
    An' th' Wise Men speakin' low,
As they tip-toed to th' manger
    On Christmas Day--
        In th' long ago.

I kin see th' Pilgrim Fathers

    As they together kneel,

To offer up th' tribute

    Thet in their hearts they feel;

With a million stars a-shinin'

    An' th' cabin lights a-glow,

Th' dear ol' mothers singin'

    On Christmas Day--

        In th' long ago.

I kin see th' ol' prairie schooners

    Drawn into a circle wide,

'Th' oxen grazin' in th' shadows,

    As th' moon drifts on it's silent ride.

Th' Pioneer's heads bowed in prayer

    While askin' God their Father

All His blessin's to bestow--

    On Christmas Day--

        In th' long ago.

I kin see th' ol' Home Ranch

    An' th' "Boss" in his easy chair,

Cowboys thet I rode the range with,

    An' my dear ol' Mother sittin' there;

Th' Sky Pilot as he thanks our Lord

    Fer his love an' pretectin' kindness,

Th' grasses an' th' snow--

    On Christmas Day--

        In th' long ago.

Th' blizzard blast is growlin',
   An' th' penned-up cattle bawl;
In th' hills th' wolf is howlin'
   In answer to th' winter call;
My good old dog is here beside me
   As I sit by th' firelight's dyin' glow,
Dreamin', jest a-dreamin'
   Of Christmas Day--
         In th' long ago.

The Cowboy's Return

Three long years had Chico wandered,
    Gleaning funds to work his claim;
By lone camp-fires he had pondered
    On an unforgotten name.
Nancy Rankin's face had shimmered
    Like the light that never fails,
Beckoning and sweet it glimmered
    Down a hundred haunted trails.

CHICO reined his nimble sorrel
    Down the dim, moon-silver slope,
Crushing clumps of mountain laurel
    In an eager, reckless lope.
Far below him, in the canyon,
    By a booming waterfall,
Lay his Gold claim, long abandoned,
    And his cabin, dark and small.

Likely Nancy had never missed him,
    Maybe it was better so.
There were others who had hissed him,
    Jubilant to see him go,
Enemies, like Charlie Griffin.
    Chico 'lighted at his shack,
Stepped across the sill and stiffened,
    With a six-gun against his back.

Charlie Griffin had waylaid him!
    Chico's hand flashed to his thigh.
But a voice like silver stayed him:
    "Stop, you jasper, or you die!
You shall never jump this Gold claim,
    Charlie Griffin   Can't you learn?
I am here to guard the old claim
    Until Chico shall return!"

Chico's voice came, hoarse and broken,
    Calling Nancy Rankin's name.
For 'twas Nancy who had spoken;
    Through the years she'd kept his claim,
Proof enough that she adored him!
    'Midst the thunder and the foam,
Tenderly he drew her toward him,
    Love had welcomed Chico home.

Prairie Dogs.

Friendly little devils, you can lay to that,
    Khaki colored, sorter, an' their bodies fat;
Always mighty nosey for they like to see,
    Bustin' every minute jest from curiousity;
Think they own the country from the way they act—
    Feelin' big as elephants an' that's a fact;

    Buildin' mounds by the dozens an' diggin' up the grass—
        When you happen near 'em givin' out a line of sass—
    Waitin' 'till you're gettin' close an' scoldin' like a shrew—
        Guess if you could understand they'd be cussin' you—
    Friendly little devils, you can lay to that,
        Khaki colored, sorter, an' their bodies fat.

Funny little cusses as ever you saw-
    Likely meanin' nothin' when they fuss an' jaw;
Like to hear the music in their barkin' tone
    When a feller's campin' on the plains alone;
Cuttin' pranks around you like a circus clown
    Growlin' like the natives in the old home town-

    Jest about as nosey as the home folks too-
        Keeps a feller laughin' at the things they do-
    Think you're goin' to ketch 'em but bless your soul
        They disappear like magic in their dog-town hole;
    Funny little cusses as you ever saw-
        Never meanin' nothin' when they scold an' jaw.

    Curious little varmints in the choice they makes-
        Bunkin' up with the fuzzy owls an' rattle-snakes;
    Scratchin' out a livin' where the ground is bare-
        Forty miles from water but they never care;
    Seems they're mighty happy jest to live an' lark
        Jerkin' up their little tails for every single bark-

Bygone Days Of The Old West

Tellin' you a story if you only knew

  What they might be tryin' for to say to you;

Curious little varmints in the choice they makes

  Bunkin' up with the fuzzy owls an' rattle-snakes.

Friendly little devils, you can lay to that,

  Khaki colored, sorter, an' their bodies fat.

THE CABIN OF LOGS ON THE HILL.

Near the pass of Palo Flechado
    Far back in the mountains of Taos,
There once stood a cabin,
    A dreary log cabin,
That served for a time as a house.

    Rough hewn were the timbers that formed it,
        And tragedy stalked at it's door;
    A hovel of hell,
        From the rafters, they tell,
    To the pit that was dug neath the floor.

    Chas Kennedy fashioned the structure
        With loopholes conveniently placed
    To cover the ground
        From the rear and around
    To the trail which the ramshackle faced.

A man of mysterious habits,
    As cold as the hard graven stone,
He toiled not a day,
    Yet no person might say
How he lived for he counciled alone.

A woman there was in the cabin --
    A woman who bore him a son;
A frail little woman,
    Who longed to be human.
She dreamed when the daylight was done.

Dreamed dreams of the babe at her bosom
    As mothers have dreamed through the years;
She cuddled her boy
    With a wild, eager joy
That shone through the vale of tears.

Still loyal was she to the master
    Who ruled with an iron-bound will;
She drudged as a slave
    Through the years that she gave
To the cabin of logs on the hill.

One night when the snow, tempest driven,
    Came down like an angry typhoon,
An object half froze,
    With flake covered clothes,
Came into Johnny Pearson's saloon.

'Twas a woman worn and weary,
    Faint from exposure and fright,
Who sank to the floor
    In the part open door,
Looked back in fear at the night.

She trembled and drank of a potion
    While the riotous crowd became still.
Weakened from cold,
    Her story she told
Of the cabin of logs on the hill.

As the tale unrolled to it's hearers,
    Men hardened in every clime,
They sickened, grew pale,
    As the woman so frail,
Recited a story of crime.

Her story was simple, straightforward,
    That brought to the blood a strange chill,
Told of the life
    She had led as a wife
In the hovel of hell on the hill.

A story of murder, full wanton,
    In numbers that reached to the score:
But seldom, they learned
    Had a traveler returned
To the world, once he entered it's door.

A shot or a blow, and another
    Was dumped in the pit full of slime
Neath the stolid log floor,
    And a heavy trapdoor
Closed down on the pitiless crime.

Then came a day when the mother,
    With blood in her veins running cold,
Heard baby lips tell
    Of that pit hole, that hell,
Of things that were cast in it's hold.

The stranger, who harked to the story,
    Was killed as he raced for the door.
The child lips that told
    Joined the vat filled with mold
Neath the gloom of the silent trap door.

That night, up the crude fashioned chimney
    She crawled, step by step, as each stone
With it's rough and soot covered edge
    Offered hand-hold or ledge,
Bit sparse, yeilding flesh to the bone.

Well she knew the master left sleeping
    Would add to his score would he wake,
But her shadowlike form
    Slipped away in the storm
Like a ghost as it fled up the brake.

With the end of the story came action.
    Davy Crockett joined in with the rest,
And the dawning of day
    Saw them well on their way;
Judge, jury and court of the West.

On a hill bleak and cold, stood a scaffold

    Where beeves had been slaughtered and hung.

The windlass would speak

    With a groan and a creak

As the rope bore it's burden and swung.

    Many years the creak had been silent,

        But the timbers stood sturdy and sound.

    Now a rope, wholly new

        From the windlass ran through

    The crown pulley down to the ground.

        And the windlass, once more creaking slowly

            Returned to it's winding in glee;

        The crown pulley sung

            As an object was hung

        In the breeze, swinging fully and free.

        The horsemen rode down through the valley,

            And Palo Flechado was still

        While eyeballs of glass

            Stared on up the Pass

        To the cabin of logs on the hill.

The Grizzly Bear

I'm ridin' down the canyon-
Fer I've nothin' much to do-
But huntin' fer some dogies-
An' a maverick er two-
It's early in the mornin',
An' I'm breathin' in th' air-
That's cool and mighty pleasant-
When I sees a grizzly bear.

He's headin' home, I'm guessin',
An' he knows he's good an' late-
An' makin' up excuses-
To be tellin' to his mate-
An' so I spurs my Pinto-
To a runnin', swingin' lope-
An' in another minnit-
Why, I loops him with my rope.

Well, I've seen th' cyclones tearin'
An' th' blizzard's blindin' snow—
I've seen a big volcaner—
Open up an' let 'er go—
But I'm sayin', pard, I'm sayin'
That there's nothin' I can tell
To give yuh half a notion—
How that bear was raisin' hell.

Th' Pinto sets to hold him—
But I'm sayin', when th' slack
Comes out that Pinto's layin'
Firm an' certain on his back—
With both th' cinches busted—
An' the saddle draggin' free—
An' then that daggoned critter
Makes a line di-reckt fer me.

Well, th' Pinto's scramblin' lively
Gettin' up all set to track—
An' me— I'm landin' pronto,
On th' center of his back;
He don't need any urgin'
As we beat it down th' trail—
That cussed bear a' comin'
Half a rod behint his tail.

Th' saddle, it's a draggin'-
Bouncin' now an' then- kerthump
Till by luck it jerks an' takes that
Crazy bruin on th' rump;
An' I never heard such growlin'-
As he wheels about at that-
An' he pounces on th' saddle
Like a terrier does a rat.

An' he cuffs it an' he paws it-
Throwin' pieces here and there-
Till th' poor old saddle's scattered
In th' ricks an' everywhere;
Then he happens to remember-
What had occupied his mind-
An' he hikes fer home a draggin;'
My rope along behind.

Well, I lost my saddle, pardner,
An' a derned good lariat-
But I've somethin' to remember-
I ain't likely to forget;
When I finds a grizzly headin'
Fer his home, I'm free to own-
That th' only thing I'm doin'
Will be lettin' him alone.

The Night Rider

Sunset - th' colors glow
    Upon th' clouds an' sky
Thar's somethin' over yander
    In th' west I'd like t' try.
I know it's night a-comin',
    An' th' trail is mighty long,
But thar's somethin' in th' evenin'
    That is like a mother's song.
An' th' dyin' shadows creepin',
    An' th' beamin' evenin' star
Keeps a-callin'-like, a-callin',
    To th' sunset - over thar.

Sunset - th' herd's asleep,
    Th' night is ca'm an' still
I know thar's rest a-waitin'
    Whar th' trail slips down th' hill.
I know thar's rest a-waitin'
    Whar th' silent evenin' sky
Paints th' glory of a somethin'
    In th' west I'd like t' try.
An' th' shadows may be stealin',
    But th' quiet evenin' star
Keeps a-shinin'-like, an' pointin'
    To th' silence - over thar.

Cupid and Cactus

We were riding after dogies
  On the Cross-Bar Lazy-B,
When the foreman Wild Hoss Charley,
  Lit a cigarette and said to me:

"Yeah, I wouldn't say as women
  May not be the proper dope-
But me, I'm more contented
  With my broncho an' a rope.
Fer I ain't knowin', pardner,
  On the species none, y' see,
But one dad-blamed adventoor
  Is a plenty, bo, fer me."

"She taught the school at Dobe,
    An' I'm statin' ca'm and wide
That a better lookin' critter
    Never crossed the great divide.
So I'm losin' all my senses,
    An' go trailin' her until,
When I axes her the question,
    Why, she answers that she will."

"But she hangs her head a-blushin'
    'Till she manages to say,
That she has no clothes befittin'
    Fer a happy weddin' day.
So I gits a hundred buckos
    From the boss, because I knows
That a woman may be lovin'
    But she's also hell for clothes."

"So I hands her out the lucre
    An' she makes me plum agree
Our engagement must be secret
    'Till her school is out, y'see.
An' we has it all considered
    We're to meet in Santa Fe,
At the Court House, an' be married
    On the twenty-third of May."

"Yeah, I showed up fer the weddin'
   Right on schedule, an' I'll say,
That there's never been so many
   Punchers seen in Santa Fe.
They was hangin' round the court house,
   So I figures they is wise
To my nupshules, an' are aimin'
   Fer to give us a surprise."

" An' then the plot develops
   That the schemin' little bait
Is engaged to every puncher
   She could locate in the state;
An' they all has paid her money,
   Each a hundred buckos cool,
Jest t' learn a woman's tricky
   An' a puncher is a fool."

" So I keeps a-waitin', waitin',
   Fer to claim my blushin' bride,
When the sheriff waves a message
   An' he calls us all inside.
It was just a little message,
   From a town in Illynois,
Readin': ' On my way to Boston.'
' Say good-by to all the boys."

" So we ambles home in sadness;
    An' I'm sayin' plain to you
That I'm all caught up on women,
    Which is meanin', I am through."

" Oh, the most of them are noble,
    Good and true, " I weakly said;
But the foreman, Wild Hoss Charley,
    Neither spoke nor turned his head.

Tenderfoot Blues

Riding a bronc as he's jumping along-
    Something is painful - he's doing it wrong,
Bumpity-bump and blipty-blup-
    When he goes down, why I ALWAYS go up.

Sore as a boil; How I rattle and shake-
    Not a square inch but's an agonized ache-
Clear from my feet to the top of my crown-
    Here he comes up - and here I GO down.

Why can't we compromise, bronc? I'll declare
    Why must I always be up in the air
When you're settled down and just ready to start
    On the ascent - we're so far, far apart-

Then, when we meet, it is awful, the jolt
    Goes through my frame like a powerful bolt-
Bouncing along like a silly old clown-
    You coming up and myself going down.

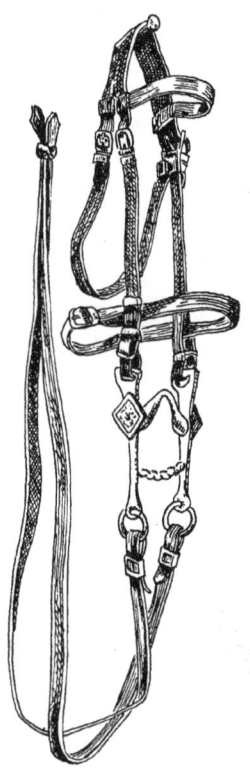

    Let's get together, or soon I shall bust;
        Why do you look like you're full of disgust?
    I'm not to blame that we look such a sight-
        It just doesn't seem that we started it right.

        WHOA! Let me off! I am weary, I say,
            Taking the bumps as I meet you halfway;
        Next time I ride I most certainly hope
            I'm blessed with a broncho that knows how to lope.

A Nature Soliloquy

I don't care much for politics
    And less for fashion's show
Society don't care for me,
    Nor I for it, yuh know.
Don't care much for business;
    Yuh gotta cheat to win.
The churches are so full of style,
    Religion can't break in.
Everything that's run by man
    Is more or less a fraud;
The only thing I've found that's true
    Is Nature, gift of God.
I've never had Her lie to me;
    Another thing I've learned,
She doesn't talk about yuh
    Every time your back is turned.

I love to get out in the woods
    As far as I can go
And watch the stately branches
    Gently waving to and fro.
I like to hear the babble
    Or the gurgle of the stream,
I like to hear the song birds
    And the mighty eagle scream;
The squirrels scold and scamper;
    The crow caw-caws in glee.

While drumming of the pheasant
    Joins in blessed symphony.
The fern-dell and the little cove,
    The rocks and tiny rills,
The peaceful green of valleys,
    The monarchs called the hills;
I sit and talk to all of them,
    My meaning well they know
For I learned to speak their language
    In my boyhood, long ago.

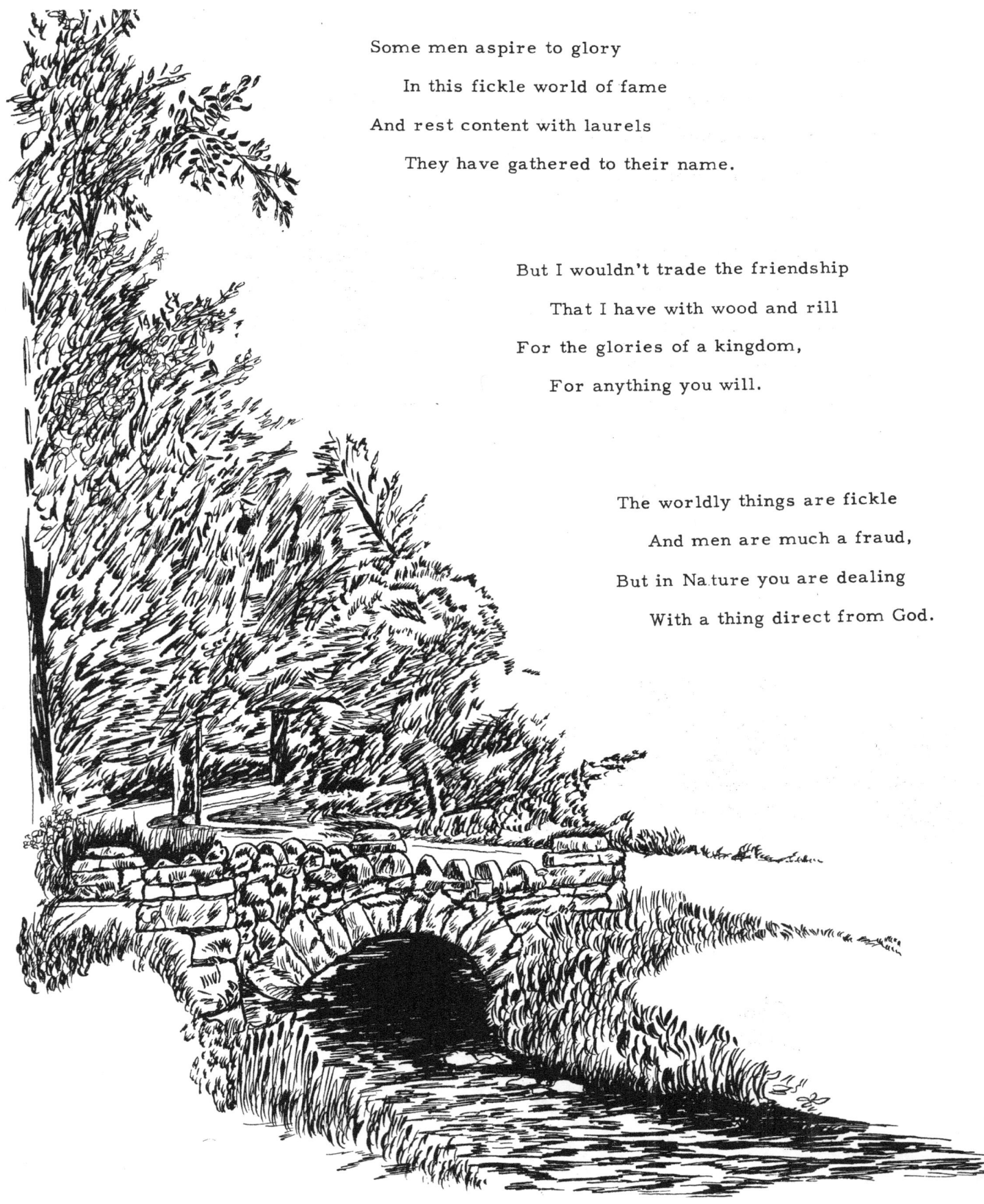

Some men aspire to glory

   In this fickle world of fame

And rest content with laurels

   They have gathered to their name.

   But I wouldn't trade the friendship

     That I have with wood and rill

   For the glories of a kingdom,

     For anything you will.

   The worldly things are fickle

     And men are much a fraud,

   But in Nature you are dealing

     With a thing direct from God.

The Mirage

In the still, grey dawn of a sun-baked plain-
    Far out where the desert rules-
Where withered grass and cactus reign
    Lies silent the lake of fools;
A mirrored spot with a silvered sheen
    That lures in it's subtle way
The traveler on to it's shores of green
    Through the drag of a desert day.

To shores of green where the horses stand
    And quaff from the waters clear-
A restful scene in a waste of sand
    To silence a mocking fear;
And so athirst with quickened pace
    You move with a sturdy tread
And hopes renewed for the God sent place
    With it's waters - just ahead.

With a parching tongue and a throat dust-dry,
    You seek the inviting spot
Where liquid pools of the malpi lie —
    You seek -- but find them not;
For always and ever they lead you on
    With pictures of cooling green-
'Till mocking, they drop from your sight, and gone
    Complete as though never seen.

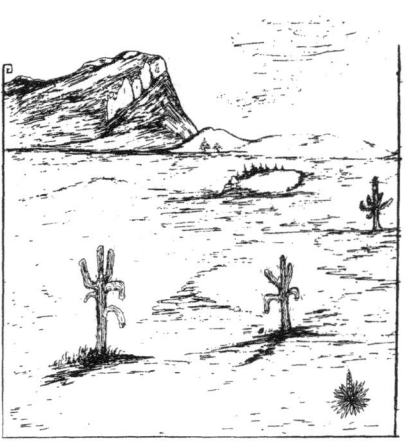

Like magic devilish, cruel, bold,
    Appears but the desert sand
Exposing thus as the truths unfold-
    The lies of a vagrant land;
Where the sun and waves of plain dried air
    Combined -- with desert rules
To form a sheen of phantom rare -
    A mist -- called the Lake of Fools.

It isn't a story I like to tell-
    The findin' of Desert Dan-
As loony as any bat from hell-
    A wreck that was once a man.
I'd never forget in a thousand years
    The day that we brought him in
For even the punchers shed some tears
    And the chink forgot to grin;

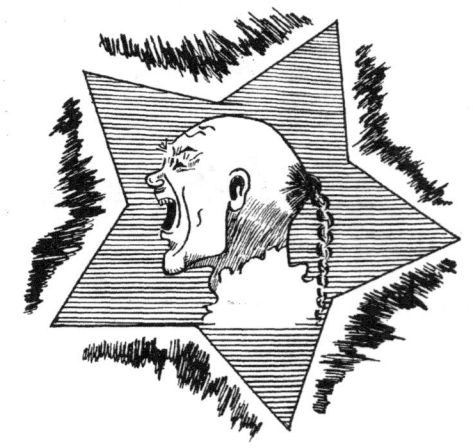

We noticed him first a movin' spot
    Close over to half-way dune-
And the sun was beatin' as stingin' hot
    As hell ought to be at noon-
Our glasses told that the movin' thing
    A draggin' acrost the sand
Was a human form - so we do a spring
    To the bronchos clost at hand

And stringin' out - each cayuse flat
    And doin' the best he can
We soon came up to the creature that
    Had onct been a handsome man.
But livin' Gods what a sight we seen
    I'll never forget I know -
His face was a sort of a sickly green
    His hair was white as snow

And his eyes were red like a ruby's red
    And his tongue was twice it's size-
His body lived but his mind was dead-
    You could tell by his bulgin' eyes;
His swollen lips could make no sound
    So we didn't know his brand
For a month or more 'till we fetched him 'round
    To talk we could understand;

And crazy? sure it was awful, pard,
    The way he would rave and make
A prayer, pleadin', and beggin' hard
    To live ' till he reached the lake;
And called the names of a kid or two
    And a woman name of Nan
And tellin' how he would get 'em through
    And to never to doubt their Dan-

(That's how we knowed what to call him Bo
    We added the desert touch
The only name he will ever know
    But a name don't amount to much).
So he kept a ravin" about the lake
    That was always a bit ahead
'Till at last we sorter commenced to take
    Some notice of what he said;

And when he'd be beggin' the woman, Nan,
    And the kids to be brave and try
To make the lake -- every cussed man
    Would sneak to himself -- and cry;
He'd never notice us men at all-
    (Remember his mind was dead)
But always to Nan and the kids he'd call,
    That the water was just ahead;

And so we started out to ride the sand
    A searchin' for what we'd find-
From Circle C into no man's land
    Where the glare nearly drove us blind;
'Twas Curley Moore that observed 'em first
    The Kids and the woman, Nan-
All huddled clost in a last embrace
    Awaitin' for Desert Dan;

All huddled clost in a last embrace
    And God what a sight they be-
The buzzards talons had left their trace
    In a way that was hell to see;
We buried 'em there in a single grave
    When the sun in the West was red
And I'm all cut up when I hear him rave
    That the water is just ahead.

No - it ain't a story I like to tell-
    Of the kids and the woman, Nan-
The Phantom Lake and the desert hell
    And the wreck with th' name o'Desert Dan.
In the still, grey dawn of a sun-baked plain
    Far out where the desert rules
Where withered grass and the cactus reign
    Lies silent -- The Lake of Fools.

The Legend of Abo Crag.

We dismounted on the rimrock
   To rest our weary nags,
When the foreman, Wild Hoss Charley
   Told me the story of Abo Crag:

" Have you ever heard the legend of Abo Crag-
   Beaver Joe with his Pinto nag
And a woman the Camp called Frisco Mag
   Well - Maybe you'd like to hear it?
It really isn't a crag at all
   But part of the Abo canyon wall
Where the rock o'er hangs - a nasty fall
   Of a thousand feet - or near it.

" He wasn't so much of a man at that
    They called him Beaver to match his hat,
A sort of a friendly desert rat
    But clean as they ever make 'em.
She wasn't a woman in any sense
    Except for sex she was all pretense,
Her life a story of vile offense-
    Her kind - may the devil take 'em.

" She heard the rumors often told-
    Of a mystic claim of desert gold
That Joe was supposed to have and hold
    And so she set out to gain it.
God knows the methods she may have used
    Or the code of morals that she abused
For Joe with his heart and mind confused
    Fell - how can a man explain it?

" An then - despite her pets and guiles
    Her tricks and traits and her painted smiles,
Her whole menu of faithless wiles
    Was met with a calm dissension.
He had no wealth of the desert gold-
    Refuted the tales that people told-
And her leopard love turned quick to cold
    Deep hate with dark intention.

" And so she raised a hue and cry

    To the half drunk mob that was always nigh-

Hag that she was - by a subtle lie,

    Inferred she had been insulted.

And so they started for Beaver Joe

    With the thing in mind that all mobs know-

A limb and a dangling form below

    And the mob-rule mind exulted.

" Far out on the point of Abo Crag

    They found him astride the Pinto nag

And the mob led on by Frisco Mag

    Advanced in a drunken fury-

He read the sense of the knotted rope

    Appraised the rabble from every scope

And knew he had neither chance nor hope

    Of hearing - defense or jury.

" He grinned a reply to the maddened yell-

    Watched the approach a silent spell

Then told them politely to go to hell,

    A contemptuous glance threw o'er them

Whispered a word in the Pinto's ear

    Then as the hag and her clan drew near

The Pinto carried his rider clear

    In a leap to the death before them.

" And out on the point of the Crag they ran,

    Frisco Mag and her drunken clan

For a view of the mangled horse and man

    And the rock from an age of sleeping

'Woke to the weight on the outer side-

    Balanced a moment - commenced to slide,

Taking them all in a dizzy ride

    Below to the devil's keeping.

" And so they claim in the desert night

    When the moon is dark and the wind is right

The Crag is bathed in a weirdly light

    And the cries from the gulf come sweeping.

I'd say the wails are a panther's cry-

    And the light - a star in the desert sky

For, aside from Joe and the Pinto, why

    Would the canyon walls be weeping?

GHOSTS OF OLD CIMARRON TOWN.

I love to sit in the gloaming,
    Lookin' down on sleeping Cimarron town;
Watching the ghosts of 2-gun men
    That go riding up and down.
The jingle of spurs are silent,
    Noise of hoof-beats cannot be heard,
Only the night breeze sighing
    Like the driftin' of a phantom herd.

Now young Davy Crockett is passing,
    Ridin' a bronc of milky white;
See Clay Allison fannin' his smokies
    As Poncho Greigo falls in the fight.
My! How Maxwell handles the ribbons
    On the team of chestnut brown,
As the moon rises in all her glory
    Over the 'Old Timey' western town.

Kit Carson, Apaches and bull-whackers
    The famous, and those unsung,
Gather again in Lambert's saloon
    As when the West was wild and young.
Cowboys and dark-eyed senoritas,
    Miners with buckskin sacks of gold,
Gather silently at the roulette wheel
    Where the game of luck is swiftly told.

I love to sit in the gloaming
    Dreamin' of the days long ago,
Watching the ghosts of pioneers
    Silently passing to and fro.
Now-- Only the ballbats dipping
    And the coyote's lonely call
Breaks the evening silence
    On the canyon's rimrock wall.

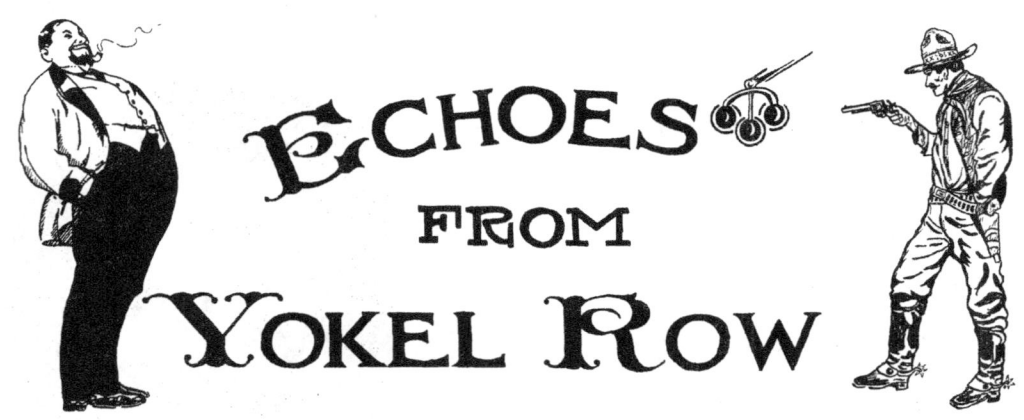

Echoes from Yokel Row

We were speaking of the cattle markets
    At the Cross-Bar Lazy-B,
When the foreman, Wild Hoss Charley,
    Snapped his chaps and said to me:

"We was shippin' out some cattle,
    An I has to make the trip
To the market with the bawlers,
    So I packs my pasteboard grip
And I lands in Kansas City,
    Where I sells 'em; then I'm free.
And I'm millin' here an' yonder
    Jest to see what I could see."

"When I'm through I starts a-driftin'
   To the deepo kinda slow,
When an hombre on the sidewalk
   Grins a bit and says, "Hello."
And the first thing I'm a-knowin'
   I have bought a suit of clothes
That is cheap at twenty buckos -
   And I need 'em, goodness knows."

"But when I reach the bunkhouse
   At the Cross-Bar Lazy-B,
I finds the sneakin' varmint
   Done the changin' act on me.
For the suit that I'm unwrappin,
   Is a brilliant emerald green,
An' was aimed to be a-fittin'
   Of a kid of about sixteen."

"Yeah, I'm mad there's no denyin',
   An' I figgers I'll go back
In the fall an' sorta amble
   To this hombre's swindlin' shack.
But one day I'm at the Junction
   Up at Dobe, an' I'll swear
If that dogie ain't a-standin'
   On the platform, waitin' there
For a train. An' when I sees him,
   Why, I'm sudden filled with hope;
And I'm driftin' down to see him;
   Then I throws my handy rope
And I brings him ca'm and certain
   On the homeward trail with me
To this very bunkhouse, pardner,
   On the Cross-Bar Lazy-B."

"And I take the clothes he's wearin',
    And I dresses him complete
In that emerald-green contraption
    That in places wouldn't meet.
For he's short, and fat, and pussy,
    While the suit of vivid green
Was intended for a youngster
    That was tall and lank and lean."

"And I heads him for the Junction,
    And t' soothe his pulsin' heart,
Why, I plunk some friendly bullets
    Near his feet t' help him start,
And the cattle gets excited,
    And they joins the merry chase,
An' he's goin', pard; he's goin'
    Like a comet eatin' space."

"With his clothes a-burstin' hither,
    And his clothes a-burstin' yon,
He ain't gone so very distant
    When he ain't got nothin' on.
But he finally wins the series
    As he rolls below the fence,
An' he tops the ridge a-runnin',
    And I've never seen him sence."

"But there ain't no fat man ever
    Made the time that hombre did,
With cows an' me a-helpin',
    Like I'm tellin' you we did."

"Do you aim to buy another
    Hand-me-down on yokel row?"
But the foreman, Wild Hoss Charley,
    Shook his head and answered - "No!"

Slowly the sun is sinking,
    Deep in the golden sea;
And as it fades I'm thinking,
    Thinking of life -- and thee;
Homeward the birds are flying
    Swift to a sheltered nest,
While in my heart I'm sighing,
    Sighing for you -- and rest.

Softly the night is falling,
    Dimmed in the evening sky;
And through its gloom I'm calling
    Longing for but one reply;
Mocking the cry, and dreary,
    Echoes but come to me--
Tired is my heart and weary
    As gulls in a storm swept sea.

Love, Honor and Away

We were heatin' brandin'-irons,
    At Cross-Bar Lazy-B,
When Foreman, Wild Hoss Charley,
    Poked the fire, said to me:

" Lots of people never figger
    That a hoss can reason, Bo,
But I'm tellin' you for certain
    There are a lot of things they know
That you'd never be suspectin'
    They had ever thought about,
Till you've found they've worked
    their thinker
    And got it reasoned out.

" I can prove it by a story
    That I mighty seldom tell;
How Apache, that's my broncho,
    Set me free o' 'Sage Bush' Nell.
She has got me locoed, pardner,
    'Fore I knows just where I'm at,
With her talk o' home and children
    And a lot o' things like that.

" So she roped me, Bo, she roped me,
    Till my soul was not my own;
So we weds in Arizony,
    And we heads for San Antone.
Now I don't mind sayin', pardner,
    When you've lived with 'Sage Bush' Nell
You have lost all fear and terror
    For the place that's known as hell.

" If I'd start right now repeatin'
    All the cussedness she knew,
I could talk until the Judgement
    And would not be half way through.
She was always raisin' thunder,
    An' I never knowed a day
That was peaceful till she left me,
    Sort of sudden, you might say.

" There was one thing I was firm on;
    She could mill about and honk,
But I'd never let her monkey
    With Apache, that's my Bronc.
An' Apache didn't like her;
    That was plain enough to see
I guess he'd heard the cussin's
    She was always handin' me.

" One day when she's a rarin'
    Like a Hopi full of Rye,
And opinin' she'd ride him
    Or she'd know the reason why,
That noted steed approaches
    Like he's crazy to be rid;
He looks me in the opticks
    And he winks at me, he did.

" So I watches as they're goin'
    Toward the canyon, out of sight;
They're not returnin', pardner,
    Though I waits up half the night.
Next mornin' Apache's standin'
    Calm and patient by the fence,
But 'Sage Brush' Nell was missin'
    And I never seen her since.

" I opine he mebbe pitched her
    In the canyon, but of course
He ain't never told me, Bozo,
    Bein' nothin' but a hoss.
Howsoever you can't drag him
    Anywhere around the spot,
Which may be a'count his conscience,
    And again it's mebbe not.

But I'd bet some iron buckos
    She's firm and fast asleep
Where the bottom of the canyon
    Is a mile or better deep.
No, I hasn't got a notion
    To go huntin' down there,
For Apache won't go with me --
    Neither one will take a dare.

" At night there's awful wailin',
    And I cannot rightly tell
If it be a pack o'wildcats
    Or the ghost o'"Sage Bush' Nell;
But the bronc will stand and listen
    At the caterwaulin' din,
Then he'll do a bit of pitchin'
    And he'll wink at me, and grin.

I opine he knows she's sleepin'
    In the canyon -- but of course
He has never told me, Bozo,
    Bein' nothin' but a hoss.

It was silent on the mesa
    At the Cross-Bar-Lazy-B,
When Foreman, Wild Hoss Charley
    Told this lovely tale to me.

Casino Sam

Casino Sam went a ridin' up the cactus trail
    alone--
His cayuse flat and runnin' like hell
    from Sanantone.
A headin' for the ranges where a trail is
    hard to find--
A ridin' like the devil, leavin' Sanantone
    behind.

Of all the orn'ry varmints ever livin'
    in the sand,
Casino Sam could give 'em spades and hold
    the winnin' hand.
A breed of border mixture one could never
    well describe--
Who made his draw behind your back--
    You know his sneakin' tribe.

And so he sought the ranges, for as
  witness of his kind
A man lay dead in Anson's place--
  Shot in the back--from behind;
And a dark eyed woman sobbin' hugged
  the form, and through her tears
She vowed a woman's vengeance though
  the trail led on for years.

Casino Sam went ridin' up the trail
  from Sanantone--
A ridin' like the devil -- but he didn't
  go alone.

Two forms came down the cactus and the
  first one lay across
The saddle like a bag of sand, roped to
  a worried hoss;
The thing was cold and stiffened -- the
  eyes a-starin' blind,
And in the back a gaping wound fired from
  a gun -- behind.

The second rider, weary, but smilin' through
> her tears
Dismounted at the endin' of a trail she'd
> rode for years;
A worn and silent woman who passed into
> the night
With eyes flashin' carbon but her hair a
> snowy white.

Casino Sam came ridin' through the sage
> to Sanantone--
Come back from out the ranges on a trail
> he'd never known--.
A headin' for a country where a trail is
> hard to find--
A ridin' like the devil, leavin' Sanantone
> behind.

The Cruise of the Espinosa.

I simply pass the story told by Narraganset Bill--
    Who sailed the Espinosa from Galveston to Brazil.
Oh! --
The wind was blowin' narsty, an' the breakers rollin' high,
    An' the lightnin' were presistent, kinda fallin' from the sky
Through the sheets of rain a-tearin' by the riggin' with a fuss
    That made the night a hellion, an' I've never seed a wuss.

So ----
    We went a nosin' careful, sort-a creepin' out the bay,
        With dynamite for Blanco and some oil for Uruguay;
    Our orders had us stoppin' at the Gulf of Guayaquil--
        Proceedin' to Bahia, in the province of Brazil.

Well ----

We hit the ocean proper with weather sort-a ca'med,

    But I didn't like the looks of things so Billy-will-be-dammed;

Fer I never seed assembled such an ugly, ornery crew

    From ev'ry port an' nation, an' ev'ry breed an' hue.

    Fer ----

    They ranged from Slav an' Polack down to mangy Portuguees --

        A noble band of cut-throats an' scum from seven seas;

    But we legged it down the channel to the Caribbean sea

        With the Espinosa steppin', sir,'s han'some as c'ld be.

Well----

We passed the ditch an' made it to the Gulf of Guayaquil

    Where we shipped ten thousan' rifles fer Bahia -- in Brazil--

Yes - we shipped ten thousan' rifles from the Gulf of Guayaquil--

    An' a lady--fer Bahia--in the province of Brazil.

    So ----

    It made me sort o' nervous with a lady in my care

        An' the dynamite an' rifles an' a pirate crew -- I'll swear

    That the only human bein' in the bunch 's I relate

        Was a Swede named Ole Jorgessen who was shippin' as the mate.

Yes ----

Ev'ry thing was pintin' fer the lightnin' soon ter strike,

    Fer the rats begin to scamper all aroun' uneasy like--

An' a gull it kep' a-lightin' on the for'ad deck that day,

    Though I done my bloomin' damdest fer to scare the thing away.

Then ----

I smelt a mess of trouble when we crossed the Capicorn,

    Beatin' down the coast of Chile fer a run aroun' the Horn--

Fer the mongrel crew were singin' of a pirate ditty bold

    That made my heart go thumpin' an' my blood run kinda cold.

"Oh! it's forty thousan' fathoms-
    Fer the Cap'n an' the mate-
Yes, it's forty thousan' fathoms-
    Be it soon, er be it late;
Fer av'ry thing's a-front us
    An' there's nothin' left behind-
So it's forty thousan' fathoms
    Fer the Cap'n an' his kind.

So ----

I run two lines of fuses from my cabin -- out of sight--
    To the caps attach'd an' ready in the hold of dynamite,
An' I kep' two life belts handy--one fer Narraganset Bill--
    An' tother fer the lady--booked Bahia--in Brazil.

And----

Things commenced to happen when we neared Magellan Strait--
    Fer they mutinied--the devils--an' they killed the bloomin' mate-
So I lit the pair of fuses when they started huntin' me--
    Put a life belt on the lady an' we slipped into the sea.

An' ----

They never seed us goin' fer it was a dirty night,
    An' we dropped astern some thankful at their disappearin' light-
An' the curses growin' fainter as they rushed the cabin door--
    Then our ear-drums fairly busted in a hell-rip-rarin'-roar.

An' ----

The good ship Espinosa with her hull all ripped an' torn
    Went to Davy Jone's locker wes' by sou'wes' of the Horn.
An' the Lady? Well, I'm happy to explain...is Mrs. Bill,
    An' we own a fine plantation near Bahia--in Brazil.

Then ----

I learned Bill is a cowpuncher forty miles from Albuquerque
    Who has never seen a breaker or been near the raging sea;
So I've formed a calm conclusion from the story he relates:
    He's the most prolific liar in these whole United Sattes.

So ----

    I simply pass the story of a voyage most forlorn,
        That sunk the Espinosa wes' by sou'wes' of the Horn.

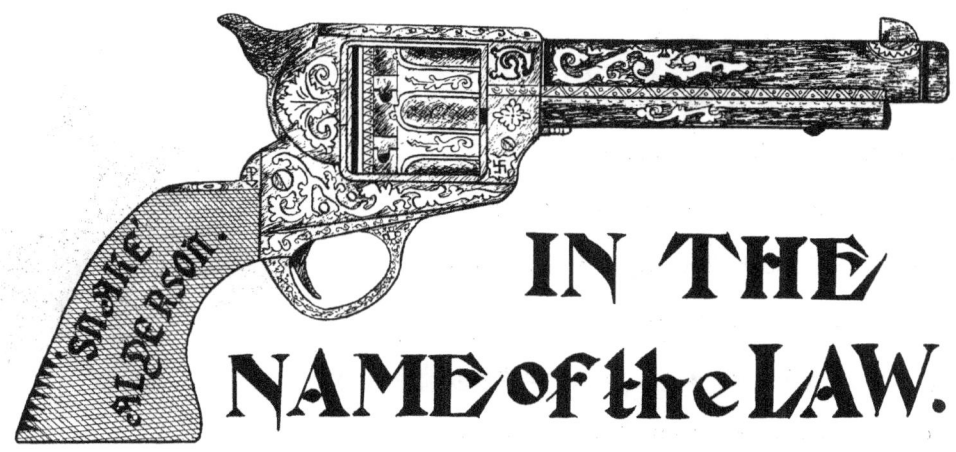

IN THE NAME of the LAW.

'Snake' Alderson watched from the side of his eyes
    And grinned like his labor was fun;
He glanced at the trail where it met with the skies-
    And filed a new notch on his gun;
He studied each one (there were seven in all)
    And showed he was bursting with pride--
As slowly his mind wandered back to recall-
    How each of his victims had died.

The first was for Williams -down there in Madrone-
    The second for Welch in Rodel;
The third for a herder near Paso del Lone,
    The fourth for a puncher named Bell;
The fifth for a youth he had shot in Sedan,
    The sixth an old codger named Vance;
The seventh, a boy - not a one of the clan
    Had ever been given a chance.

He slowly arose, looked around him and strode
    To the bronc that was waiting near by-
Then mounted the tough, little, pinto and rode-
    Up the trail where it met with the sky;
With a short, easy lope he swung over and down-
    The slope to the valley below-
And racing his bronc he swept into the town
    Like an arrow twanged swift from a bow.

Straight on to the place where he knew he would find-
    A drink for the thirst of his breast-
A killer by choice that sometimes had their kind-
    In the old fashioned, gun-slinging West;
"Wake Up!" he yelled out--"I have rid all th' way
    This day from th' Paso del Mar;
Back Up! Every hombre -- I'm aimin' to say-
    Th' 'Snake' drinks alone at th' bar."

" 'Snake' Alderson speaks --If there's any kaint hear,
    Or thinks that I'm mebbe in fun--
I'll tickle th' drum of his slow workin' ear,
    With th' crack of my favorite gun;
I'm rarin' to shoot and I'm rarin' to kill,
    I'm drinkin' alone at th' bar;
'Snake' Alderson, gents, who's a hell of a pill
    And comes from th' Paso del Mar."

A man sauntered in through the wide open door-
    And stopped while he glanced through the room-
Then slowly advanced down the uneven floor-
    To the bar and it's threatening doom;
"Stand back!" Yelled the 'Snake', "ain't you heerd me declaim?
    "I'm rarin' and set fer a draw!"
The other man spoke --"You are under arrest-
    I come-- IN THE NAME OF THE LAW."

The room was as still as a tomb at the word-
    The 'Snake' watched his man like a cat;
He made no reply, like perhaps he's not heard-
    And the rest of us wondered at that;
The stranger was slight but his manner was cool-
    His guns hung far back and too high-
It seemed he was taking that chance of a fool-
    Who came on the scene just to die.

'Snake' Alderson grinned;" So you're aimin' to take
    Me pard --is that what you demand?
Th' hombre that's takin' th' person of 'Snake'
    Ain't borned --so yo're law can be damned;"
"**I'm sayin'**", the stranger spoke quiet and low-
    With a queer little jerk of his head-
"I've come for your person--I reckon you'll go
    Along with me peaceful - or dead."

He stood like a man who's not aiming to fight-
    His thumbs sort of hooked in his vest-
His guns still behind hanging high and too tight
    For the game he was aiming to test
Then 'Snake' shot his right to the gun that had dealt
    Out death to the seven before-
But it never moved out from it's place in his belt-
    For he fell, like a rock, to the floor

Two shots rang out but they sounded as one-
    The stranger stood easy, at rest,
While the slow, curling smoke drifted up from his guns
    He'd drawn like a flash from his breast.
"You'll witness," he said with a slow, easy drawl,
    "I beat Mister 'Snake' to the draw--
While he was resistin' - in front of you all-
    Arrest -- IN THE NAME OF THE LAW."

ALKALI PHIPPS

I'd pen the sad story of Alkali Phipps
    Who toted a smoky on each of his hips
And spread consternation on annual trips
    From Carson to old San Jacinto.
A killing to him was a time honored joke
    He simply delighted to see people croak
And, leaving behind him a trail of blue smoke
    He cantered along on his Pinto.

He'd ride out of line any time, any day,
    To scrape up a rumpus or stage a gun play;
And boy - how he'd perforate gents in the fray
    Was something quite foreign to reason.
You could very near follow the route he essayed
    By the newly made mound or the freshly used spade-
A certain result of this man-eater's trade
    Who knew neither mercy nor reason.

An' bad?

    Gracious lad;

        With the habits he had

No person was safe from this lead slinging bad

    Gazook of the plains who, with debonair air

Loped along while the wind sighed it's way through his hair-

    And his mustaches streamed from his tan beaten face

Like a seal in the desert - somewhat out of place.

    But sad was the day

When he wended his way

    And swooped like a cyclone on Old Santa Fe.

With his horse running flat and his guns smoking free

    He came into town like a flying banshee -

And spying a bar with a wide open door

    Rode cockily in and leaped down to the floor;

Rode jauntily in and leaped down to the floor-

    Nor dreamed that in the leaping his prestage was o'er;

Ah Alkali Phipps, adios, au-revoir.

It chanced that a party named Terrence O'Dade-
  Who sold baby ribbon in Spigels' Arcade-
(A mild little whiffet the color of jade)
  Was eating his lunch plain and frugal-
Cared not for the wrath of this menacing foe-
  And liked not the tread of Alkali's show-
So -- fully decided he planted a blow
  Smack-dab on the wild actor's bugle.

And Alkali sat-
  Unbecoming and flat-
He wonkled his winkers and felt for his hat;
  While O'Dade threw the smokys out into the street-
Helped the man-killing demon up onto his feet
  And planted a kick where a kick should be placed
And again on the highways of Santa Fe raced.

One Alkali Phipps - but this time in the lead
  And but one thought posessed him,
    'twas speed--damit--speed.

And run---

   Did he run?

      Why the son-of-a-gun

Threw sand thirty yards to the rear by the ton;

   It ended when Terrence went back to his frills

And Alkali Phipps gained the sheltering hills.

   He wouldn't come back for his horse it is said

But paid a young greaser to get it instead-

   And the horse gave a horrified snort of disgust

When he looked at his master--

   And fled through the dust.

So now in the Army one Alkali Phipps

   Goes booming along with a song on his lips;

A song on his lips and his mouth full of gum-

   In the Salvation Army he beats the bass drum;

With a aboom-ta-da-boom

   He inveigles the scum

Of the streets by the boom

   Of his mighty bass drum;

The boom-ta-da-boom

   Of his trusty bass drum.

The Relay

Old Jepp Todd, the faithful, rode a relay with the mail;
    Ridin' west from Larned on the old Santa Fe trail,
Ridin' west from Larned toward the town of Santa Fe,
    Goin' down through Syracuse, he took it on it's way.
Changin' mounts at stations designated on the trail,
    Keepin' up a relay with the U. S. Mail.

Took a man of iron and a copper-bottomed hoss,
    Ridin' out the coulees and the prairie far across;
Fightin' heat and blizzards, thieves and Injuns too,
    Took a man of iron if the mail kept goin' through;
Took a man of nerve and iron on the Santa Fe trail,
    Keepin' up a relay with the U. S. Mail.

Used to hear 'em tellin' it. He'd come swingin' in,
    Ridin' like the mischief with a quiet sort a grin,
Springin' from the saddle for a transfer of his trust.
    On again and gone again amid a cloud of dust,
On again and gone again down a dusty trail
    Keepin' up a relay with the U.S. Mail.

Half a dozen Injuns from Abo canyon pass,

    Sneakin' to an ambuscade, reptiles in the grass,

Hid their wiry mustangs in a coulee out of sight,

    Stealthy in their movements as a shadow in the night;

Hidin' in the coulees for a dash upon the trail-

    Waitin' for a relay with the U. S. Mail.

When the fight was over, half a dozen Injuns lay

    Dead and dyin' on the trail that led to Santa Fe.

Riderless, their mustangs roamed searchin' all the plain,

    Waitin' for their masters who'd never ride again.

Watched a single horseman disappearin' down the trail,

    Ridin' to the Westward with the U. S. Mail.

Old Jepp Todd is comin' along, swingin' into town,

    Swayin' in the saddle with his head a-hangin' down;

Swayin' in the saddle, 'till it seemed he'd lose his place,

    Ridin' to the station with a sickly grinnin' face;

Crimson red a-drippin' to the sands along the trail--

    Dyin' in the saddle with the U.S. Mail.

Mistah Buzzahd Explanes.

Mistah Buzzard flew long—
   Mistah Buzzard flew high—
Till he's only a spec'
   In de blue ob de sky;
An' de uther birds axed
   Mistah Buzzard jes' why
Dat he sails so fer up—
   In der top ob de sky?

An' he wink an' he wonk—
   An' he woggle he's haid—
An he preened ob hisself—
   Den he ruffl'd an' sed—
" Ah sails mase'f up
   An' ah sails mase'f high—
Caus' ah wants ter innspec',
   An' dats' how an' dat's why.

An' each bird what heard—
    Shook a shake ob de haid—
At de wisdom ob what
    Mistah Buzzard hed sed—
Which was only der way—
    He was usin' ter say—
" Ef ah wants ter sail high—
    In de blue ob de sky—
Ah haint sayin' when—
    An ah haint axin' why—
Ef ah rabbit dodge in—
    Er a rabbit dodge out—
Ah haint axin' him—
    What he's dodgin' erbout;
When de hawk's sailin' low—
    Er he circl's an' wheels—
Ah haint axin' him—
    What he's got in he's heels;

" As frien's, ah erknowledge
    Ah like yo all fine—
But— ten to yo bizness—
    An' ah'll ten ter mine;
It's moughty ol' sayin'—
    Ah'm quotin' ter yo—
Ef yo min' yo own bizness—
    Yo've got plenty ter do."

DRIFTIN', JEST A-DRIFTIN'.

I miss the silver jingle of your spur
    And th' sweet mountain winds of home.
My ol' hoss is longin' for th' home corral
    Yes - lonesome - I kinda hates to own.
Oh the prairie dogs aire barkin'
    And th' buffalo grass is gettin' green.
Mavericks and slick-ears all are tallied -
    Sech a bunch of long-horns you never seen.

White bleached bones th' desert's toll,
    Down here in th' sage brush and sand.
The rattler curls in th' yucca' shade,
    As buzzards circle the Rio Grande.
Chili Pickers from over th' border,
    With grinnin' teeth an' coal-black hair,
Rangin' like a pack of lone coyotes
    Lookin' fer eats and a hidden lair.

Th' boss is smilin' rather sum'tious
    As he sniffs at th' mornin' air.
Mought be a little rain in th' offin'-
    Gilas aire a-sunnin' here an' there.
Yu ringtails stop your millin'
    Fer I'm feelin' pretty wolfish now.
Hev lost the makins' in th' shuffle -
    With ol' Buckskin lookin' fer a row.

There's no use of yu a-snortin'-
    On hatred an' loco yu seem to be fed.
I'ma sure gona try and ride yu,
    A sun-fishin' an' a duckin' yore head.
There's no use of yu a-rompin'
    Like a fat yearlin' on th' range;
I'll wrap these rowels aroun' yu till yu
    Look like a Chihuahua-dog with th' mange.

Guess I'll be headin' fer th' home ranch.
    Pard, don't yu weep no tears fer me.
Goin' back to th' land of Diamond hitches
    Th' mountains blue and th' pinon-trees.
Yu kin play aroun' with th' rattlers,
    Herd your longhorns in th' chapparral.
But me an' my ol' hoss is driftin',
    Jest a-driftin', back to th'
        ol' home corral.

The Coyote's Lonely Call.

Evening alone on the prairie--
    The last faint ray of light.
Slowly the stars in heaven
    Peep forth from the depths of night,
With only the whispering breeze,
    And the coyote's lonely cry.
I seek my blanket and saddle
    And wrapped in gentle slumber lie.

Gone are the lonesome trails,
    Gone are the cares of day,
Nighthawks dip in the turquoise sky,
    As I dream the hours away.
A horde of phantom riders
    Spur across the starlit waste.
Herds of ghostly longhorn cattle
    Stampede in a misty haste.

    Dew drops gather on the yucca blade,
        The moon rises in all her glory,
    Touching the coulees with mystic tone
        The camp-fire embers whisper a story.
    The bronc browses on the grama green.
        Again the coyote's lonely cry,
    As I gather closer my blanket
        And wrapped in gentle slumber lie.

Jog On, Jehoshaphat!

Road gets rougher every mile;
   (Cluck) Jog on, Jehoshaphat, an'
      show some style.
Mule gone lame an' hens won't lay;
   Corn's way down an' wheat don't pay;
Hogs no better, steers too cheap;
   Cows quit milkin', meat won't keep;
Oats all heated, spuds all froze;
   Fruit crop's busted, wind still blows;
Sheep seem puny, an' I'll be durned,
   Rye fields flooded an' the haystacks burned.
Looks some gloomy, I'll admit--
   (Cluck) Jog on, Jehoshaphat, we
      ain' down yet.

Coal's in high an' crops in low;

   Rail rates doubled, got no show;

Money's tighter, morals loose;

   Bound to get us--what's the use?

Sun's not shinin' as it ought to should;

   Moon ain't lightin' like it could if 'twould

Air seems heavy; water punk;

   Tests your mettle; shows yer spunk;

No use stoppin' to de-bate--

   (Cluck) Jog on, Jehoshaphat, it's

      gettin' late.

   Wheels all wobble, axle's bent;

      Dashboard's broken, top all rent;

   One shaft splintered, t'other sags;

      Seat's all busted, end-gate drags;

   May hang t'gether--believe it will;

      Careful drivin' I'll make it still;

   Road's some better--not so rough--

      TROT! Gosh ding ye! That's the stuff.

   Old trap's movin' right good speed--

      (Cluck) Jog on, Jehoshaphat, you're

         some good steed.

   Road's smoothed out 'till it don't

      seem true--

      (Cluck) Jog on, Jehoshaphat, you

      pulled us through!

The Rattlesnake

I live my life in the desert
    I bask in the morning sun-
I sleep in the shade of the cactus blade
    When my search for food is done.

    I pal with the dogs of the Mesa-
        Along with the solemn owl-
    Queer friends are we--as assorted three-
        Of quadruped, serpent, fowl.

    We live in the self-same shelter
        Nor dream of a tenant's strife
    No jealous care may enter there
        To rule our domestic life.

I am hated, despised and stricken-
    A reptile of dire offence-
But my rattlers tell of fluid hell-
    In the fangs of my one defense.

I am blind through the heated summer
    And long for the cool return
Of days to be when again I'll see
    Those foes that I sense and spurn.

Hate on as you've always hated
    And curse me with every breath
But step with care in my humble lair-
    For the price I exact is death.

I live my life in the desert
    I bask in the morning sun,
I love the shade of the cactus blade
    When the cool of the day is done.

The Ranger's Old Six-Gun

I sleep in rust neath a coat of dust
    Hanging over the old fireplace at rest
For my owner's gone with the countless throng
    And the "tough ones" who tamed the West;
But I dream on anew those old days through
    And only wish they might return to me
With an old bowie, **holster** and cartridge belt
    On the self same peg to share my sympathy.

The coyotes yelp from the sage-brush hills
    That skirt the Sangre del Cristo base,
And the cresent moon awakes from gloom
    The old black bear's trysting place;
I muse again on the hunting, when
    The white-tail deer moved in bands
And the mule-tail roamed 'long the Cimarron
    By the edge of the silvered sands.

And the turkey-hen's broods in the cottonwoods
    That fringe the wild-oat fields?
      The catamounts cry in the chilly fall night
When the hoar-frost nips and steals?
    The bald-eagle soars as in days of yore
Above old Cimarron canyon's dark rim,
    And the bull-elk graze 'mid the mountain haze
On the Rockies ragged, tall and grim.

Bygone Days Of The Old West

I have seen the West when its days were best,
    I've heard Cimarron's gun-battles roar,
And I've followed the rustlers o'er many a trail
    I surely long for those days once more.
I've camped a spell in a mountain dell
    Where plain and mountain meet,
Where the gray wolf howls, the bob-cat prowls
    The slopes of the timbered steep.

From the Rio Grande down to "No-man's Land"
    Led countless old cattle trails,
In thousands strong this mighty throng
    Once tramped the river swales,
This golden time of my youth and prime
    Through the dimming past I see
My master's hand and a winning smile
    To share my sympathy.

THE CIMARRON CANYON.

A great, long range,
    In formation strange,
A thousand tints in its hue;
    With peaks so high
They touch the sky
    And silence comes to you.

A crystal spring,
    Where mosses cling-
A bird sings soft and sweet;
    A fragrant flower
In a shady bower
    That's safe from human feet.

A cliff, deep down,
    Where shadows frown,
And a scrub-pine tall and drear;
    A lake; a grove;
A river cove,
    With rapids cold and clear.

An awesome sight,
    Mixed with delight,
A glimpse of the Great Recall;
    There's thought sublime
In this work of time,
    And a mystery over all.

ROCKY MOUNTAIN CANARY.

Sometimes I git to thinkin'
    Thet they mebbe made yuh wrong.
Yo're body short an' stumpy,
    An' yo're ears so cussed long;
Yo're allers kinder wooly,
    An' yo're allers half asleep
An' eatin' weeds an' cactus
    Like yuh might been born a sheep.

Sometimes I git t' thinkin'
    Mebbe yuh air mighty wise,
An' seein' more'n I do
    Out yo'r drowsy lookin' eyes.
Mebbe yuh air knowin'
    More'n folks at twict yo'r age,
Whilst a-browsin' in th' cactus
    Er a-leanin' on the sage.

But whenever I'm a seein'
    Sech a funny, lazy bein',
Lookin' like yuh ain't carin'
    If th' world is out o' plumb,
Why, I allers start grinnin';
    Fer it's recent I'm beginnin'
T' admit yo'r ways air winnin' –
    Yo'r so careless like, an' dumb.

An' so, when I'm a-seein'

    Yo'r lazy, sleepy bein' -

Lettin' on yuh ain't a-knowin'

    Of a thing, I know I'm wrong

If I'm thinkin' yuh ain't keerin';

    Seein' everything an' hearin'

With them ears so cussed long.

Sometimes when I get lonesome,

    I'm free t' own an' say

I'm allers mighty thankful

    When yuh opens up to bray.

It's like a band o' music --

    T' drive away my care;

T' hear thet 'hee-haw-honk-ee'

    Come a-floatin' thru th' air.

An' so when I'm a-hearin'

    Yo'r voice, my mind gits clearin'.

I wanter keep yuh, pardner,

    Jest t' lissen to yo'r song;

I like t' know yo'r gazin'

    At th' cattle whilst they're grazin';

An' yo'r list'nin down th' canyon

    With yo'r ears so cussed long.

Silver Plume

    Long before the white man
        Sought the valleys of New Mexico
    Came a tribal people
        And established their Pueblo-
    Came a tribal people
        With their Chieftian Standing Buffalo-
    In a fertile valley
        Neath the range tops capped with snow.

Thunder Bird was kindly,
> Sending rain to make the grasses grow—
Golden maize and chili-red
> Waved in the breezes to and fro—
Smiling on his people
> Was the God of Mercy--Manitou--
Smiling on the valley
> Where the crystal waters flow;

Silver Plume, the mighty,
> Swiftest runner in the tribal band—
Son of Standing Buffalo
> And suitor for a maiden's hand—
E'en the hand of White Deer
> Fairest creature in the valley land—
Pride was he of every one
> Within the council stand.

Princess maid was White Deer
> In the lodges of the San Juan—
Lithe of limb and graceful
> With the carriage of a leaping fawn—
Glad indeed the suitor
> She would deign to smile with favor on—
Glad indeed was Silver Plume—
> As birds are glad at dawn;

On the Rio Grande

    They would sing the Indian lover's song-

Minor strains of wildwood

    As he drove the bark canoe along,

Skimming o'er the waters

    Lined with banks where blooming roses throng

Or forming sturdy moccasins

    From tanned doe-skin and thong.

Dream on man and maiden

    While the sun of day is shining bright-

Thrill with fervent glances

    In the mystic of lover's light-

From the silent mountains

    With their lofty tops of gleaming white-

Soon will come a shadow

    That will change the dawn to night.

THE UNREST OF STANDING BUFFALO.

TOM TOM TOM TOM TOM TOM TOM -

    Assemble the council-too long have we waited-

    In peaceful pursuits will we linger no more;

    The lust born of conquest has never abated-

    'Twas born in our fathers so long gone before;

Assemble the warriors - the braves of my people-
The war dance is on - let no hand feel restraint-
The Totem Pole trembles from ground to the steeple-
My braves dance in scalp-lock and feathers and paint,
Then off to the hills and the valleys surrounding-
No matter if conquest be near us or far-
We follow the paths of our fathers confounding
The tribes who would battle--our council is WAR.

THE FAMINE AND PLAGUE.

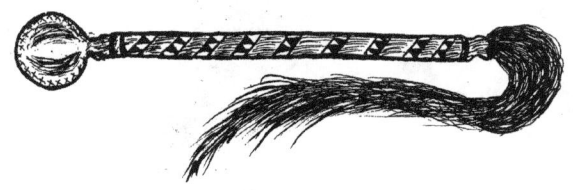

No longer the maize in the valley is growing-
No longer the roses bloom out on the hills-
No longer the ripple of clear waters flowing
In musical rhythm from turbulent rills;
The grasses are brown and the horses are dying-
The earth void of life as a hard beaten crust-
The loam of the fields lying dormant and drying
The wind driven volumes of powder-like dust;
The water holes fail and the game has retreated-
While famine and want through the valley attend-
And pestilence stalks down the trail undefeated-
The wrath of the Gods seem to on htem decend.

BIG MEDICINE.

TOM TOM TOM TOM TOM TOM TOM -
   In the council chamber sat the
Chiefs of Standing Buffalo.
   Sat in solemn council -
Faces drawn in matters grave;
   Starting on a mission
To the mighty man of medcine
   In the mountain fastness
Was a young and sturdy brave;
   Silver Plume, the runner,
Was intrusted to the finding
   And to learn what sacrifice
The tribal rites must show
   To atone for war-like deeds
That brought drouth and famine
   And provoked the wrath to fall
     From mighty Manitou;

When the second sun had passed
    Across the valley staggered
Silver Plume, the runner,
    With an answer from the scribe-
The angry God demanded
    That a human life be offered
From the mighty warriors
    Of the erstwhile erring tribe;

And the one their wrath demanded
    Pay the debt of sacrifice
Would be chosen in a manner
    Such as this--
The fairest of the maidens-
    Knowing not the price it meant
Should greet the one to pay it
    With a kiss.

Then Silver Plume and the chieftians
    Left the tribal hall
Each one in thoughtful silence
    Deep, profound-
And lo — the mighty runner
    In a stumbling manner fell
Exhausted as he sank upon the ground.

(And the mighty man of medcine

    In the fastness of the hills

Brewed mystic herbs

    That cast a magic spell-

And muttered incantations

    As the kettle seethed and boiled

At the moment when the sturdy runner fell.)

THE KISS.

Ah--White Deer, it were better

    Had your wig-wam hid from view

The fallen lover lying

    Like a beacon calling you-

How could you know the greeting

    That you placed upon his brow

In worried love would mark him

    For the sacrifice and now--

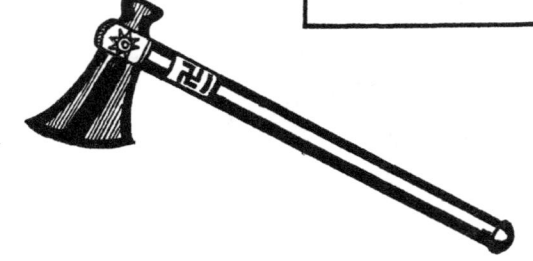

The Chieftians grave have turned away-
　　The light of day has flown-
And for a lingering, blissful hour
　　Your love is all your own-
Enjoy then for as the sun
　　Shows in the East at dawn
The flashing blade will claim it's own
　　And love's sweet dream be gone:

TOM----TOM----TOM

　　Slowly the moccasined feet to the altar
Step to the time of the Tom-tom's refrain-
　　Lighting the East came the sun or the morning
Bathing in splendor the mountains and plains.
　　Silver Plume, straight as the shaft of an arrow,
Son of a chieftian and worthy the part-
　　Stood like a statue to pay the atonement-
Taking the swift flashing steel in his heart.
　　Came then a cry from the rock over the river-
Timed to the stroke of the death dealing blow-
　　White Deer sprang clear and the graceful leap ended
Deep in the waters that gurgled below.

Bygone Days Of The Old West

If you should chance to be passing at evening
    Near the place of the leap and the blow—
Out on the waters when shadows have fallen
    You should be hearing their love song I know;
In the canoe, phantom like, they are drifting
    On through the night to eternity's shore—
He who gave life for the good of his people—
    She who gave life for the love that she bore.

"Mex" From Over The Border.

"Mex" from over the border
    Was yellow, the boys all bet,
He and his Pinto pony
    That answered t' Cigarette.
He hired as extra rider
    To carry the U.S. Mail,
When the Pony Express was makin'
    The old Santa Fe trail.

"Mex, look out for the 'Paches
    In the canyon; don't forget."
"Senors", replied Martinez,
    "Me, I have Cigarette!"
He swung to the western saddle;
    Say, boys, how that pony ran!
He entered the walled-in canyon;
    The race with death began.

For the 'Paches were lyin' in waitin'
  With bowstrings strained and taut,
Half hidden behind the boulders;
  That's how the Apaches fought!
Like a part of the horse he was ridin',
  Crouched to his pony's mane,
"On faster," he urged, and faster
  The arrows sung again, again,

Twas a sudden lurch in the saddle
  That tugged at the bridle's bit,
Twas a half-sobbed word to his pony
  That snowed the man was hit.
Then over the blue camisa
  There trickled a crimson stain
That dripped from the dusky fingers
  Grippin' the bridle rein!

But closer he sat in the saddle,
    Plyin' the spur and quirt;
Thought of the mail he carried
    And scorned the mortal hurt,
For, though they had dubbed him "yellow",
    Noble's the ride he made,
With the point of a 'Pache arrow
    Under his shoulder blade!

As they sat in the father station,
    Awaitin' the comin' mail
And the relay pony was ready
    Facing the Western trail,
They heard the horse a-neighin,
    Gallopin' hoofs sound tread
Then "Mex" from over the border
    Fell from the saddle dead!

THE PINES

Did you ever hear the pine trees singin'
    In the dreamy quiet of the evening moon,
Their murmur in tones subdued,
    As they whisper their mountain tune?

    Playing to the summer sunshine,
        Defying the long winter storms.
    Giant sentinels of the mountains
        Carryin' on their everlastin' charms.

In boyhood days I have wandered
   Beneath their towering shade,
And listened to their droning --
   ·Sweetest mountain music ever made.

   They would strum a love song,
      Swayed by rhythm of breezes divine.
   Needles sparkling in the moonlight,
      The cones gently keepin' time.

   They sleep in peaceful silence
      'Neath the sky of turquoise blue.
   Monarchs of the mountain forest,
      My love dreams are all for you.

THAT DAD-BURNED LITTLE PEA

The Chink was washing windows
    At the Cross-Bar Lazy-B,
When the foreman, Wild Hoss Charley,
    Pulled his queue and said to me:

"I was ridin' fence one winter
    Fer a ranch down Cimarron way,
An' I'm savin' up my buckos
    Fer a trip to Santa Fe.
Had a plumb good stake, I'm tellin',
    Fer a puncher, when I quit,
As I'm gettin' tired an' aimin'
    Fer to mill around a bit.

"So I hits the sage an' cactus,
    Feelin' fine an' ridin' free,
Cravin' action, pard--fence ridin'
    Never did agree with me.
So I bumps into a circus
    Down at Albuquerque one day,
An' it sorta gets me goin'
    When th' bands begins ter play.

"So I figures I'm a-stayin'
    Fer the show; an' so I went
To the lot out on the commons
    Where the outfit had its tent;
An' I sees a crowd a-standin'
    At a table where a zeek
Is rakin' in the lucre,
    So I sorta takes a peek.

"An' he's got a pea a-rollin'
    With a funny little shell;
An' he's bettin' not a bozo
    In th' bunch of us c'n tell
Where the little pea's a-hidin';
    But, I'm watchin' clost, I swear,
An' I bets him fifty buckos--
    But the dam thing wasn't there.

"Well I keeps a-tryin', tryin',
   'Till I've lost three hundred men;
An' I'm gettin' sorter leery
   Of his game right there and then;
So I tells him Ca'm and certain--
   Nothin' showin' in my tones--
That I'll go him one more bingle
   Fer a cool six-hundred bones.

"An' his grin is sorta leerin'
   As he nods he's takin' me;
Then he starts a-doin' capers
   With that dad-burned little pea.
So I pulls my "smoky" easy
   From my belt, and when he's done
I opine the one it's under
   With th' muzzle of my gun.

"An' remarkin', sorta casual
   That I hope it's there, because
I'm gettin' sorta nervous--
   And, by thunder, pard it was!
Yeah, I got my roll, I'm sayin',
   And a lot of sad abuse!
Fer the elephants stampeded
   And the tigers all got loose.

When the fight was goin' noble,
    An' I sees my chance to go,
I mounts my bronc, Apache,
    And we heads fer Mexico.

A form went out the window
    With the quickness of a wink
As the foreman, Wild Hoss Charley,
    Threw a saddle at the Chink.

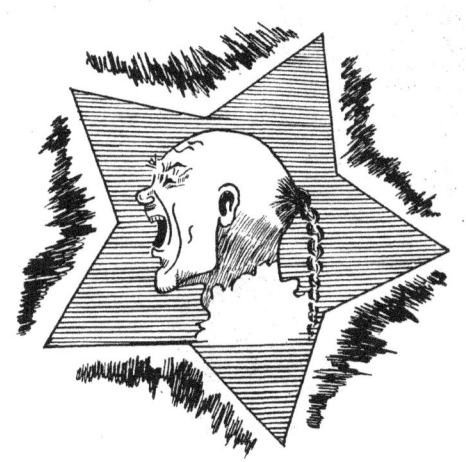

THE COYOTE.

We was making rawhide ropes

At the Cross-Bar Lazy B,

When the foreman, Wild Hoss Charley

Took an extra hitch and said to me:

"It ain't so much of a tale at that,

But it tickled the folks of Medcine Flat,

And rid the town of The Coyote Bat,

A killer from down the Pecos;

It only shows you never can call

The way the cards in a game may fall,

And bluff won't win in a fight a-tall,

When it comes to a two-gun fracas.

"The coyote lit in the town one day,
   With an ornery look and a sneerin' way
And shows he's achin' to make a play,
   For the white of his eyes are showin';
And any one in the place can tell
   He's mighty tough and as mean as hell,
For the guns he wore had a deadly smell
   With their sixteen notches showin'.

"He wouldn't pay for a cussed thing
   That he ate or drank and he had the swing
Of a man who knew his skill was king,
   And killed for the love of killin',
So the months went by and his ugly face
   Took up too much of the open space
And kept the folks in the little place
   Afraid of their lives and millin'.

"A stranger ridin' from Abo Pass,
   Dropped in one day for a social glass,
He looked as awkward and as green as grass,
   While takin' his drink of likker;
The coyote, thinkin' as I suppose
   He'd run a bluff, to the stranger goes
And reachin' out to his sun-burned nose
   He twists it and gives a snicker.

"And then he reaches to make his draw,
    But pardner, lightnin' is slow and raw,
For the killer opens his mouth and saw
    Two guns that were surely aimin'
Direct and straight at his heavin' side,
    And the muzzles, pardner, were deep and wide
And the stranger behind 'em satisfied
    The way that his mouth's declaimin'.

"I DON'T know, skunk, if you'd really fight,
    But I'm aimin' to stay in this town tonight--
An' it's too damn' small--now get me right,
    Fer I'm awfully shy on jokin';
You've just ten minutes to hit the street,
    An' then I'm comin', so shake your feet,
An' lissen, pard, you had better meet
    Me heeled--and your guns a-smokin'.

"And so they met as the thing was planned.
    The Coyote, pardner, had filled his hand,
But the stranger walked in the yellow sand
    His guns in his belt, I'm tellin'.
But all at once like a lightnin' flash
    They both tore loose with a single crash,
And the killer's guns were knocked to smash
    And the Coyote skeered and yellin'.

"And then the stranger, as ca'm and free,
    Tossed both of his smokin' guns to me.
And speakin' low to the crowd, sez he,
    I'll show y' a bit of brandin'.
Then walkin' where the killer stood,
    He soaked him, pard, like a fighter would,
And knocked him clear of the sand a good
    Ten feet from the place he was standin'.

"And mebbe you think the crowd ain't wide
    And free a-takin' the stranger's side,
With The Coyote whipped 'til he sobbed and cried
    And begged for his life, I'm tellin';
The stranger told him to face the West,
    Then gave him a kick where it fitted best.
And pard, I never could hear the rest
    For the crowd and their crazy yellin'.

"No... it ain't so much of a tale at that,
    But it tickled the folks of Medcine Flat,
For that was the last of The Coyote Bat
    And that was the thing worth knowin';
And the stranger grinned as he rode away,
    And we've never known to this very day
Just who he was, but I'm free to say
    We wished him luck with his goin'.

The treading of the life-line--
We enter it at dawn--
With joyous youth we carry
The journey on and on;
With hope we reach the noontime--
Refreshing is the rest--
Then on and on and onward
We travel toward the West.

Oh, some are on the high road;
    Others take the low;
And some are crowned with lustre,
    While some but dimly glow;
It matters not the brilliance,
    Or brightness of the flame,
The high road or the low road,
    The ending is the same.

The treading of the life-line--
    We enter it at dawn--
The youth we spurned--behind us--
    And years are creeping on;
With shattered hope--and weary--
    We cling unto the flight,
Commencing with the dawning
    And ending with the night.

Don't know why I feel so lonesome,
    Moon is shining clear and bright;
Cattle are all resting easy,
    But I just can't sleep tonight.
There's no cactus in my blankets,
    Don't know why they feel so hard,
Maybe because Rambling Jim is singing
    Annie Lowery on the guard.

Oh, how I wish he'd quit it;
    Couldn't sleep now if I tried
Makes the night seem long and lonesome
    And my heart is stilled inside.
How my darling used to sing it
    And it sounded sweet and gay,
Nights I'd take her home from dances
    When the East was turning gray.

Her brow was like a snowdrift,
    Oh, her eyes a heavenly blue
And her face I still can see it,
    Smiling like the morning dew.
Her hands were soft and trembly
    That night beneath the trees;
When I told her that I loved her,
    That she was all the world to me.

Her folks thought I was wild and reckless,
    And unsettled, guess they were right-
For I went to punching cattle
    And I'm still at it tonight.
She finally married old Gambler Jim
    Who cared only for drink and cards
Wish Rambling Jim would quit singing
    Annie Lowery on the Guard.

I cannot stand his singing
    Of things that happened then,
The good old days have passed me
    Which will ne'er return again.
"Cook, wrangle up a little hot coffee
    It's my watch, I'm comin' Pard-
I'll stop that fool from singing-
    Annie Lowery on the Guard."

The Rustler's Last Retreat.

I reined my bronc at the rimrock's edge,
    Made camp in the grey mesquite.
White bleached bones, the desert's toll,
    Showed plain the rustler's last retreat.

Rusty bits and a booted spur,
    A winchester half buried in the sand.
Bullet marks on the rimrock wall—
    Another unwritten story in cattle-land.

    A running iron with a broken shank,
        Empty shells in the pack-rat's nest;
    A rawhide saddle deep with dust.
        A message scrawled on the rimrock crest.

"I gambled with Fate and lost,
    Looks as though my race is run.
Three shells left, a dry canteen,
    Old Pinto dead and a red-hot gun."

I sit by my campfire dreamin',
    Coyotes howl in the grey mesquite.
A picture appears on the rimrock wall,
    Showin' plain the rustler's last retreat.

HORSE SENSE

We were ready for the round-up
At the Cross-Bar Lazy B,
When the foreman, Wild Hoss Charley,
Ropes his bronc and says to me:

"There's a horse among a thousand,
   An' I'm cravin' to relate
That he's smarter, bo, than any
   Dad-burned puncher in the state.
An' there ain't no other reason
   I'm a-standin' here todya,
But because of his effection
   An' his foresight, as they say.

"He ain't usin' all his talent
    Jest to herd a bunch o' steers,
But excuse me, pard, a minit,
    While I wipe away my tears.
When I'm thinkin' what I owes him,
    An' of how he worships me,
It gits me, pard -- dawggonit--
    An' the weeps start flowin' free.

"For a friend like him, that's stickin'
    To a man through all his strife,
Is a jooel, bo, a jooel,
    When he up an' saves your life.
It happened in Arizony--
    When a blond, called Cactus Nell,
Rounds me up jest like a yearlin'
    An' she ropes me fer a spell.

"An' It's settled we'll be married,
    So I hits the tall mesquite
Fer t' go an' git th' license
    Over at th' county seat.
An' everything is bunko
    Till I'm ready to go back,
An' I mounts my bronc, Apache,
    Speakin' words t' make him track.

"But he's actin' sorter funny--
    Like he mebbe ain't agreed--
An' I'm worried, thinkin' mebbe
    That he's sorta off his feed.
But I keeps a-urgin', urgin';
    Then he heads th' other way
An' he braces out his pinons
    Like he's meanin' fer t' stay;

"So I finally lose my temper
    An' I digs him with a spur,
An' he's raisin' hell now, pardner,
    While I'm combin' out his fur.
An' I never seen sich pitchin'
    In my whole young life a-tall;
He does th' sunfish wiggle
    An' th' rest--he has 'em all--

"An' he's showin' me some others
    I opine is all his own.
Then he flops me, bo, an' kicks me,
    An' he busts my collar bone,
An' it's while I'm convalescin'
    In a hurry to get well,
San Antony Sam, from Texas
    Runs away with Cactus Nell.

"An' the honeymoon ain't over
    'Till he mounts his horse an' rid
To th' canyon, with his lasso,
    An' he hung hisself--he did.
So I figures that Apache
    Musta knowed how things'd be,
An' he showed his real effection
    By th' stand he took with me.

It was silent for a moment;
    Then Apache took a bite
From the leg of Wild Hoss Charley,
    When he cinched the saddle tight.

The Pack Rat

I sorter like a pack-rat--
    Comic little cuss--
Gathers up the pinons
    Without a bit of fuss.
Gathers up the pinons
    And stores 'em in the ground
I sorter like a pack-rat
    A caperin' round.

I sorter like a pack-rat;
    He allers leaves a sign
To tell me where the pinons
    Is buried - which is fine.
It takes him all the season
    To pack 'em to the hole
I sorter like a pack-rat,
    Bless his little soul!

I sorter like a pack-rat,
    They look so mighty wise;
An' somethin' like affection
    Comes shinin' from their eyes.
I never get so lonesome
    With one of them in sight
I sorter like a pack-rat
    When campin' out at night.

I sorter like a pack-rat;
    He's allers on the swap
He'll take what suits his fancy
    An' then he'll never stop
Until he brings you somethin'
    To take its place; I'll swear
I sorter like a pack-rat,
    They tote so cussed fair.

I sorter like a pack-rat;
    He's such a friendly cuss
A tendin' to his business
    Without a bit of fuss.
He gathers pinons fer me
    And stores 'em in a hole
I sorter like a pack-rat,
    Bless his little soul.

 # A Preacher of Cimarron.

It was in the early '70 a stage coach crossed the Ponil bridge
    Skirting along the foot hills just adjacent to the ridge,
Skirting along the foot hills with the ponies on the run-
    And they headed up the only street laid out in Cimarron.
With a flourish born of practice that bespoke the driver well,
    They stopped with due precision at the Old St. James hotel;
As the strangers alighted there was one whose dress proclaimed
    Him a servant of the gospel, from the East, as he declaimed,
And he wore a lid of beaver and a collar that was white-
    And he also wore a pleasant smile that told you he was right;
But his very first impression of the West was hard to tell-
    So we'll step along beside him as he enters the hotel,
Where we find some noted characters engaged in having fun--
    This, then, was his introduction to the town of Cimarron.

The first thing that fell on his most startled glance
  Was the striking nude form of a brother
On the top of a pool table giving a dance-
  One hand held a pistol, the other
A bottle of whiskey, the spectacle made
  Would startle tradition, (or shock it)-
Clay Allison danced, and the music was played
  On a mouth organ, blown by young Dave Crockett.
The dance being ended and Allison dressed
  The crowd with a whoop took it's place
At the bar, where each person with gusto expressed
  His pleasure with more or less grace.

The door softly opened and there in the frame
  The form of a greaser appeared-
A killer of note and one Ponchoe by name,
  A personage much to be feared.
For a moment a deep silence invaded the room
  Then Allison spoke to him, clear,
And his words sounded like a message of doom-
  "You hunting me, Ponchoe? I'm here."
The hands swiftly reached for the guns that they wore
  When a form stepped between them and said--
"There may be a way that you can settle this score
  Without any blood being shed"

'Twas the parson that talked and the guns were returned
   To their holsters and Ponchoe went out,
Securing his horse which he mounted and turned-
   Then suddenly wheeling about
He rode through the door where the tables were set,
   Dismounted and pulled up a chair-
And Allison promptly accepted the bet
   And likewise rode in on the dare.

At opposite sides of the table they sat-
   A game where the stake was their lives-
And each stirred his coffee, complacent, at that,
   With the barrels of their big 45s.
Their horses stood by while the meal was consumed
   Then each led his mount through the door
That led to the bar of the St. James saloon--
   Where the parson had stopped them before.

Then Crockett cut loose and shot out the lights;
   And Ponchoe and Allison fired;
And the crowd quickly rushed through the door
      from the fight
   And the guests sought their rooms and retired.

The bar-room was closed and locked up for the night
> Without more inspection, but when
Lambert opened next morning, the dawns early light
> Showed dimly the forms of two men;
The one was the cook, badly scared but alive,
> 'Neath the stove where he'd wedged himself in;
And Ponchoe, erect, with a big 45
> Against a chair, with a queer foolish grin;

> They went to his side, half expecting a shot
>> But stopped with a look of surprise-
> For the killer was dead and a neat little spot
>> Showed plain midway of his eyes.
> And this was the how-do-you-do handed out
>> To the Parson that witnessed the fun;
> So we only may guess his opinion about
>> The habits of gay Cimarron.

> But a sky-pilot in the old Western days
>> Must needs be a man to conform to it's ways;
> And just such a person was Tolby; his grace
>> Finally won him respect, and the smile on his face
> Was known on the range and the lowest of dives,
>> Bringing sunshine to all, speaking God to their lives--
> And rare in his presence was evil proclaimed-
>> Or the God of his teachings reviled or defamed;

In sickness or trouble no ride was too long;
    No sun was too hot or no typhoon too strong;
No night was too dark or no blizzard too cold;
    No trail was too dim or a message too old
To keep the sky-pilot from pallets of woe-
    (Such pallets as only the far places know)-
With words bringing comfort and deeds giving cheer-
    With many a cnnfidence poured into his ear,

Well knowing it safe for a secret expressed
    Was looked for all times in the cells of his breast;
And so he endured that the good might attend-
    Known only as a counselor, brother and friend-
A servant indeed, this prince of the plain
    Lived on in its glory, sung loud its refrain-
And died as the servant of man--we are told,
    At the hand of a Judas for pieces of gold.

On a day in September, the fourteenth, it is said,
    In eighteen hundred and seventy-five-
The sky-pilot rode from Ponil country head-
    The last to be taken alive.
Some where on the trail he discovered, first hand,
    Two cattle rustlers at work; and the two
Were changing Long-H to their own private brand.
    One Longwell and Sam Donohue
Were the rustlers; and fearing the parson would peach
    They started a man on his trail,

A low-sneaking Greaser, that hung like a leach,
    'Till the chance opened up to assail,
It came in the canyon and taking his aim
    He shot him and started to hide
His corpse by the stream that now bears Tolby's name,
    In a drift that was piled at it's side.

The stage happened by and the driver was paid
    To forget what he saw in the vale;
But later, when the cowboys were out on a raid
    For strays found the corpse and their tale
Aroused all the punchers who gathered and caught
    The driver and hanged him until
He sudden remembered the things he forgot
    And told what he knew of the kill.

Then over in Taos the greaser was found
And returned for his trial but before
The day on the calendar happened around
He died; which was strange they all swore.

Oh, above the sage and pinons rears a granite shaft today
To the honor of the pilot who in passing on his way
Spoke a kindly word of greeting--proved a friend in time of need
Emphasized his God and Master in every word and deed;
Battled sun and storm and censure but a righteous vict'ry won;
Love and honor to thy ashes -- Tolby, of the Cimarron.

LARIAT JOE

Lariat Joe riding fence for McCarty,
    Was thought to be "queer", and the Lazy Bar-Z
Had harked to his voice which was husky and hearty
    And groaned with his songs -- always off key.
His favorite theme was a freak composition
    With words that were drivel and tune that was worse;
He kept all the punchers in bad disposition
    And even the Chink in the chuck house would curse.

Snag Tooth Dave went a ridin' into Reno--
    Kickin' up the gravel down the street he sailed,
Rode his old cayuse into Diamond Joe's Casino,
    But they laid him out in Reno
        When his six-gun failed.

The coyotes would howl in honest derision
    When calmly he'd ride with his voice booming out-
The cattle would stalk to another division
    Of pasture whenever he'd amble about.
The fence knew naught of his art of repairing,
    But far too much of his boomerang voice;
And many new kinds of up-to-date swearing
    Were heard as he carolled the song of his choice.

Snag Tooth Dave had a lady up in Reno
    Every day a letter to his love he mailed;
Took her to a dance down at Diamond Joe's Casino,
    But they laid him out in Reno
        When his six-gun failed.

The Lazy-Bar Z voted solid to kill him,

    And chased him with gusto clear out of their sight.

They pumped leaden bullets in effort to spill him

    But he fled from the range and vanished in flight.

Straight into Reno he dashed, and the people

    Stood silent, amazed as his bugle rang out

In discordant song over housetop and steeple,

    While they listened in wonderment, agony, doubt.

    Snag Tooth Dave held four aces up in Reno

        (They tried to stop him but his voice prevailed)

    Meant to get the fifth one down in Diamond Joe's Casino-

        Then they hushed his song in Reno'

            When his six-gun failed.

Fool Around and Fish.
F. Lambert

Oh, the days are getting balmy
And the grass is showing green,
While the leaves are all awakening,
Fine as I have ever seen;
And I've got the same old feeling
That comes o'er me every spring,
When the brook begins its calling
And the birds begin to sing.

Its a lazy-hazy feeling,
Couples with a fervent wish,
Not to do a dog-gone thing
But lie around and fish.
Just to find a quiet place,
And lie around and fish—
Just to sorter shake my troubles off
And fool around and fish.

There's a silv'ry pool that's hidden
Well from anyone I know,
Where the sentinels are giants,
With their branches hanging low.
There no sign of habitation—
There no sign of sordid quest,
But the peaceful slumbering quiet,
Where a man can truly rest.

Oh its' calling, calling, calling,
For it knows my every wish
Is to dabble in the waters
And just fool around and fish.
Not to do another blessed thing,
But lie around and fish—
Just to get out in God's garden once,
And tinker 'round and fish.

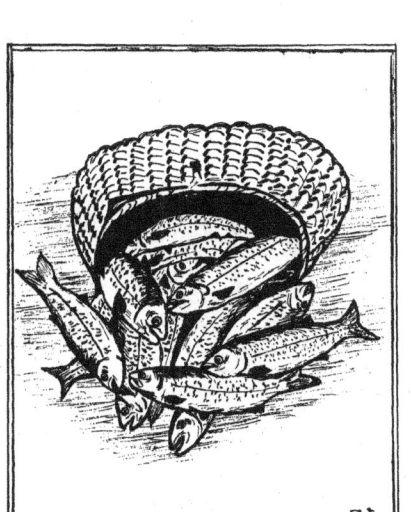

Juan Espinosa
A Tale of the West

Juan Espinosa lived much as a grandee
    Or yet as the Dons or Muy Ricos of Spain;
With gun and machete he was wonderful handy
    And ruled as a monarch his rancho domain.
"Twas just at the time when New Mexico's keeping
    Was being proclaimed by the states, and his name
Held terror for those--either waking or sleeping--
    That came within sound of his scurrilous fame.

"EL RANCHO"

The Peons who crawled at the master's commanding
    Were ready (and eager) to further his will,
Be it rustling of steers in the valley, or banding
    Together for robbing the mails--or to kill.
The mountains of Sangre de Cristo protected
    This red handed villian, and deep in their shade
His raiders assembled to ride -- unexpected--
    And strike on the plans that their leader had made.

And woe to the Peon who ventured complaining-
    To ears that were deaf and heart made of stone;
Such walked with their chief down the canyon explaining-
    And then - Espinosa returned, but always alone.
And woe to the maiden whose graces had pleased him;
    He held for ransom or barter or gain;
Their fate, fore-ordained by the fancy that pleased him--
    A prisoner of hell on his rancho domain.

"THE MAIDEN"

His sister--A dark eyed Senorita of beauty-
    Held not to his ways, and so, living apart,
Denounced evil deeds -- her conception of duty-
    Still keeping a place for him deep in her heart.

And then came a Gringo from Poncho Pass riding
    Straight into her life as it seemed, and the thrill
Of passionate love she declared without hiding
    Was as pure as the rose blooming there on the hill.

At happy fandangoes they danced, and their dreaming

    Were dreams of the future, rose colored and gay-

A shack in the valley, with mountain tops gleaming

    Snow covered--and gaily the time passed away.

But soon Espinosa discovered her lover-

    Had gold - and he planned in his own stealthy way-

A stab in the dark and a hurry to cover-

    The Gringo was dying, but yet as he lay

He fired, slightly wounding Espinosa, who in turning,

    Faced fury incarnate, a tigress in form--

A dark eyed Senorita, with eyes flashing, burning;

    And crouching in fear he waited the storm.

He rather expected wild manifestations--
   Hysterical words, demonstrations of woe-
But tense she stood, glaring, and then imprecations
   Like thunder-bolts came, hissing, earnest and low.

"May you roam unattended with hate soaring o'er you-
   Despised by your people, alone in the hills;
May hunger be with you and death stalk before you,
   And be haunted forever by the ghosts of your kills;
And then at last, with your arms spread in pleading
   May swift speeding bullet pierce straight through your heart,
And the wolves of the mountains gulp down their greeding
   The flesh from your bones as they rend you apart.
But your head shall return--with its evil thoughts stilled-
   And then I shall know that my curse is fulfilled."

With his band Espinosa fled into the ranges
   Of Sangre de Cristo in fancied retreat,
But the tide of his fortune reverses and changes-
   The curse fell upon him in fullness complete.

The Kiowas, using the upper trail, wended
    Their way in seclusion, and struck with a vim
The band; Espinosa and brother decended
    Their way to escape o'er the canyon's sharp rim;
Far back in the mountain's wild range they retreated,
    The only men left of the villianous crew,
And though for a time they were beaten, defeated,
    They planned other crimes from their new rendevous.

    Joe Lamb of the punchers, with shot well directed,
        Brought death to the brother when out on a scout,
        For the two, whom the Alma stage driver suspected
        Of trying to hold up the stage coming out.

Juan Espinosa, alone, never faltered,
>   But drove his career from a secret retreat-
His murders were stealthy, his plan never altered,
>   The Gringos must die--and his records complete
Showed thirty-two souls he had sent to accounting-
>   A record of blood seldom equalled before-
But proved by the names and the direful recounting
>   Of facts in the raw-hide bound book that he wore.

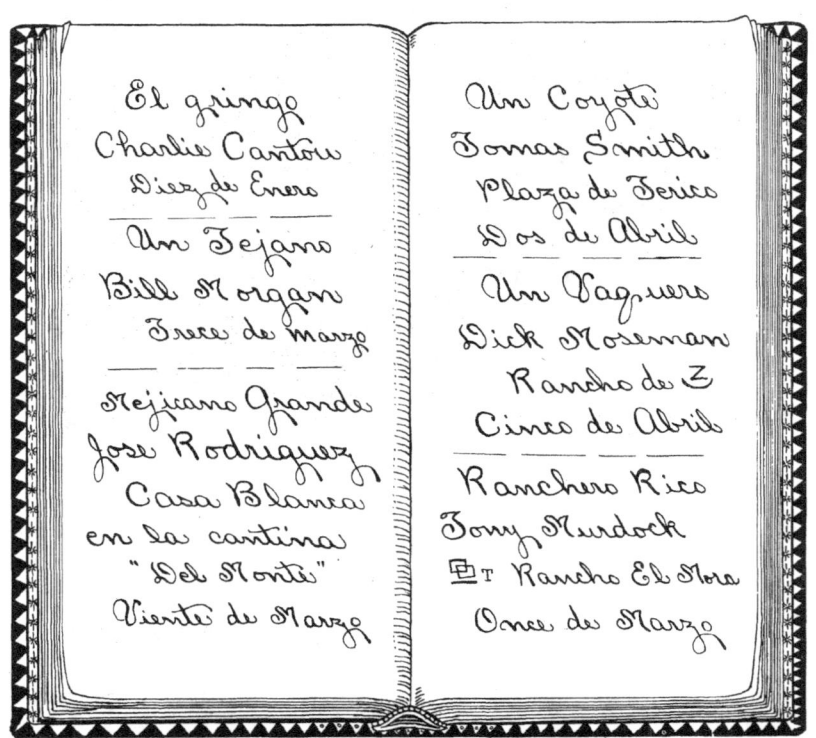

Juan Espinosa, remember the setting-
>   The dark-eyed Senorita, the curse, and the pale
Young Gringo she loved, have a care in forgetting-
>   A shadow, alert, finds its way on your trail.

Tom Tobin smelled smoke, and his nostrils dilated
    With joy, for it told him his quarry was found;
For days he had stalked in the passes and waited
    With patience and fortitude not to be downed.

In a moment the wisp curling up was detected,
    A detour was made that consumed near a day,
But the fire light was doused that he hoped
    and expected
Would show him where the murdered lay.

OLD TOM TOBIN

    Just then came a beam through a sky cloud revealing
        In dim silhouette the transgressor at stand,
    His arms wide extended- (as though in appealing)-
        He leaped for the bluff which was closely at hand.

A shot spat it's note, and the mad leap was ended

    While yet in mid-air, for straight as a dart,

The bullet went true and the bandit descended

    To earth, with a great gaping hole in his heart.

    The wolves of the mountains had feasts to their liking

        As told by the satisfied howls of the pack;

    And Tobin returned with his proof, which was striking,

        The head of the bandit rolled up in a sack.

And the fair Senorita looked on in disdain-

    With a laugh that was either of hell, or insane.

The Buffalo Hunt

Oh, come with me to long years ago:
    The West was wide and the buffalo
Roamed o'er the ranges, to and fro,
    With the will of their free endeavor.
Naught but memories now are found:
    A horn, a bone, some skulls around
A wallow hole in hoof-beat ground,
    For the herd has passed forever.

Oh, once the time these ranges knew:
    The pounding feel, of the swift tattoo,
Of a thousand herds that thrived and grew
    On their billows wide and sweeping.
And once they knew the tingling thrill
    Of flashing lance, the deadly skill,
When hunters drove their shafts to kill,
    To the thump of the wild herd's leaping.

Bygone Days Of The Old West

Oh, once the crack of a rifle spoke
    Through clouds of dust, with spurt of smoke,
And a racing, plunging creature broke
    The swinging pace, and tumbled.
His mates swept on in headlong flight
    (For the foe hung close on left and right)
And disappeared from his blinded sight,
    Nor cared when to earth he tumbled.

And at the close of a hunter's day
    A hundred forms might sprawling lay
Along the path where on its way
    The frightened herd had wended
Its wild stampede o'er brake and swell,
    Retreating from the reigning hell
Of slaughter, until darkness fell
    And for a time 'twas ended.

Oh, fated breed; no more there be
    Your browsing herds, on wide range free,
Nor the coming generations see
    Or know your presence, ever.
No more fear ye the hunter's zest
    Nor wild alarm disturb your rest,
For with the old, the golden west
    You've passed away forever.

Oh, naught but memories may be found --
    A horn, a bone, some skulls around --
A wallow hole in hoof-beat ground --
    For you have gone forever.

Calling

Can't you sense a spirit sort of speakin' in the trees,
   Just a sound of sighin' in the whisper of the breeze,
Smoky haze a lyin' down the valleys an' the leas,
   And the fragant breath of new mown hay?
Don't you feel the thrillin' and the tingle in the air,
   Busy birds a trillin' and a-drillin' here and there?
Nature is callin' from the skies, and everywhere--
   Callin' happy summer, far away.

Leaves commence a-curlin' and a-fallin' all around;

    Here and there a furrow showin' fresh the broken ground;

Geese will soon be honkin' as they travel south'ard bound;

    Squirrels are busy storin' day by day;

Corn is golden yellow, like the evenin' sunset hue;

    Stars begin to twinkle like the steel of autumn dew;

Everything preparin', as the call comes siftin' through

    Nature callin' summer, far away.

THUNDER BIRD

Tom-tom-tom-tom-tom-tom-tom!

    Beat the tribal drums in the vale of the Pueblos;

Wake the God of Thunder in the hills of the Pueblos;

    Baking in the sun is the tribe of the Pueblos;

Tom-tom-tom-tom-tom-tom-tom.

    On the cliffs of the Pueblos
        An image you will find
    Of a bird revered and holy
        To the symbolistic mind
    Of the people who proclaim him
        God of Thunder and of rain
    And the lightnings in the heavens
        And the tempest of the plain;

Weird the legend of the people;
    Strange the image of the bird;
Stranger still the old Taos story
    Told by sign and broken word
At the camp-fire in the valley
    By a grave-faced Taos chief,
Of the idol which is painted
    On the cliffs -- and his belief.

And the setting of the story
    Was complete; the heated plain--
Evening--and the camp-fire glowing--
    And the clouds portending rain--
With the coyotes in the distance
    And the chief in silent thought
Gazing at the glowing embers
    Made a picture not forgot.

Then I spoke the word "Lluvia"
    (Meaning rain); and at the word
He responded with the legend
    Of the mighty Thunder-bird.

THE LEGEND
AS TOLD BY THE TAOS CHIEF.

Way up high in the mountain snow,
    Heap much higher than eagles go,
Close to the great God Manitou
    Where heap big spirits be,
Thunder-bird he live like rest
    In wigwam built the very best.
He watch-um east, and look-um west,
    To see what he can see.

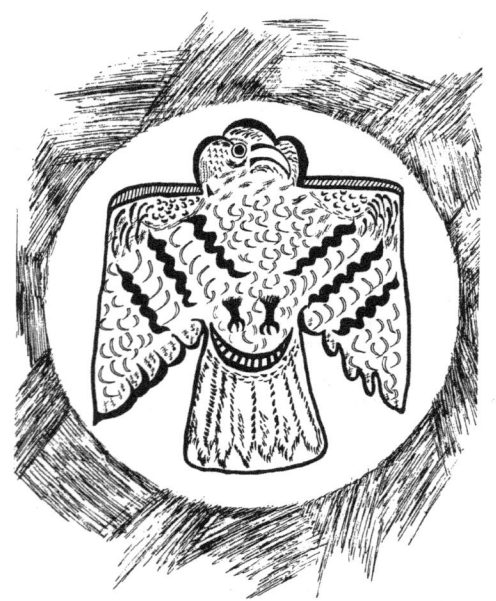

White man call um lightning--so--
    Taos chief he say um--no, no--
Heap big flash -- it come and go
    When Thunder-bird make-um wink.
Much big fire come from his eyes
    When he wink-um, and it flies
Here and yonder when he tries
    Great big hard to think.

White man say big thunder sound
    From the lightning; Injun found
Thunder-bird he beat and pound
    Winds on mountain top;
When he great big thunder make
    He have fight with rattlesnake;
Heap much shiver, heap much shake,
    Then sometime he stop.

Thunder-bird sometime fall asleep
    Into slumber heap much deep.
Ground dry up -- so Injun keep
    Tom-tom beating loud.
Then old Thunder-bird he wake,
    Send Lluvia from the lake
On his back while white man make
    Foolish talk of cloud.

All things good in Thunder-bird;
    Watch-um Injun, watch-um herd.
Make big listen, speak no word;
    Watch-um close and see.
Him way up high in mountain snow,
    Heap much higher than eagles go,
Close to the great God Manitou.
    Thunder-bird him be.

Thus runs the ancient legend
    Of the spirit of God and rain,
As told beside the campfire
    While the lightning lit the plains
As the thunder crashed about us
    And the rush of storm was heard,
I almost believed the story
    Of the sacred Thunder-bird.

    I could fancy that the lightning
        Was the flashing of his eyes;
    That the beating of his giant wings
        Woke echoes in the skies;
    And the crash of earth a-tremble
        I could easily mistake
    For the onslaught of a rain-god
        On a giant rattlesnake.

But the grave Taos chief in silence

   Gazed impassive in the light

Of the campfire -- then, upstanding,

   Nodded me a short good-night.

Tom-tom-tom-tom-tom-tom-tom!

   Happy is the tribe on the vale of the Pueblos;

Rain and peace and plenty be the lot of the Pueblos;

   Rocks and the estufas tell the praises of the Pueblos;

Tom-tom-tom-tom-tom-tom-tom!

The prairie wind whispers to the dunes
    As they shift the bright diamond sand,
Building new ridges and valleys,
    Glistening white in the desert land.

The cactus smiles in the sweltering heat
    As a rattler seeks its shade.
Sun flowers droop their weary heads,
    The Sand Gods polish the yucca blade.

An old miner stands by his fallen beast,
    Buzzards circle in the sunset rays.
Coyotes call to their wary mates
    The coming feast at the break of day.

The dunes drift and the sands shift
    As the old miner seeks a water hole,
Knowin' well, if not found ere another day,
    He will pay the desert toll.

The moon comes up in all her glory,
    Sand dunes drink in the silver rays.
The bull-bats dip in the gray mesquite,
    As the miner plods his weary way.

Off to the east the trail is plain,
    Leadin' to the living land,
With mountains high that are lookin' down
    On the glistening white desert sand.

The old miner sobs a thankful prayer,
    As he kneels beside a lake of liquid gold.
The prairie wind whispers a cheering tune,
    The sand dunes build on as of old.

THE LEGEND OF A GUARD OF EL DIABLO.

Somewhere out in the broad expanse
    Of hills and desolation
To the South and East of Albuquerque
    In the desert's drear formation
Is cached a fortune of Spanish gold--
    The Gran Quiviras' treasure--
A million or more in its bed of sand
    Awaiting the finders' pleasure.

A document found in Madrid, Spain
    Recounted in full the story
Of slaughtered priests by Indian hands
    And the rawhide pages hoary--
Contained a map in crude design
    Supposing to point the way
Through cactus, sage and hell itself
    To the place where the millions lay.

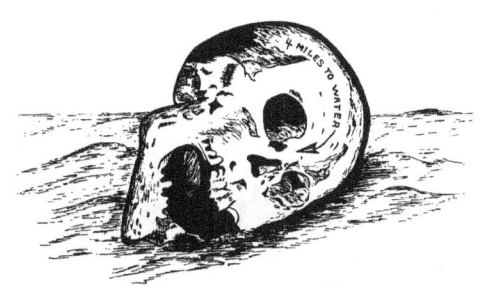

And many a man has sallied forth
    Full in the desert's reaching
To find the gold and his story's told
    By the bones on the sand wastes bleaching—
So maybe you'd like to hear the tale
    Of the guard who has its keeping
And never allows a single soul
    To learn where the wealth is sleeping.

Bygone Days Of The Old West

In the depths of Canyon Diablo
    Death stalks in a thousand forms or so
And only the men of the malpi know
    The danger it holds - and dread it.
You run the gauntlet of poisoned springs
    A million fangs, a million stings--
Creeping, crawling repulsive things,
    And few are the feet to tread it.

But where is a land so rugged, bold,
    That men forego in their search for gold?
And so a guard was placed we're told
    O'er Gran Quiveras' treasure-
A lady fair on a steed of white
    Whose robes reflected a phantom light
Plain to be seen the blackest night
    That the season had in measure.

A woman as light as a bounding fawn
    Who smiled and beckoned you on and on
'Till hope and strength and will were gone;
    And then, with her wild laugh playing,
She left you there with the fangs and stings
    Your choking thirst and the poisoned springs
While the cold, hard sound of her laughter rings
    On your ears like the devil praying.

The Indians whisper a wierdly tale

    Of the spirit sounds that at night assail

The ear with a long-drawn hellish wail

    From the walls of the canyon soaring;

And tell of the braves who the warning spurned

    With fates unknown (for they never returned)

Nor aught of their passing was ever learned;

    But the sounds from the depths keep pouring.

And always the horse and rider appear

    On the edge of the rimrock, plain and clear,

And always the cold, hard laugh you hear--

    The laugh of a semi-human--

That leads you on, but in truth away

    From the point where the silent millions lay,

Then casts you off when she'd had her say--

    The way of a vampire woman.

And so if you long for a wealth of gold,

    Go out in the depth of the desert hold,

To Diablo with its poisoned springs,

    Its million fangs and its million stings,

And meet the lady in raiment light

    Of a phantom horse of milky white

And ask her to kindly point the way

    Where the Gran Quiviras' treasure lay.

And it might be well when you don your pack

    To say good bye -- for you won't come back.

I'm driftin' back to Old New Mexico,
    Ridin' free in the spring-time air -
Where there's cactus, thorny chapparral,
    Sage brush and prickly-pear.
Buffalo wallows in the sun-kissed hills
    Where the bald eagles cut the blue,
Gentle prairie wind fans your face,
    All nature smiling a welcome to you.

I'll soon be where open range is plenty,
    Where the greenest grama grasses grow;
In the land of Squaw and Diamond hitches-
    Where the cool mountain water flows.
Mountains are a-loomin' in the distance
    As the ball-of-red sinks in the West,
My old hoss longin' for the home corral
    And stompin' grounds we like best.

Bygone Days Of The Old West

I'll start my camp-fire glowin'
    In the shadow of the rocky bluff,
Where the cedars and pinons mingle
    And the trail is getting rough.
Soon bacon and the Arbuckles aroma
    Fills the cool evening air,
A coyote calls from the distant rimrock
    To its wary mate sulkin' there.

Night-hawks dippin' in the gloamin',
    A million stars twinkling overhead—
With my old Frazier saddle for a pillow
    Fragrant buffalo grass for a bed;
All my thoughts are on a rampage
    As I lie beside the firelight's dyin' glow,
Dreamin' of the ranch and loved one
    My boyhood happy days in th' long ago.

In the east the daylight is breakin'
    Old Cayuse - time to be on our way—
Little sassy prairie-dogs are barkin'
    We'll reach the old home range today.
How I love these old hills and prairie
    And true friends that never grow old—
'Tis the land of love and promise
    And sunsets of bright burnished gold.

THE MAID FROM DURANGO

In the dreamy old town of Sabina--
    One night in the long years ago,
I sat in the La Joya Cantina
    And harked to the gamesters "Cacho"-
The soft southern night and its droning;
    The breeze, with its rhythm and swell-
And the tide with its dull, ceaseless moaning-
    Cast o'er me a half conscious spell;
And then through the haze of my dreaming,
    Above the dead lilt of the sea,
A melody rare found its way on the air,
    And the singer was smiling at me--

Amigo mine, Amigo mine,
    Don of the Paso del Mar,
The maid from Durango
    Will dance the fandango
If Senor will play the guitar;
    La Luna shines bright on the water
Where the waves ripple over the bar;
    And the maid from Durango
Will dance the fandango,
    If Senor will play the guitar.

Oh; Fate, cold and cruel, that brings us
    To flower-laden pathways of spring,
And then like a wicked gnome flings us
    Far back to December's smart sting!

Her smile to me was as the showers
    Must be to the roses in June,
But it always had taken me hours
    To coax a guitar into tune.

Bygone Days Of The Old West

Oh beautiful maid of Durango,
    You make a mistake in the call;
No more could I play the fandango
    Than the theme of the Dead March in Saul.
Oh fain would I follow thee, ever,
    And glad would I be of the chance
With nothing to do but hearken to you,
    And plunkety-plunk while you dance.

    Amigo mine, Amigo mine,
        Don of the Paso del Mar,
    The maid from Durango
        Will dance the fandango
    If Senor will play the guitar.
        La Luna shines bright on the water
    Where the waves ripple over the bar;
        And the maid from Durango
    Will dance the fandango,
        If Senor will play the guitar.

I sought out skillful musicians
    As tutors, who tried to portray
The numberless slants and positions
    And practiced them day after day;
My life settled down to a dreary
    Routine with its plunkety-plunk,
'Till the tutors in turn, growing weary,
    All quit me, pronouncing me "punk"-

And so I kept on for a season

    Ker-plunking my way all alone,

But my fingers smacked strongly of treason,

    Refusing to fashion a tone.

So I lost the sweet maid of Sabina

    For never an air did I plung-

And my heart gave a sigh when she told me

        good-bye,

For I knew what she meant when she sung--

    Adois, Amigo mine, Adois, amigo mine,

        Dunce of the Paso del Mar,

    The maid from Durango

        Would dance the fandango

    If someone could play the guitar.

        La Luna is dark on the water

    Where the sea surges over the bar,

        And the maid from Durango

    Will dance the fandango

        But no one can play the guitar.

THE PENITENTES.
A RELIGIOUS SECT OF NEW MEXICO.

The worship of God as discerned by man
Has varied in ways since belief began.

Hermanos de Luz have mysterious ways
   And strange belief of the clan.
Their fervent religion dates back to the days
   Of old Pagan times -- thus it ran
Through the era of Christians, it's teaching
    we trace
   To Padus, St Anthonys' creed
Was founded, the self-whipping brotherhoods' place
   Was formerly in Spain and it's lead
Spread into Old Mexico, thence o'er the line
   To our borders -- and this will explain
The Brothers of Light and the means they divine
   For remission of sins -- super pain.

To imitate the Saviour's Crucifixtion-

    To suffer as the man of destiny-

Is their religion -- fervent the conviction

    To lead a people through it's misery.

In the dark hours of night with the watchers in place

    The Penitentes--stripped to a black cap and clout-

Appear with their leader, will ready to face

    The tortues of hell that their sins be wiped out

With a knife called the 'picada' - three edged and keen

    In the hands of the leader, on backs that are bare-

The gashes are cut and the blood courses clean

    From meaning slashes he executes there.

Then fast to their ankles are iron locked chains-

    A needed percaution, devised, so they say,

If the devil should chance in their sacred domain

    To carry a Penitente off and away.

Bygone Days Of The Old West

And then in procession, in solemn accord-
    They march with their voices raised loudly in song
Self-flogging, the cactus root whip, like a cord,
    Cuts deep in their flesh as the conclave moves on.
Three Moradas, distant apart half a mile,
    Are known as degrees on the Penitente road-
(There are crosses, by stone neatly placed in a pile)
    Great timbers that add to the Penitentes load.

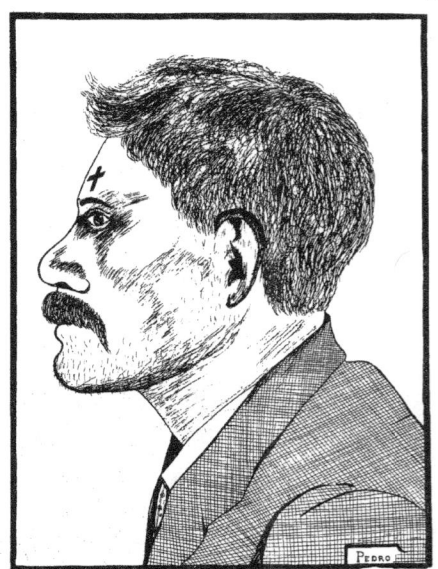

    The ones more advanced take the greater in size
        And heft them along on the way to the goal-
    Then falling exhausted each Penitente tries
        To last to the end and atone for his soul;
    The weird sounding song like a wail of distress
        The leaders with crucifix -- holding a light--
    The sin weary forms o'er the sands onward press--
        Hermanos de Luz--seeking God in the night.

At the end of the road certain brothers are tied
    To their crosses with thongs of wet raw-hide
        and high
They hang through the long weary hours, crucified-
    The thongs cutting deep in the flesh as they dry
Retard circulation with suffering and pain
    Beyond understanding they seek to atone
Their sins and transgressions -- and just where the plain
    Rounds up to a hill -- on their crosses, alone
In bold silhouette on the sky line they stand-
    The crosses that bear them in drastic relief-
A custom most strange to be found in a land
    So boasted in learning -- so sure in belief.

For hours they hang thus--then loosed and they fall
 To earth--some to rise and return as they may
While others lie still have given their all
 That their sins be forgiven and taken away.
And so on Good Friday of each year such a scene
 Takes place on many mesas in New Mexico-
With other strange customs no white man may glean
 With other strange customs no white man may know.

Hermanos de Luz--Brothers of Light-
 Sincere in their faith and conception of right.
And the worship of God, as discerned by man-
 Has varied in creed since belief began.

Lonesome Land

A-ridin' down the cactus

Through the shiftin', driftin' sand,

A-huntin' for a dogie

In a God-forsaken land;

A-huntin' for a dogie

That had wandered far, like me,

A-driftin'--just a-driftin'

In a silent sandy sea.

A-ridin' down the cactus
In the teemin', gleamin' glare--
With none to come a-trailin',
For there's not a soul to care;
A-dreamin' as I'm ridin'
Of the days that used to be--
A-huntin' for a dogie
That is better off than me.

A-ridin' down the cactus
To a nearin', clearin' pool--
A cottage just a-showin'
Through the trees invitin' cool;
It's nothin' but the lyin'
Of the sand mirage I see--
So I'm trailin' for a dogie
That is better off than me.

I love the lure of the open way.

Would I were as a gypsy king
    To wander the face of the earth and sing
My roundelay as the seasons bring
    A zest to my mild endeavor;
To the tinkling strain of your sweet guitar
    I'd raise my song to the silent stars--
Restraint aside, I would leap the bars
    To follow the road forever,

(Ker-plinkety-plinkety-plank--Plink-plank)

(Ker-plinkety-plinkety-plank--Plink-plank)

You'd find us together in all kinds of weather--

    Like birds of a feather--(ker-plinkety-plank)

We'd know the tang of the sea--the sea,

    The plains and the mountains so free--so free,

In all kinds of weather you'd find us together--

    For birds of a feather we'd be.

I love the lure of the open way,

    And the sunset's glow at the end of the day,

The shimmering light of the milky-way,

    The peace of a quiet gloaming;

'Tis then the chord of the strumming strings

    Sends forth its strains till the wild-wood rings

With a thousand symphonies and brings

    My heart to go forth a-roaming.

(Ker-plinkety-plinkety-plank--plink-plank)

(Ker-plinkety-plinkety-plank--plink-plank)

Though lightnings be flashing and thunders be crashing

    And the winds begin thrashing--(ker-plinkety-plank)

It speaks to the wild in our strain--our strain,

    The thunders, the tempest and rain--and rain,--

Though thunders be crashing and wild winds be trashing

    It answers the call in our strain.

OLD PAL "BETSY"

"Old Pal Betsy, we've been pards
    For nigh on to forty years,
Trackin' down killers and rustlers
    For changin' brands and rustlin' steers.
Yes, you're old, battered and scarred,
    And notches numbered with care;
But your trigger pull was ever true-
    And safety played when you was near.

"Oft times we left our bronc behind
    When death was lurkin' nigh;
From rock to rock and brush to brush
    Waitin' THE CHANCE - You and I.
Glimpsin' a shadow in the grey-mesquite
    As nerve and muscle answered the call,
Never knowin' how the deal would end--
    Or how life's cards soon would fall.

"Oft times in storm-swept, pitchy-darkness

    No moon or stars to be guided by,

We would circle-ride and softly singin'

    Get the herd bedded-down and peaceful lie.

Soon we knew the stampede was comin',

    As thunder rolled and lightnin' played

Static jumpin' from horn to horn --

    As the leaders run, reared and swayed.

"With our bronc runnin' with the leaders,

    You and I on the Death Ride --

You belchin' forth lead and brimstone,

    Till the millin' started on the inner side.

Soon up the trail they went a-grazin',

    The sun come up in all its glory --

The Punchers forgot the troubled night,

    Aroun' the chuck-wagon just another story.

"You and I have had our fling together,

    Think of the deals we've pulled through;

Law and Order was always our motto --

    Old Pal Betsy, 'How I love you.'

As I sit here in the bunk-house

    Holdin' converse with my soul,

I grip your old pearl-handle--

    And live again.....THE DAYS OF OLD.

Mother of mine;

When the shadows were falling

Deeper and deeper as they crept to the West,

Soft came the strains of your lullaby calling,

Calling my soul to its haven of rest--

"Hush-a-bye, honey,

Shadows be gone,

Cradle your head

On my breast 'til the dawn;

Mother will guard you

All of the way;

Hush-a-bye- honey

Sleep 'til the day."

Mother of mine;

Like the sun in its glory,

Or as the tear in the heart of a rose,

So was your love, and its wonderful story

Lightens the burdens, the heartaches and woes--

"Hush-a-bye, honey,

Down through the years

Mother will cradle

Your sorrows and tears;

Follow and keep you

All of the way;

Hush-a-bye, honey,

Sleep 'til the day."

Mother of mine;

How the shadows confound me,

Deeper and deeper as they creep to the West;

Oh! could I fly, when with night they surround me,

Back to the God-given love of your breast.

"Hush-a-bye, honey"--

Oh, could I be

Kneeling once more

As a child at your knee;

Love, as God meant it,

Wholly divine--

(Hush-a-bye, honey)--

Mother of mine.

LITTLE BALLY

Straddle my saddle, Little Bally,
    I'll take yu down to the Home corral.
Yu' poor little orphan critter,
    Th' coyotes won't get yu, Little Pal.

No use of yu a-bawlin' and a-kickin'--
    Yu've got a mighty lot to learn
About these long snowy winters,
    An' runnin' irons thet burn.

Now you're ridin' nice and docile,
    And I know we'll get along--
The trail is rough and windin'
    So I'll sing yu a little song.

I'll giv' yu leche a-plenty.

    Sure sorry thet yu lost your Maw.

Soon with sun baths and alfalfa

    You'll be big an' sassy like your Paw.

Your Dad done yu'uns sorter dirty

    When he up and left your Maw,

Rangin' alone in the breaks and coulees

    Down on the lower Currumpaw.

    Gee! your fur is soft and silky,

        Your eyes aire big and brown.

    A white spot on your forehead,

        An' built right up from th' ground.

Here's where we stop, Little Bally,

    This is th' old home corral

Where we'll get leche a-plenty

    Don't worry anymore, Little Pal.

THE MEXICAN SHEEP HERDER

I lika de mounts de caps with snow,
    I lika de river where ever she go;
I lika for myself to smella de pine -
    To shoote de coyote an' readie de sign.

De trail she leads down frum de mounts so high,
    I no gota fraid 'much' - for the wolf when she cry;
De wind she blow -- de snow she cum --
    De Burro he singa de Home Sweet Home.

I sheepie de camp on de side of de hill,

    I runa myself so fast I can't keep a still;

De babie sheepie de mama no can find -

    She cry lika hell, I thinka de girl I leav behin'.

De wood she wet, de fire I no can make,

    I gota cold for de feet an' maka de shake;

De hands she gota freeze -- de eyes maka de cry -

    I maka go for de carpa an' kissa myself good-bye.

De dogie he cum an' licka de hands all he could,

    I looka in de carpa, I finda de pichie-de-wood;

De fire she burn - de coffea she gita de hot -

    An' de chili an' de tortilla she hita de spot.

I lika for de sheepies to lay down by de side,

    I lika to huggie de doggie for sava de hide;

I lika for myself to see de snow she bring --

    For I gotta mor' grassie for the sheepies

        in de spring.

The Plow-Handle Ruminations of Hiram.

These city fellers furnish me
    With a lot of--p'tu, by gee.
They like ter have their merry shoots
    About the way I grease my boots,
And laugh about the subtitoots
    I wear fer linen collars;
They pester me with golden bricks,
    An' lots of other 'tarnal tricks
They're tinkered up to hand to hicks
    And get their hard-earned dollars.

But I just mosey on my way,
    A plantin' wheat an' corn an' hay.
They like ter call me country jake,
    An' every consarned fool'll take
A crack at me an' try to make
    A joke about my habits;
They say I've hayseed in my hair--
    That moss hangs on me everywhere
An' that my whiskers are a lair
    An' hidin' place fer rabbits.

Bygone Days Of The Old West

But I jest sorter go ahead
    A raisin' hogs an' beef an' bread.
They send their politicians out
    To smile an' prance an' rant about,
An' think they're pesky sharp, no doubt,
    A puttin' somethin' over;

A sailin' round in fancy cars,
    An' handin' out their cheap seegars,
A leavin' open gates an' bars,
    An' trampin' down my clover.
But I jest let 'em think they're wise,
    A grinnin' at their dratted lies.

There's a lot of fellers spoof at me
    That's goin' downright hungaree
To keep in punk societee
    An' all it's gaudy trimmin',
They rack what little brains they got
    With some dod-gasted shyster plot
That's crooked, jest as like 's not,
    Ter eat an' dress their wimmen.

But me an' ma have beef and lamb

    An' fresh laid eggs an' country ham.

I've noticed that the farmer folks

    Ain't worried none about the jokes

That's handed 'em by city blokes

    Who've never earned a dollar;

We have our fun, though, anyway,

    When things ter eat climb day by day

An' they must dig like heck ter pay-

    Gee whiz, but don't they holler!

    But Ma'll wink at me and say--

        We'll have fried chicken, eh, ter day.

    These city fellers furnish me

        With lots of--p'tu -- fun, by gee.

THE MOUNTAINS

There's somethin' sets me thinkin',
   Tho' I'm sorta half afraid,
When I get to ruminatin'
   On the time when you was made;
Cause I seem to hear the crashin'
   An' the groanin' of the sphere–
When the mighty force of nacher–
   Reared your lofty summits here.

There was shakin', an' some quakin',
   Like the end of time was come.
There was flashin', smashin', crashin'
   That would strike a human dumb.
There was moanin', plenty groanin'
   An' a rumblin' of the earth,
As a planet writhed in labor
   When it stopped an' give you birth.

A firey stream was flowin'
    From the depths no man can tell,
Like they mebbe might be pourin'
    From the fountain head of Hell;
An' the night was shot with lightnin'
    An' the day was filled with fear,
When the earth was in convulsion
    As it raised yo'r summits here.

Oh, the majesty of mountains
    I can feel and hear and see.
I jes thank the Power that placed you
    Like a picture here for me;
I can glory in your beauty
    As my bein' throbs and thrills
At the majesty of mountains
    And the friendliness of hills.

The Pioneer's Thanksgiving

There was snow in the clearing
and frost in the air,
The cupboard was empty,
the table was bare,
He reached for his belt with its powder and ball
And the clumsy old musket that hung on the wall.
In ambush he lay 'mid the bushes and rocks,
Hearing only the wind and the bark of a fox,
Till a bronze colored bird,
still a stranger to fear,
Ran out in sight of the young pioneer.

A flash in the woods -- and a volley of sound,
And the king of the gobblers was sprawled on the ground -
His featherly dames in the chilly gray eves
Found only a spatter of blood on the leaves;
But the walls of the cabin were bright with glow
From the logs of the cavernous fireplace below,
And he whistled a love-ballad tuneful and clear
As he roasted the turkey - the young Pioneer.

A wish for his sweetheart
    To brighten the board
Arose with the thanks
    That he gave to the Lord.
The snarl of the wolf
    In the forest was heard,
As he feasted alone
    On the flesh of the bird.
But the dangers behind him,
    The hardships before -
The wind in the chimney,
    The storm at the door,
The moccasined feet
    That forever were near
Disturbed not the dreams
    Of this bold Pioneer.

Where they molded his grave in the dark spruce's shade
    The streets of a Western town are laid,
On the site of the cabin a Spanish manison has grown
    With columns and arches of adobe and stone;
But spare him a thought who remembered to pray
    In fervent thanksgiving that desolate day,
May his spirit immortal abide with us here,
    The pride of the nation, the brave Pioneer.

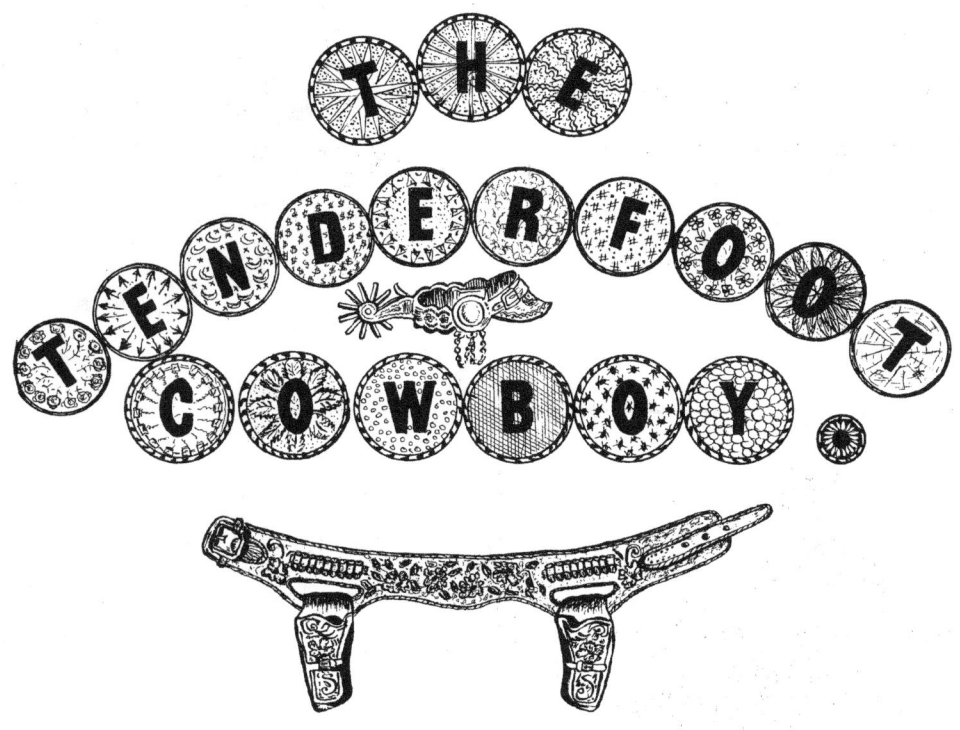

The Tenderfoot Cowboy

By their brands ye shall know them
   On any range they may feed or roam
By their ear-marks ye shall tally them
   Be they longhorn, whiteface or roan.

      When ye find a slick-ear maverick
         It's rangin' in the brakes all alone
      Go ahead and ear-mark and brand it
         And tally it amongst your own.

      When ye find an animal driftin'
         Wearin' some other outfit's brand
      Be sure and get word to the owner
         This is the code in cattle-land.

Bygone Days Of The Old West

When ye find a lonely little dogie
    With its mammy dead or gone
Jest lift him in your saddle
    And bring him right along.

When ye find two old range bulls
    Kickin' up dust in a head-on bout
Jest sit down in the shade of a cactus
    And let the darn fools have it out.

When ye rope a cow or yearlin'
    And give 'em a turn and fling
Quickly slip from your old saddle
    And use your piggin-string.

When ye ride the fence line
    See all wires are good and tight,
Read trail sign of any rustlers
    That had crossed the range at night.

When ye ride up to the chuck-wagon
    BE SURE - Don't kick up any dust
Or the old camp-cook with his pot-hook
    Will treat you with blows and disgust.

When ye find a sheepman encroaching
>   An' he says he's come to stay,
>   Jest shake your slicker near the herd
>   It'll set 'em stampedin' on their way.

When ye find a rustler busy
>   Be sure your trigger-finger's true,
>   Try and get him the first shot
>   Or it's an even bet he'll get you.

When ye hear a rattle in the bushes
>   Your ol' hoss snorts and starts to rear
>   Tighten on th' reins and set your saddle
>   For it's nothin' but a bear.

When ye hear a hail-storm a-comin'
>   There's no shelter where you're at,
>   Just unsaddle your ol' hoss
>   And use your saddle for a hat.

When ye make up your bed-roll
>   And the tarp is wet with dew
>   Very likely you'll find a rattler
>   That has spent the night with you.

So listen to what I'm sayin'
>   And when us old waddies are gone
>   Just follow the code in cattle-land
>   I'm sure you'll never GO WRONG.

A Character Sketch of the Border — A Ranchero of Mexico.

Oh what if you were a mighty Ranchero-
    With a million acres of land or so-
And host to whoever might come and go
    As they willed or as fancy might lead them-
Oh wouldn' you sort to want to know
    The why and where of the steady flow-
If you were a mighty Ranchero
    And knew that your larder fed them?

Maxwell Mansion, Cimarron, N.M.

Have you ever heard of Maxwell and his 'dobe palace grand
    On the Cimarron? It seems a fairy tale-
But the character had being in the old romantic land
    When the Santa Fe first blossomed into a trail;
A man of marked appearence -- certain origin unknown-
    Except that he named St. Louis as the town
He hailed from down to Mexico -- for reasons of his own-
    And back of that the record closes down;
With his high-heeled boots and sombrero drooping low
    He was known to every Mexican, Red and White
From Larned to the Capitol down to old New Mexico,
    As an hombre who would play you square and right.

MAXWELL'S ADOBE RANCHO

In his mansion made of 'dobe he was host to every man
    That would care to seek his table or his bed-
The tribes of every color, creed or fashion, breed or clan
    Were welcomed to be sheltered and be fed.
No pay would he consider nor a tinker's dam he cared
    If you stayed a year, a month, a week or day--
If you kept the simple rules; If not--you'd have to be repaired-
    And lucky if you made your get away;

When it came to business dealings he exacted to a cent.
    As the tenants of his acres could attest;
He was generous in privilege but collected up his rent
    With precision coupled up with earnest zest;
And the gold that he collected was disposed of carelessly
    In a bureau drawer half open; not a dime
Was ever taken from him, though it stood where all might see
    For the bedroom door was open half the time.

But the party that endeavored to evade the master's toll-

    Paid the debt--no matter where the trailings ran;

Once it led to Dodge City and this picturesque patrol

    Followed on--and so to speak--he got his man.

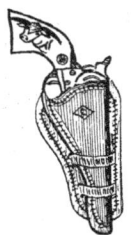

    They relate that once in Cimarron a scheduled pony race

        Brought the populace for many miles around;

    And the day found Maxwell ready with his horses in their place

        For he boasted of the best that could be found.

    When a braggart puncher stated he would cover any pile

        That his horse could beat the field, he set a pace-

    For Maxwell called the ante, raised and re-raised with a smile

        'Till the stakes reached into the thousands on the race.

Then the puncher bribed the rider to lay down and let him win

    And in some way Maxwell sensed the double cross-

For he told the crooked jokey with a meaning sort of smile

    The speed he expected from his hoss--

And pointing to a certain rock almost beneath the wire

    He idly tapped his rifle as he said--

"If when you pass that dornick you are not ahead--I'll fire

    A 30-30 through your wooden head.

The race went into history and Maxwell's pony won

    By many yards, which was as Maxwell willed--

For he watched the match in silence as he fingered his gun

    And the shady rider kept from being killed.

    He'd gamble on the weather or anything at all,

        A wager high or low as you might choose;

And with a sport's abandon he would let you make the call

    For it seemed the lucky devil couldn't lose.

His cattle doubled, trebled, he was richer than a king-

    He shot a gun like lightning--quick and true--

He was monarch of an empire with the Mesa for a fling--

    This capable old western buckaroo.

Bygone Days Of The Old West

A trapper once out shot him and it made him sad at heart-
    For slick and clean the trapper neatly drew
His smoky and shot a swallow 'twas flying like a dart--
    A thing that Maxwell couldn't seem to do.
And that's the only record of a bet he ever lost-
    This gay gambolier of Old New Mexico-
Who kept his doors wide open to the people, free of cost-
    And welcomed both the highest and the low
Free hearted in the Western Way he left a trail behind
    Of deeds both good and bad--as records go--
In battle he was heartless but by nature he was kind--
    This gay gambolier of Old New Mexico.

    Oh what if you were a Ranchero-
        With a million acres of land or so--
    Would your doors be open wide? -- Ah no--
        We'd term if a fools endeavor.
    You, (or I), might devise a sign
        Forbidding the world to cross our line-
    (And the world would forget your name - and mine) -
        But remember the fools forever.

Sculduggery

We were smoking after dinner
  At the Cross Bar Lazy B,
When the foreman, Wild Hoss Charley,
  Grinned a bit and said to me:

"See that skull hangin' yonder
  Sorta careless on a nail?
Well, that there's the skull of Yorick--
  An' it landed me in jail.
It was down in Sanantonyo
  Where I pays a bucko flat
To a side show jest fer lookin'
  At a crazy thing like that,

"Which they claimed belonged to Yorick
  (Though I never knowed him, pard,)
But I'm aimin' to be friendly,
  So I ambles in their yard
An' I sees this thing you're seein',
  An' I ambles out content
That I've sorta done my duty,
  Though I never knowed the gent.

"Well a couple of weeks had flitted
    When I'm down in Santa Fe,
An' this same contraption's showin'
    (And I'm friendly, as I say,)
So I spends another dollar--
    Which has made the total two--
Jest to honor Mr. Yorick
    In a kinda howdy-do.

"But the skull they're showin', pardner,
    Ain't the same, or I'm deranged;
It ain't half as big or ugly,
    An' I wonders why he's changed;
So I calls the man's attention
    To the one in Sanantone,
An' he's claimin' that was Yorick's
    After he was done full grown,

"But the one he's usin' now, pard,
    (That's no bigger than a toy)
Was the skull of Mr. Yorick
    When he was a little boy.
Well that sorta made me nervous,
    An' it riled me up, it did,
To be payin' for a grown-up
    An' get nothin' but a kid.

"So I asks for half a dollar
    As a rebate on th' deal,
An' they guys me, pard, an' snickers
    Jest because I made a squeal.

"So I plumb forgets my talkin',
    But my action's good and strong,
An' I busts 'em; then I'm leavin',
    Takin' Yorick's skull along.
Then the sheriff gets me later,
    An' I'm up for quite a spell
While they're waitin' to discover
    If the show folks all git well.

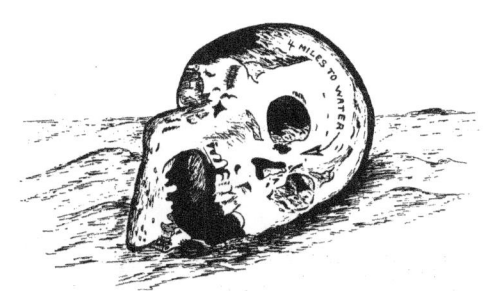

"So I'm keepin' Mr. Yorick--
    As you see him--on a nail,
An' I always think he's grinnin'
    At him gettin' me in jail.

"That's no human skull", I ventured,
    "It's a plaster-paris thing,"
But the foreman, Wild Hoss Charley,
    Only grinned, and tried to sing.

BROKEN TRAIL OF LIFE.

A driftin' cowboy was old "Bill Dupree",
    Roamin' far from his native home;
He hired out to the Cross-Bar-Lazy-B,
    And rode the trails but always alone.
The only thing that he possessed
    That he could call his own,
Was an ol' double-rig Frazier saddle,
    And his bronc "Old Strawberry Roan".

He would top him off at daylight
    With the oak brush as a stage,
And set the punchers whoopin'
    As he tore up the cactus and the sage.
Then he'd head him down the trail --
    Out across the alkali and sand;
Ridin' all the salt-licks and water-holes
    From the rancho down to the Rio Grande.

When the golden sun was sinking
    Beyond the foot-hills in the west,
And the last beams had faded
    Over the mossy-hill crest;
Bill would sit by the camp-fire
    And in the embers dyin' glow --
See many things pictured there
    That happened in the long ago.

How those fantastic figures are movin'
    Across the broken trail-of-life;
There's the old home ranch in Texas
    Two lassies and a golden-hair wife.
Then the prairie wind fans the embers
    There's the saloon, gamblers, cards and rum,
Cheatin' and arguments in the makin' --
    Two men fallin' before his smokin' gun.

Then the long night ride to cover,
  Dodgin' the Rangers and the Law;
A long and lonely winter's trappin'
  Down in the breaks of the Currumpaw.
Goin' North with the trail-herd,
  Ridin' under the name Bill Dupree
Reachin' the lower Cimarron country,
  Hirin' out to the Cross-Bar-Lazy-B.

Now he's softly singin'--
  Annie Lowery on the guard,
As he gazes in the distant shadows
  Dreamin' amongst the mountain flowers.
Ol' Strawberry Roan is quietly grazin',
  And the bull-bats dippin' near,
As his heart turns back to Texas --
  With the fallin' of a tear.

There's a look of lonely longin'
  In the eyes of faded gray,
As he places his saddle for a pillow,
  Gazin' at the clouds driftin' on their way.
In one, there's a golden-hair maiden,
  Beckonin' on with a winnin' smile;
In another, two black-eyed lassies--
  Jest mirages, the heart to beguile.

OLD SANTA FE.

Winding street for trudging feet,
    Dog fight in the alley;
Sunshine on the snow-tipped peak,
    Canyon and on valley.

    Plaza green, walls that lean,
        Around the dim Placita;
    Breezes blow to and fro --
        Guitar strings wail "Juanita"

Picturesque and grotesque,
    Beautiful, historic --
Double palaces of old
    Politics caloric.

Bygone Days Of The Old West

Archaology and mythology,
    Clique and Coronado's clan;
Now a lynching, ne'er a pinching --
    Music by the band.

Clear bright air, gardens fair,
    Mystery, intrigue --
Artists rave, old roofs cave,
    Statesmen talks fatigue.

Cigarettes, election bets,
    Henchmen, and office holders;
Ancient churches, relic searchers,
    Boulevards and boulders.

Faction fuss, scandalous,
    Tales of men and maidens;
Piety and propriety --
    Burros pinon laden.

Wild carouse, frequent souse,
    Pests and prohibition --
Investigation and revelations,
    Graft and high ambition.

Legislature, love of nature,
    Trail, cliff and pine;
Beads devout and sauerkraut --
    Chili, native wine.

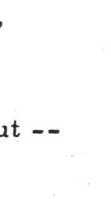

Tourists gape, entrancing shape,
    Pioneer and puncher;
Cathedral bells, New York swells-
    Enchilada munchers.

Splashing fountains,
    Same old charm always;
Fancination, recreation,
    Such is Santa Fe.

BLACK WOLF

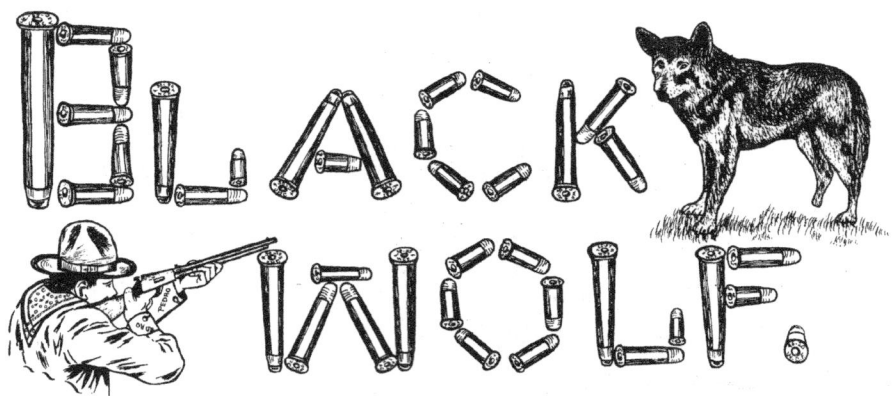

Now this is a tale of a varmint
    And part of the race he run;
He knew the feel of a trapper's steel
    The curse of a snare well done.

A wolf of mongrel breeding
    That trailed with a mongrel pack-
He went his way with a tribe of grey
    Though he wore a coat of black;
A giant of bone and sinew-
    A creature of mad desire-
With the stealth of his half-caste mother,
    The hell of his savage sire
And the cat-like tread of a panther-
    And scent that was super-drawn -
And jaws with a snap like a steel sprung trap
    With knife-like molars on.

The passing of days brought wisdom
    As silently, one by one,
The grey of the pack diminished
    Until as a pack 'twas done;
And so on a winter morning,
    The hills he had always known
Threw back the cry of his bold defi
    And he went to his kill--alone.

With a step that had long grown weary
    He skirted the canyon wall-
Nor once did a friendly greeting
    Respond to his anxious call;
So, silent as any shadow,
    He crept to the vale below
And followed the bent of a wild doe scent
    On a trail that he did not know;

And losing his sense of caution,
    And careless of time and place-
He felt but the hunger knawing
    And eagerly drove the chase
Far up in the mountain places
    And down through a sheltered glen
He loped on the deer-trail driven,
    Close to the haunts of men

And just at the very moment
    When victory seemed complete-
He felt the tang of jaws that sprang
    From the velvet beneath his feet;
Oh-the crush and crunch and biting-
    And the pain of the tortued bone-
And the quiet that seemed to chill him
    As the doe sped on alone;

Then wild with the fear within him
    He leaped like a thing insane
Each time with a strength and fury
    That tested the anchored chain,
Each leap and the flesh was rended-
    Yet never a cry gave he
'Till the fight in the night was ended
    And bleeding - he whimpered -- free;

And then as he limped to the mountain,
    Far back in his mongrel mind
He planned revenge for the mangled foot
    He'd left in the jaws behind;
Planned though he scarcely knew it,
    The way he would take his toll
And vowing hate for man's estate
    To the depths of his very soul;

Limped on to the mountain places-
    Torn by pain and strife-
Limped on to the mountain places
    Mangled and marked for life.
When spring came down to the valley
    And the melt of the snows began
His trail led down from the ranges-
    Led down to the haunts of men;

And three of the tracks behind him
    Were perfect, entirely whole,
But the fourth could well be taken
    For the marks of a prod, or pole;
And soon there were tales of terror
    Told all the valley through-
Excited words of the throat-slashed herds
    Each morning was told anew;

And many a man that ventured
    Went forth to return no more
But the tale was told in the track
    marked mole
    And the gash where the molars tore.
He carried the war relentless
    Creating a nameless dread
'Till a purse was made for the man
    that laid
    Sure proof of the Black Wolf --- Dead.

And a hunter of skill and cunning
  Slipt out from the troubled vale
With his gun and pack on his sturdy back
  He followed the queer marked trail.

In the long drawn days that followed
  Were tests of a super-skill
The hunter and the hunted sparring-
  Each for his chance to kill;
And each respected the other -
  Gave credit for nerve and grit-
So the wolf re-crossed and doubled-
  But the enemy never quit;

At times they were close together
  And often a longing eye
Would watch the pursurer trudging
  The intricate trail close by;
But always the guard was perfect
  And never a chance found he
For the swift attack on the sinewed back
  And the slash that would leave him free.

At night when the foe was sleeping

    He circled the camping spot

But always the leap was menaced

    By a fire that was bright and hot;

At times he was sorely puzzled

    When the scent of the man was plain

And somehow a recollection

    Was brewed in the mongrel's brain;

    He knew in a way uncertain

        That back in the days of yore

    He had whiffed the tainted savor

        As the same man-scent before.

And the man would wake with the dawning

        And smile at the signs he read

And think of the purse and honor

        He'd claim with the Black Wolf--Dead.

The end was as unexpected

    As ever a man might tell

The trail led down from the mountain

    And into a broken dell;

The wolf - in a sudden fury

    Stopped short with a practiced care

He raised his head to the windward

    And sniffed the polluted air

And gone was his sense of caution-
    And gone was his doubts and fears-
His rage would have been a credit
    To the hate of a thousand years-
No longer the thing uncertain-
    He knew in his soul and mind
He had nosed that scent on the jaws of steel
    Where he left his foot behind.

And so an astonished hunter
    Was met by a swift surprise;
A charging, bristled demon
    With death in it's glowing eyes;
A smile - as the rifle leveled-
    A curse - when the hammer fell-
For the gun with a blameless record
    Had harbored a faulty shell-

And the teeth of the mongrel slitted
    A gash that was deep and wide
As the flashing steel of the hunter
    Sank swift in a heaving side;
And thus did they find them lying
    Mute proof of the others art-
The man with a fang-torn wind pipe-
    The Wolf with a severed heart.

Now this is a tale of a varmint
    And part of the race he run
That cursed the feel of a trapper's steel
    To the day when his trail was done.

Water Bound

It was rainin' slow and gentle
    At the Cross-Bar-Lazy-B,
When the foreman, Wild Hoss Charley,
    Pointed out--and said to me:

"See Apache standin' yonder?
    Gettin' soaked--doggone his hide.
Two short years ago this summer
    He'd a crinkled up and died;
For I'm tellin' truthful, pardner,
    That until the time I state,
He ain't never seen a raindrop
    Nor a cloud--at any rate.

"Bein' born in old Arizony
    On a sandy mesa plain,
He ain't never seen a sprinkly,
    Let alone a soakin' rain.
When he crosses into Texas
    It starts pourin' down one day,
An' he starts to runnin', pardner,
    Like the very hell's to pay.

"An' a buckin' an' a pitchin',
    An' a squealin' every breath;
For I'm tellin' you for certain
    He was mostly scared to death.
An' I'm honest plum astonished
    At the way he behaves,
For I'm knowin' certain, Bozo,
    That he's nearly fell to staves.

An' I think a little soakin'
    Would be somethin' he'd adore;
But I plum forgot Apache
    Never seen a rain before.
An' I'm sayin' when it's over
    There was not a bit of doubt
That he was a sorry Broncho
    An' was plenty tuckered out.

"Course in time he doesn't mind it;
    But for months he'd buck and crowd
An' go buckin' like an outlaw
    Every time he seen a cloud.
An' come rearin' to the bunkhouse
    Where he'd right away begin
To kickin' on the door, pard,
    'Till I'd have to let him in.

"Now he loves a rain, I'm sayin'
    Watch him dozin' - ain't I right?
For his ribs don't rattle, pardner,
    An' his skin is soaked plum tight;
He's the best darn Bronc in Texas;
    You may search it far and wide.
See his standin' peaceful, pardner,
    Gettin' soaked doggone his hide!"

It was raining nice and gentle
    At the Cross-Bar-Lazy-B,
When Apache looked up calmly,
    Switched his tail--
        and winked at me.

"TEXAS LOU — THE LAW WANTS YU".

I stood on a rim-rock at twilight
    After-glow of the western sun;
One hand held my bridle reins,
    Th' other resting on my gun.
In my pocket was a Criminal Warrant
    Readin', bring in Old Lou alive or dead,
Wanted for the rustlin' of range cattle
    From the XIT, LAZY-G an' th' ARROW-HEAD.

Texas Lou was a fightin' man,
    Sudden and sure on the draw;
A dead hip shot, who'd cast his lost
    With killers and rustlers agin' th' law,
Cut in th' grips of th' gats he wore,
    Were notched th' deaths he delt.
His pals knew and feared Old Lou
    An th' six-guns swung at his belt.

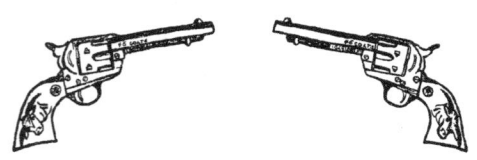

In th' shadows of th' canyon
    Just after darkness came.
I crouched in lonely silence
    In that tense and waitin' game.
A hoof-beat sound in th' canyon draw--
    A rustle of oaks near the rocky trail--
A shadowy form of horse and man--
    Th' time had come to assail!

"Texas Lou, th' law wants yu".
    Like a flash his right hand fell;
"These words", said he, "sound strange tu me---
    Yu kin go straight to hell."
Crash! roared both our guns
    As of in a single sound.
I felt a searin' tinge on my cheek;
    Tex slumped an' slipped to the ground.

Calmly I went over an' knelt at his side,
    Th' one who'd defied th' law.
"Texas Lou," I called; but Tex was dead,
    Beaten at last to th' draw.

THE CROSS-BAR-LAZY B ✧-B

The lamps of the old Rancho are burning
    Soon the canyon with darkness will fill
The cowboys from the prairie are returning
    Snow clouds showing dark over the hill.
The cattle are all under shelter
    Call of the coyotes, long and shrill,
Fireplace in the bunk-house inviting and hot
    And the heart of the puncher thrills.

The lamps of the old Rancho are gleaming
    Out over the trails and glistenin' snow
In the cook-shack the rays are beaming
    From cook-stove to rafters low
Old cook busy with pots and pans
    Singing a song of the long, long-ago
Cowboys sigh as blue-smoke rings rise
    With their happy faces all aglow.

The lamps of the old Rancho are greeting
    New range boss, wife and daughter fair
Soon they will be visiting the bunk-house
    Casting shy looks here and there
All of the cowboys are now busy
    Washin', shavin' and combin' their hair
Hangin' up their Stetsons, chaps and spurs
    Making up their bunks with extra care.

The lamps of the old Rancho are burning
    Wind and snow-flakes filling the air
Cowboys singin' and strummin' th' old guitar
    Smell of the pitch-pine logs beyond compare.
Fantastic figures showing in the firelight
    Bring back thoughts of other years,
Such are winter nights at the old Rancho
    The cowboys their joy and sorrows share.

VACATION DAYS.

Come on Pard to the deep pine wood
    Softly the robin is singing,
The chipmunk is feasting on the rose bud,
    The jay from limb to limb is springing;
Here you may sleep--
In the grasses so deep--
    While the sunshine makes you so weary,
And you sweetly awake--
As the sun through a brake--
    Bids you sing again of life, so cheery.

The buck-brush is tufted with blossoms of white
  And throwing its perfume around it,
The fawn replies to the doe's low call
  For the joy again she has found it;
The camp-robber's breast--
Peeps over the nest--
  In the midst of the Indian Bells blushing,
The call of the Coyote---
In a short, sharp note---
  While the rivulet over the stones is gushing.

Love of nature is tugging at your heart
  And pleading for you to answer the call,
As the aspen leaves play in the breeze
  Where the evening shadows fall;
Sweet charms love to enfold you--
To charm and to hold you--
  Clouds driftin' along in the sky so blue,
With deep mystery that prevails--
In her ruff, rugged trails--
  And sweet silence comes to you.

IN THE LAND OF MAÑANA.

A TALE OF THE NEW MEXICO MOUNTED POLICE

A letter came in the Springer coach mail
    To Paradise Station, commanding in tone,
That started a Ranger, alert on the trail
    To never return - if he came back alone.
The Ranger came back in two months and a day
    With one Andre Aragon, victim of fate,
And the doors of the prison at Old Santa Fe
    Closed on him forever - a prisoner of state.

Josefita, a sister of Andre, was plain;
    Carmelita, another, was fair as the rose;
Josefita a slave in the household domain;
    Carmelita a lady, with butterfly clothes;
And the husband of plain Josefita -- a cur
    Deserter from Villa - decided that he
Would rather have gay Carmelita than her
    And laid out a plan that he might become free.

So, hiding in wait by the spring side, he fired

    And killed--Carmelita--whom fate decreed

To go for water most strangely attired

    In the garb of her sister; and stunned by the deed

Juan Montoya fled from Auga Caliente

    With lithe Andre Aragon close on his trail

On through Durango with hardships a plenty

★ CARMELITA ★

    The fire of his vengance must surely prevail;

        He entered the States with his pockets depleted

    And killing Bill Crozier -- (Diamond-A man)-

        With a blow from behind, he robbed him, retreated-

    And here the long trail to Manana began.

        The sheriff at Juarez wired that Aragon was landed

           So I beat it to the Capitol of Mexico and tried

        To secure extradition but the Greasers sort of handed

           Me the technical refusal -- it was up to me to ride

        Back to Old Juarez returning, I was what you called set-back

           When I found he'd sawed the bars and broken jail

        So I traveled to Chihuahua where I fitted up a pack,

           On a pinto I started down the trail.

THE TRAIL
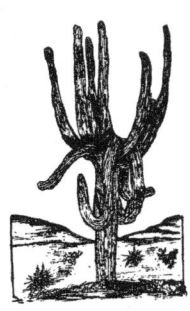

Through the dreary sage and cactus that was lonlier than hell
   'Till the fourth day my Pinto shied
From a ledge along the rimrock -- and together down we fell
   And the plucky little devil groaned and died;
So for forty odd kilometers I hiked it with my pack-
   My weary feet afire it seemed to me-
I dreaded to go forward but be damned if I'd go back
   With that greaser I was after running free.

Well--I finally found a herder and I slept the clock around
   Then I bought another pony and supplies
And I rode the God-forsaken always watching 'till I found
   The signs that told their story to my eyes:
A slaughtered deer and booted tracks down near a water-hole -
   The ashes of a camp-fire, plain to see,
Were evidence in plenty that some other weary soul
   Was roaming through the cactus same as me.

I knew him for a Mexican by the signs that told me plain--

    No Injun would have left the carcass there--

No Gringo would have cut his steak except across the grain-

    My Chili-picker must be near -- but where?

The water-holes were far apart -- one night I camped it dry--

    It chanced to be in loco weeds and so

I had to kill my pony that went locoed -- I must try

    To make my way afoot if I could go.

    A solid week I hoofed it when an Injun camp I found

        And I asked of them (in Spanish) - if they knew

Of a pesky Chili-picker who was gallivatin' 'round

    And they answered me by signs I'll give to you;

They pointed to a water-jar -- then held two fingers out-

    And signaled at the moon as Injuns can--

Which meant two days and night aback at somewhere near about,

    The last live water hole they'd seen my man.

Two weeks more I found him and I posed as one who'd fled
    From the laws up in Arizona -- all was fine-
But I dare'nt show my hand until in some way I had led
    Him on to soil across the boundry line;
For weeks we stayed together and he told me all the tale
    Of the murder of the puncher for his roll-
Working, riding, sleeping, eating, seeking always to prevail
    On the Greaser to approach my cherished goal;
We worked in the mines together and one evening Andre sez-
    I'm going to rob the pay box -- Amigo mine-
So you beat it out ahead and I'll meet you in Juarez
    Or better still, Nogales on the line.

Well, the thing worked out exactly as the wily Greaser planned
    For he met me as he said, but do my best
He was wary as the devil of your Uncle Samuel's land,
    And dreaded crossing over he confessed.
So I bribed two Senoritas on the north side of the line
    To hand us out a handsome flirt or so-
And the trap was sprung as outlined for they done their vamping fine
    And we walked across the line into Arizona.

Then I sudden slipt the smoky from his belt and made a draw
    While the sheriff, who was waiting spoke his piece--
That a certain Andre Aragon, a breaker of the law,
    Was a prisoner of New Mexico's Mounted Police.
The day we left for Santa Fe the smoking car was filled
    With Mexicans and it seemed a likely chance
That a meek and humble servant was in line for being killed-
    If one could judge from muttered threat and glance;
So I clamped an iron on his leg where everyone could see
    And snapped the other one on mine -- 'twas plain
That we would stay together -- then I held aloft the key-
    And flung it through the window from the train.

And thus for hours--some twenty-four we twain were made as one-
    I'll not forget the gladness of the day,
When the irons loosed their gripping and the long, long trail
    was done-
    And the prisoner safe at last in Santa Fe.
When I said good bye to Andre I was sort of sorry too-
    For he shook my hand and sort of leaning close--
"You only done your duty, so I hold no grudge at you
    Old Timer of the Mesa -- Adios".

The Ranger's tale is finished and I only wish to add

    That Juan Montoya crossed the Great Divide

Way down by Silver City -- if the tidings make you glad--

    The Ranger will be more than satisfied.

    And the man who trailed the desert,

        Foot by foot and piece by piece

    Was a lad they called Kid Lambert,

        Of the New Mexico Mounted Police.

GALLO DAY

A rooster, some broncs, and a straightaway,
   Some Mexicans to play it -
Make up the game on Gallo-day -
   (As Mexican people say it.)

    The rooster placed in a shallow pit
       And the earth tamped tight about him
    Allows the head to protrude a bit -
       (The game would be stale without him.)

    The riders decide their turn by lot
       And then with their rowels clinking
    Retire with their broncs to the starting spot-
       (What think you the rooster's thinking?)

Now here they come, their ponies race
    For the head that is barely showing,
Each in his turn at proper space -
    (No rooster would feel like crowing.)

And swinging low each rider tries
    A grasp for the head respondent -
No easy task, sir, I'll advise -
    (The rooster is sad, despondent.)

And soon a skillful hand will bring
    From pit, the fowl grown dizzy,
And now the game is in full swing
    (With the rooster exceedingly busy.)

Excitement rife is high indeed
    The game grows wild and thickens
About the man who holds the prize -
    (It's fun, but hard on chickens.)

Each tries to loop his reins about
    The hapless fowl and land it -
While the welkin rings with laugh and shout-
    (No bird on earth could stand it.)

The player wins who keeps his seat
    Though worn and torn and battered
And still retains the rooster's feet-
    (The other remainders scattered.)

And the victor gathers his laurels in
    Unto and around about him;
(But the rooster never has a chance to win-
    Though the game would be stale without him.)

Ruminations of a "Buster"

The Chink was serving dinner
   At the Cross-Bar-Lazy-B,
When the foreman, Wild Hoss Charley,
   Sipped his coffee and said to me:

"I ambles into Pecos,
   Where I hears they had a quid
They opine is jest too cussed bad
   An' ornery to be rid;
An' the local aggregation
   Voiced their sentyments and doubt
As to me a-gettin' on him,
   Let alone to ride him out,
An' they backs their poor opinions
   With some good old iron men.
Did I ride him--DID I RIDE HIM?--
   Bo, you ask 'em how and when.

Yeah, of course he done come pitchin';
  Never seen his beat, I guess,
But I'm coppin' all his tacticks
  Till I had him in distress.
When I finished he was standin'
  Sad and wobbly on his legs
And grandma could have topped him
  With a basket full of eggs.
So I grabbed my hard-earned sheckels
  An' I beats it where the Kid
Is dealin' out some faro,
  An' I sings to him, I did:

"DEAL 'EM HIGH AN' DEAL 'EM HANDSOME--
  FOR AT FARO I'M A BEAR;
DEAL 'EM HIGH AN' DEAL 'EM LOWLY--
  DEAL 'EM SWIFT, BUT DEAL 'EM SQUARE."

Yeah, they cleaned me good and plenty;
  Sent me out again to roam;
Jest a lonesome bronco buster,
  Broke, a thousan' miles from home.

Bygone Days Of The Old West

Then an ornery, two-gun killer,
    With four notches on his gun,
Started in to get insultin'
    With his sneerin' kind of fun.
Now, I seldom packs a smoky,
    But, I've notions of my own,
An' he riled me, pard, he riled me
    With his mean and leerin' tone;

So I landed swift and sudden,
    Square and certain on his back;
Dug my spurs into his bein',
    Grabbed his guns and made him track.
Round an' round the room I rid him,
    Shootin' now an' then--I did,
With the whole cabooddle laughin'
    At the varmint as I rid.
Yeah, I told him plain I'd kill him
    If he tried a-layin' down--
So I rid him out the doorway,
    Down the street and out of town.

Every jump he makes I'm shootin',
    While each tinklin' shiny spur
Was a doin' noble duty
    As it dug into his fur.

And I'm stickin', Bo, I'm stickin'

   On this Hell-rip-rarin' ride,

Till he lost his heart entirely

   An' he plumb broke down and cried.

So I kicked him once, impartial,

   For I still was sort of mad--

Get the hell quick out of New Mexico

   'Fore some bucko hurts you bad!

       So the punchers and the others

          Makes a pot for me at that,

       Makin' him the most prolific

          Varmint I have ever sat.

       I was jest a bronco buster,

          But I don't mind sayin' here

       It's the best dad-gummed profession

          On this blamed old hemisphere;

       There's nothin' else could give me

          Half the thrill as when I rid

       That insultin' two-gun killer

          Out of Pecos like I did.''

              It was silent in the chuck house--

                 Not an eyelash made a wink--

              As the foreman, Wild Hoss Charley,

                 Threw a biscuit at the chink.

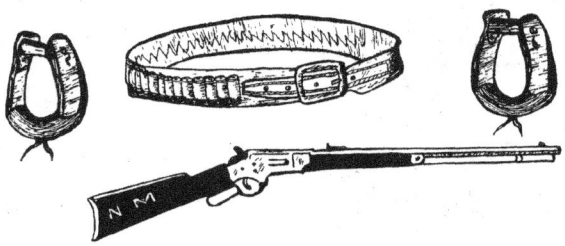

The Old Camp Cook

When water and wood is sighted
    And th' sun sinkin' in th' west,
Th' old chuck wagon comes to a stop,
    Hear th' old camp cook above all·th' rest,
"Waddie, wrangle up th' water--
    Waddie, rustle up th' wood--
Hand your Uncle Tom down th' shovel,
    Pick out th' spuds that are sound and good."

Soon th' fire is kindled
    Th' smoke begins curlin' in th' air,
The chuck-box lid is lowered,
    Pots and pans scattered everywhere.
"Waddie, put th' bed rolls out yonder--
    Waddie, don't yu raise any dust--
Hand your Uncle Tom down th' pot-hooks,
    See that th' skillet is minus rust."

Th' sour-dough biscuits are brownin',

    Th' dutch-oven an' lid is pipin' hot,

And th' son-of-a-gun is boilin'

    In th' old, black iron pot.

"Waddie, round-up th' tools an' cups--

    Waddie, put th' wash-pan on th' log--

Hand your Uncle Tom down three contented cows,

    See thet th' wheel-mules don't get in th' bog.

Evenin' shadows are fallin'

    Th' Arbuckles aroma is befittin' to th' air.

Th' cowboys have reached the water-hole,

    Ball-bats flyin' here and there.

"Waddies, come an' get it--

    Waddies, don't you hear th' call--

Your Uncle Tom is th' camp cook

    On th' western slope this fall.

THE LAND OF THE SETTING SUN.

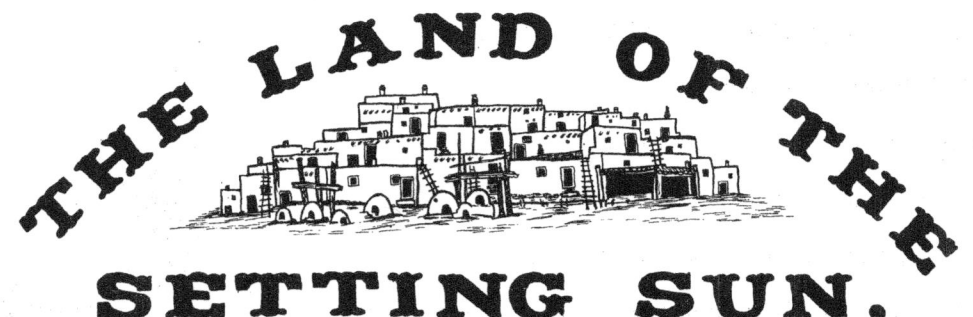

Oh land of the west, the golden west
    Thy triumphs have but begun
The favorite land by nature blest
    The land of the setting sun.
Your rocks and rills, your stately hills
    Your billows of virgin soil
Are vaults of wealth whose doors swing wide
    To the key forged from honest toil.

The rat-a-tat-tat of the mustang's feet.
    The whir of the rope through the air.
The buzz of the rattler grim and low
    That speaks to the man "beware!"
The she wolf's cry as she watches nigh
    Where the whelps snuggle down in their den
Makes the red blood leap with a gladsome rush
    Through the veins of men who are men.

Where nature unbosoms her secret heart
    And communes unreserved with you
Where hand meets hand with an honest grasp
    And the words of her sons ring true
Where men are judged by their actual worth
    And the sort of race they run
And not by the limbs of a family tree
    Or for the deeds their fathers done.

When winds swoop down from the mountain's crown
    To roar o'er the vast domain
'Tis nature's broom that sweeps the gloom
    Of disease, from thy fertile wing.
Where life is a grand and glorious song
    In a land where you live it free
And man is near to his God above
    As a man on earth can be.

So here's to the land of the golden west
    Who's trimuphs have but begun
Here's how -- to the land I love best
    The land of the setting sun.
Here's how -- to the west when famine strikes
    Here's how -- when her people feast
I would rather be buried deep under your sod
    Than alive in your seething east.

THE LONG LONG TRAIL.

There's a trail a leadin' somewhere
    And I'm ridin' it today-
It may be near the endin'
    Or it may be far away;
Each day it is growin' rougher-
    Dimmin' down to just a track
That is blotted out behind me-
    So -- I won't be comin' back.

It may be leadin', leadin'
> To the mountains or the sea—
Or the valley where the mists hang;
> There's no other way for me.
But to follow where it's takin'—
> Searchin' out the dimmin' track
That is blotted out behind me—
> So -- I won't be comin' back.

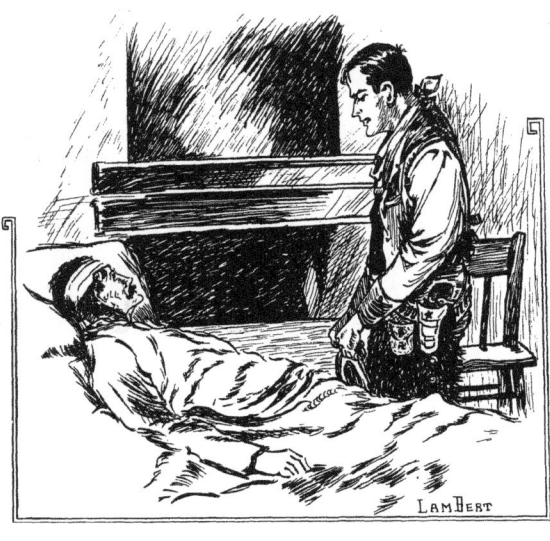

And I'm hopin' when it's finished
> At the endin' there will be
Loved ones who have solved its windin',
> Waitin' there to welcome me;
With my old cayuse a restin',
> Free of saddle, rope and pack,
May there be no wish or longin'
> For to come a trailin' back.

When Billy the Kid Went Out.

It wasn't spectacular as you'd suppose—
    Though many have twisted the story—
To fit their fancy when they would compose
    A tale of prowess and glory;
As a matter of fact, the passing was tame,
    No fervor of battle or shout--
A step in the night--and a swift spurt of flame--
    And Billy the Kid went out.

    They say he came from Boston,
        It is conjecture more or less,
    But it is safe to say
        Twas somewhere in the East-
    Just a kid--he sought the places
        Where adventure teemed, I guess
    And the chance of the prosiac seemed the least;
        Oh he learned the lesson early
    As the mind of youth will do
        And he chose the path that erring youth will go;
    Though he paid the debt before his years
        numbered twenty--two
    He was Outlaw King of Old New Mexico.

At a lake called Los Portales is a spring and cliff of rock
  With a stone corral and camp house close at hand,
Where the gang of cattle rustlers had headquarters, and the stock
  Were driven and an expert changed the brand.
As the leader of this thieving crew he gained great renown
  From Santa Fe on down to Angelo;
If they sought to stop him he would shoot the party down
Cold-blooded; and uncertain records show,

  Not counting in the Injuns and the Mexicans, 'tis said,
That the total numbered up to twenty-two;
  For a lad of twenty summers he'd a reputation red
Never equalled in the borders' grim review.

But the course he run was drawing to a close; his wild career
  Was destined to be short--the laws demand
Keep silent but the vengance of it's claim drew ever near
  Until the day of payment was at hand.
And here's the final chapter of the out-law as is otld
  By men who knew the way it came about;
Commencing in December on a morning bleak and cold
  And ending in July, when he went out.

Bygone Days Of The Old West

Tom Emery, Jim Sweet and Lon Chambers were three
    Cow-punchers from Panhandle land;
Pat Garrett was sheriff; as officer he
    Was leader and held command
To break up the stealing of cattle and so
    We found the discerning trail
That leads up a snow covered arroyo
    To a little stone house in the vale.

Their horses were tether they crawled through the night
    'Till the house was plainly in view-
And waiting — they lay 'till the slow coming light
    Of dawn had begun to peep through;
Then one Charlie Bowda stepped forth from the door-
    "Hands Up" was the sheriff's command-
But he reached for his gun and they plugged him before
    His belt had been touched by his hand;
He staggered inside and his chieftain-the Kid,
    Advised him his moments were few--
And sent him back out with a gun and he bid
    Him pick off a 'lizard' or two
Before he crossed over, and Bowda went back
    To try at his chieftain's behest
He staggered and fell just in front of the shack
    With his face looking out to the West.

Then out of the chimney the barrel of a gun
    With a message of white fluttered there--
And the march of the bandits was quickly begun
    Through the door with their hands in the air.
One Tommy O'Folliard, the last in the line,
    Made a dash for his freedom in vain;
For the shots of the posse drawn deadly fine
    Fell near him and on him like rain.

Then on to Ft. Sumner the rest of the band
    Were taken; a stop of a day
Was made for fresh mounts, then the little command
    Rode on to Old Santa Fe;
And Billy the Kid was at once put on trial
    For his record so ruthless and red-
Found guilty, and sentenced within a short while,
    To hang 'till his carcass was dead.

Two guards were assigned him, Bob Ollinger and
    The other a party called Bell--
Instructed to keep, at all hazards, the bland
    Desperado confined in his cell.
One morning, Bob Ollinger, placing a tray
    Of food for the prisoner, leaned down--
And the Kid, like a flash, snatched his pistol away,
    Killed them both and walked free through the town;
Securing a horse from a hitch-rack he strode
    Through the broad open light of the day
From the two silent forms in the cell house and rode
    From the noose and Old Santa Fe.

On July Thirteenth, in eighty one,
    Pat Garrett got a tip
That the Kid was near Ft. Sumner
    So he planned a little trip
That ended in the finding
    Of the layout where he hid
In dogged, watchful silence
    For the coming of the Kid.

And 'twas never known exactly
    What took place but it is said
That the moon shown through the window
    Where the bandit lay in bed—
And the door was standing open
    For the night was sultry hot—
A favorable condition
    For a sure and certain shot;
At any rate Pat Garrett
    Brought the bandit's end about—
Probably the only witness
    When Billy, the Kid passed out.

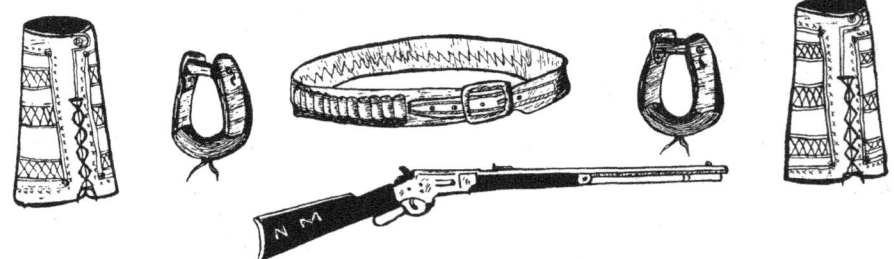

He was buried at Ft. Sumner
    Near O'Falliard- and today
The green alfalfa's waving
    O'er the places where they lay;
The wooden boards that marked them
    Fell to dust many long years ago--
Where the bandit king is sleeping-
    Down in Old New Mexico.

No---It wasn't much spectacular
    As fiction stories tell---
But a matter of precision
    That was business like as hell;
Just a hardened proposition
    Figured down to leave no doubt
That the end was accomplished--
    And the Kid---passed out.

Uncle Tom Curtis on a Calico Trail.

"Calico" said Uncle Tom,
Wall, here's the pint with me--
A puncher ort to stick to steers
An' let the wimmen be;
Oh yes, I had a little fling
With one some years ago,
And that's the reason I (p'tu!)
Consider thet I know.

It happened back in Santa Fe
When I was browsin' down
About a dogie car-ni-val
Thet chanct to be in town;
She kept a stand with pocket knifes
An' other tarnal things
Thet you could win by ropin' 'em
With little wooden rings.

I spent some dough a-tryin' it,
But not a cussed one
Would wrap itself around a knife;
I couldn't see the fun;
An' so I sorter cussed (p'tu!)
About their little graft,
She kinder sized me up a bit,
An' then the critter laffed.

(P'tu!) not mean y' understand,
But pleasant like -- and low--
The way a woman always laffs
When anglin' for a beau--
An' me, I ain't got sense enough
To drift on down the street,
But stays and talks until I'm derned
Nigh locoed pard, complete.

We makes a date to meet that night
An' have a little talk;
An' so we did, and started out
To take a (p'tu!) walk;
I must of spent a dollar, pard,
Fer candy; an' I hope
To choke to death -- I ups and asks
Thet female to e-lope.

She seemed to like the idy like,
An' hinted kinder low
She'd have to have some money,
So I gave her all my dough.
An' then she let me kiss her--onct--
I'm telling you, the taste
Of that there kiss was mighty like
Old flour-and-water paste.

She said she'd pack her duds next day,
An' then tomorrow night
We'd meet again, and we'd e-lope;
An' I agreed all-right;
But when I went to town, I'll swear,
The car-ni-val had flew;
An' with it went my female love
An' all my money, too.

(P'tu!) she left a letter that
Explained she couldn't go
E-lopin', cause her husband
An' the kids would miss her so.
It made me mad as thunder,
But what was I to do
To get my money back again?
So there y'are --(p'tu!)

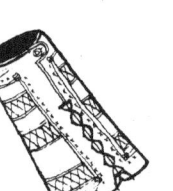

Y' can't tell when they're married, pard,
They lie like all get-out.
They sorter get you locoed
Till yer kinder mill about.
Yes calico may be all right,
But here's the pint with me;
A puncher orter stick to steers
An' let the wimmen be.

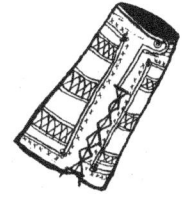

LITTLE PAPOOSE.

LITTLE PAPOOSE

Of what are you thinking, grave little Papoose,
    Tied fast in your buckskins like mummies of yore?
Do you know the legend of Old Mother Goose
    Or the five little pigs and the sleepy-time lore?
Dark shadows abound in your beady black eyes,
    As black as the strands of your wonderful hair;
And the sun glistens down in your face as it tries
    In vain to discover a smile hidden there.

Swing high in the shade where the breeze whispers low;

    The coyote's weird cry is your lullaby tune

A smile steals upon you and eyelids droop low--

    The sandman, the sandman will be with you soon.

And the squaw mother comes for a spell from the field;

    The buckskins are loosed as she pauses to rest;

The glad moments fly, as reluctant they yield

    The time she may cuddle you close to her breast.

    Your father returns from the hunt with his kill;

        The light, silent steps of his moccasins fall;

    A song finds its way from the turbulent rill,

        But deep is your sleep, unaware of it all.

    Dream on in the arms of your mother; the low

        Soft sigh of the wind lulls you deeper to rest;

    For Manitou guards wee papooses, I know,

        When the sandman has found them

            'way out in the West.

DESERT SHIPS.

Ho, for the West and promised lands-
Desert ships through desert sands.

Oh, the sad, glad tale of the pioneers,
   And the gruelling race now run,
The heartaches born of the early years,
   The sting of a bleaching sun;
The tortured way of the long, long trail,
   Where the white-topped schooners plied;
A noble cast for a gruesome tale,
   Where the actors fought and died.

The dangerous road, by perils crust,
   Stretched on through the shifting sands;
The agony of unquenched thirst-
   The thieving red-skinned band;
The lying beck of the plains mirage-
   The winds with the heat of hell-
The viper's nest and its camouflage-
   The feel of the desert's spell.

The dread of a poisoned water hole-
    Or a desert well gone dry--
The call to God from a mother's soul,
    As she watched her offspring die;
The vigil on through the lonely night-
    For the foe that was always near-
The call to arms and the lusty fight
    Filled the day of the Pioneer.

The buzzards wheeled in circles wide,
    High over the deadened plain,
Where a driver faltered or turned aside
    And was lost from the wagon train.

Bygone Days Of The Old West

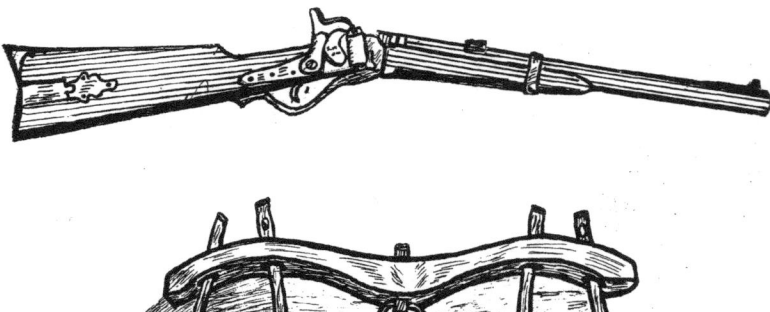

A speck of white in the setting sun
   In the days of the used-to-be-
A footsore team and an antique gun-
   A ship in a sand-swept sea-
A weary man and a woman pale-
   The brood of the luckless twain-
Their all-in-all on an unknown trail,
   Adrift from the wagon train.

Ho, for the West and promised lands-
   Bleaching bones on the desert sands.

Old Fort Union

FRED LAMBERT

Out in the sage-brush on western prairies,
    In the Sunshine state New Mexico,
Stand the ruins of old Fort Union,
    Built of rock and adobe long ago.

Oh, what a halo of history hangs o'er you
    'Round and about your illustrious name!
Oh, what a mission the fates placed before you!
    Well did you carry, and just is your fame.

At a distance your myraid of tall chimneys

Rise out against the blue western sky,

Like a line of old timey soldiers

Ghost guarding the cattle grazing nearby.

Oh, ragged are the corrals and walls of adobe,

Marked and scarred are the old stone cells.

Dark and dingy-looking the powder house

Of bygone days that only story can tell.

The heavy wooden arches are going to decay--

Cisterns full of water murky and cold.

Window frames broken and splintered away--

Roof timbers covered with mildew and mould.

Nearby cut hub-deep in the prairie adobe,
  Ruts of the Santa Fe trail stand out today;
Lasting memories of pioneer hardships endured
  As brave hearts plodded their weary way.

Rest ye in peace, brave soldiers and scouts,
  Neither rushing wheels on the open thoroughfare
Or droning engines in the sky of blue,
  Can disturb those that are slumbering there.

THE PACK TRAIN

The first faint streaks of the coming dawn
    Lighten the eastern sky;
The cunning coyote homeward slinks
    To his den in the gulch near by.
The grasses bow their tasseled heads
    To the sun-kissed summer breeze,
While the birds are singing their roundelays
    From the top of the swaying trees.
Then echoing sharply o'er the hill,
    And whispering through the dell,
Like the silvery voice of an elfin king
    Comes the sound of a tinkling bell.

And winding around the time-worn-trail--
    A trail of a bygone day --
Comes an old bell mare and her train of mules,
    Sorrel and brown and gray.

Now snatching a bit of the tall bunch grass,

    Then casting a look behind --

It's little she cares that on her back

    Is dynamite for a mine.

Far down below in the river's gorge

    Where the water sparkles clear;

A dozen men are driving stakes,

    In charge of an engineer.

For a railroad soon will bridge the gorge,

    And circle the canon's rim;

Then wind away, twin belts of steel,

    Till lost in the distance dim.

And the old bell mare with her train of mules

    Must push on farther still,

To seek the land of the setting sun

    Beyond the distant hill.

For, yet untrodden, new trails await

    The stanch, the true and bold,

While grimly smiling and desolate

    The desert guards her gold!

A Bunk-House Tale

We were loafing in the bunkhouse
   Of the Cross-Bar-Lazy-B,
When the foreman, Wild Hoss Charley
   Twisted his mustache and said to me:

"Sometimes I get to thinkin',
   And I wonder now and then,
If there's any fools are more loco
   Than the common run of men;
An' I'm jest about concludin'
   Every man has times that he
Ain't exactly compus-mentus,
   Or it seems that way to me.

"I'm thinkin' of a weddin'
  That took place in San Bernal,
When a 'tarnal' fool was married
  To Josiah Sander's gal.
She was pretty, mighty pretty;
  Hair the tint a sunset throws,
An' her cheeks were blushin', pardner,
  Like the petals of a rose.

"An' she laughed and sang and fluttered
  Like a lark in early spring,
Till it sorter made me joyful
  Jest to listen to her sing.
Yeah, they lived t'gether, pardner,
  Happy as the day was long;
He, content to have her near him,
  Jest to listen to her song.

"Then one day she gets a letter--
  Cunnin', pard, an' worded well,
An' concocted by a devil
  In the lowest depths of hell;
Full of pizen as an adder,
  Intimatin' clear and plain
That the writer was a lover
  Claimin' her in part again.

"Yeah, she showed it to the critter
  Who she married, an' the fool
Plum believed the lyin' varmint.
  An' she listened ca'm an' cool,
Not denyin' nor explainin'
  That no word of it was true,
But a-standin' white an' starin'
  Lookin' at him through an' through.

He's a-talkin' plum accusin'-
  But her lips are firm an' set.
Then he left her with a name, pard,
  That a woman can't forget.
Yeah, it killed her, pard, it killed her,
  An' the poor fool wandered back
To her grave out on the Mesa
  By the little 'dobe shack.

The Lure

Where is the man who will ride with me
    For the good that a man may do,
Down scented paths to a crystal sea
'Neath skies of a friendly blue?
    To carry cheer to a breaking heart--
Or hope to a soul despaired--
Oh where is the man who will do a part
    Of the work that his God prepared?

Remember the end of the path will bring
The glory of earth and sun,
    And perfect peace to the hearts that sing
From the joy of a deed well done;
Oh where is the man who will ride with me
    For the good that a man may do
    Down scented paths of a crystal sea
'Neath skies of a friendly blue?

And silence fell -- nor a man replied

To the challenge weird -- for a foolish ride.

Oh where is the man that dares to ride
    To the desert depths away
On the Western slope of the Great Divide,
    Where the Gila monsters play
And bones peep forth from burning sand,
    Where vipers dare you pass
And the sun beats down on the barren land
    As it floats in a sky of brass --

Where sand-dunes mock and throats gulp dry
    And tongues fantastic loll
All swollen, fearful as they cry
    And curse their Maker's soul ---
Where hell abounds and buzzards wheel
    And wait their biding hour ---
And strong men choke and nerves of steel
    Lose all their fancied power ---

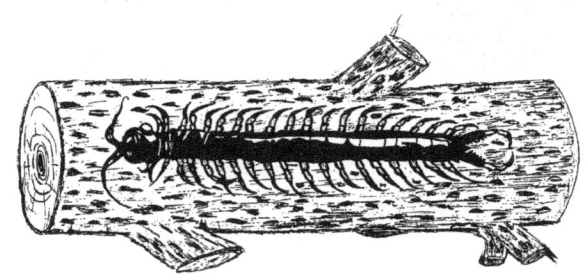

And phantoms, specters, God knows what

    The trails for you may hold ---

But they say, perchance, there may be a pot

    At the end, well filled with gold;

Oh where is the man who dares to ride

    To the desert's depths away

On the Western slope of the Great Divide

    Where the Gila monsters play?

And a hundred million men replied ---

Lead on to the gold -- we dare to ride.

Swan Song of the West

Empire supreme in a world full of vastness,
    Romance and tragedy, legend and lore,
Unto itself as a world in its fastness,
    Passing each day to return never more.

    Bold were your days as the mountains, high soaring,
        Bold were your plains and the canyons cut through;
    Deep were your coulees, the blizzard winds roaring,
        Bolder the people you fostered and knew.

Bygone Days Of The Old West

Gone are the days of the trail and its glory,
    Clear comes the call, but there's none to reply;
White covered trains wend their way from your story,
    Men of the ranges rode hither and by.

    Slow your retreat, but as sure as the dawning:
        Leaving but memories, strive as you may.
    Looms the abyss of eternity yawning:
        Into its maw and forever away.

    Sing me a song with a chivalrous themeing,
        Courage and love and a weird saddened strain,
    Bold in its tenor but soft in its dreaming,
        Soft in its dreaming of sorrow and pain.

Sing me a song with a wonderful story,
    Sing me a song filled with pathos and rest,
Sing me good-bye for an empire of glory,
    Sing me through tears Adios to the West.

Old Pal Of Mine

You're jest a poor old lonesome wreck,
    As far as I can see;
An' you're a dog and I'm a puncher--
    The road ahead is free.
I've nothin' left on earth but you,
    What more could I--indeed?
No kin or friend could e'er replace
    Your own unselfish creed;
You're jest a poor old hungry dog,
    As far as I can see,
But darn your flea-bit ornery hide,
    You're everything to me.

You're jest a lean, old hungry dog,
    But I can mind a night
That you jumped in and saved my skin
    When I had lost the fight;
And on another day you braved
    The waters swift and brought
My fair-haired baby from the flood;
    Exhausted, still you fought--
You're jest a lean, old hungry dog
    Till I look into your eyes,
Then -- dam the man 'at says 'at you
    Ain't human --dog, he lies.

You're jest a poor old hungry dog,
    As far as I can see;
Not worth a dollar bill--
    No hoss or pedigree;
Some lazy like and not as spry
    As other dogs I know,
And always taggin' me around
    No matter where I go;
You're jest a poor old hungry dog,
    As far as I can see--
But, darn your ornery flea-bit hide,
    You're everything to me.

In Santa Fe

There wasn't a man in Santa Fe

Who'd go to the mat with Shag Bronte.

He could ride a horse and shoot a gun

    Like the devil himself, and the deeds he'd done

Would put him in jail for a thousand years-

    A changin' brands and rustlin' steers

And killin' men on the least pretext

    Whenever his one-track mind was vexed.

    His lineage ran in a tangled strain

        To English, French and a dash of Spain-

    With a trace of Scotch; and Indian tones

        Were manifest in the high cheek bones-

    The--pure hell and unrefined--

        A nonescript with a mongrel mind.

He was hated and feared in every place
    That knew his voice or evil face,
And even the ones that formed his clan
    Cursed and despised him to a man.
But the curses never were voiced or heard
    By so much as the sign of a whispered word.

    But there came a night when Shag Bronte
        Made a mistake in Santa Fe.
    A stranger leaned on the long-horn bar
        And slowly puffed a mild cigar-
    A tenderfoot you would say at least,
        Who ought to be back in the quiet East;
    A man not meant for the turbulent way
        Of frontier times in Santa Fe.

He dressed the West, but his clothes betrayed
    To a normal mind they were tailor made;
And the guns that hung in the belt he wore
    Were nickel-plate of a minor bore.
He paid no mind to the jibes and jeers
    So plainly meant to reach his ears.

Then Shag walked in; and he quickly saw
    The Tenderfoot, and a loud guffaw
Boomed from his chest as he neatly drew
    And shot the stranger's cigar in two.
But the stranger neither moved or spoke
    Except to call for another smoke.

Shag stood watching the play begun,

    His right hand holding the smoking gun;

The stranger placed the cigar with care

    In his mouth; and then with a careless air

Made a motion as though to scratch a match,

    In the masculine way, a ready match.

And all looked on--nor a soul devined

    The move the stranger had in mind.

As his hand swung up, a nickel gun

    Crashed its shots and the game was done;

For Shag Bronte was dead before

    His body fell to the barroom floor;

And he never knew he had matched his brains

With the man most feared on the Western plains.

And Billy the Kid rode on his way

    To the Texas line from Santa Fe.

THE INDIAN LOVE SONG

When Running Bear, a Kickapoo
    And temperamental soul,
Met Rising Dawn, the dusky pride
    Of every Seminole,
He courted her with eagle claws,
    With gaudy beads--and, worse,
He wrote her many, many reams
    Of Seminolic verse
Proclaiming that his simple love
    Was lasting, firm and true,
And offered to the Seminole
    His heart and tepee, too.

Her father, a prosaic man,
    Insisted Rising Dawn
Must realize that social lines
    Were very closely drawn,
And locked her in the council house
    Without ado or talk,
Then whetted up his hunting knife,
    His rage and tomahawk;
No wedding drums should ever beat
    Their jubilant tat-too,
Announcing that a Seminole
    Had wed a Kickapoo.

And every night poor Running Bear
    Would sing a sad farewell
With agony of sorrow that
    His lips could never tell.
And from the mountain fastness
    He would sound his tragic notes
That wailed of grief in volumes
    As it gurgled from his throat
To tell the woods surrounding
    That his wedding was taboo,
Because she was a Seminole
    And he a Kickapoo.

The night was strangely silent --
    And the woods resound no more--
With echoes from the hillside
    To the council chamber door.
A shadow sought the fastness
    When the song was going good--
A subtle shadow stealing to
    The singer in the wood;
A thud--a crash of bramble--
    And the chant of love was through--
The drastic, senior Seminole
    Had kicked the Kickapoo.

RANGE REVOLUTIONS.

I SIMPLY pass the story
   Told to me by "Cactus Bill',
Who planned a revolution
   In the province of Brazil.

I'd rid the ranges, pardner,
   For a good round dozen years,
And listened to the coyotes
   And the bawlin' of the steers;
I wants to be somebody
   In this grand old hemisphere
But I'm about concludin'
   That there ain't much chances here.
And ridin' buckin' bronchos
   In the cactus and mesquite,
Ain't doin' much to land you
   Square and certain on your feet.

So I happens to remember
    That a year ago last spring
A fortune teller warned me
    I was born to be a king;
And I gets my head to workin'
    With my plannin', pard, until
I hits on revolutions
    And I trails it for Brazil,
Where revolution's easy;
    And I figgers out, towit:
I'll confiscate a country
    And be president of it.

There ain't no trouble, pardner,
    When I landed at the docks,
I gets my revoulters
    From the populace in flocks.
They're mongrels from the cities,
    And mangy Portuguese,
Some loafers from the shippin'
    And riff-raff of the seas.
I buys a dinky cannon,
    My noble men can drag,

I takes some old bandanas
    And rigs me up a flag;
We has our secret meetin's
    When I address my crew
With revolution' phrases
    And they cheers me frequent, too.
I writes up a song that's aimin
    To cheer 'em up a bit,
The tune we use is "Dixie
    And certain makes a hit.

We've set our minds on revolution
    Soon our cannon we'll be shootin'--
Get away--get away,
    If you don't want to be crippled,
GET AWAY.

It finishes by statin'
    That we're aimin' to be free,
And the words that's plain explainin'
    Their President is me----

We'll march right through the jungle,
    We will, we will,
We're goin' in this thing hell-bent
    With Cactus Bill, our President,
Get away, get away, for the revolution
    arm-ee.

Yeah,--I'm just about to open
    With some interestin' scenes,
When a mangy mongrel Judas
    Has to go and spill the beans.
And the first thing I'm a-knowin'
    They had landed me in jail,
And not a hombree, pardner,
    In the place to go my bail.

I overhears their plannin'
    For to shoot me, so I makes
A plum ferocious leavin'
    And I beats it for the brakes.
Yeah, I heads across the country
    To the mountains where I hid;
For them wild Brazilian Grandees
    Chased me clear into the Andes
Where I stayed for half the summer
    And I nearly starved, I did.

Well, I finally goes a sneakin'
    To the Gulf of Guayaquil,
Leavin' all my revolution
    Ca'm and quiet in Brazil.
And I shovels coal, I'm tellin',
    To Galveston for my fare,
For I'm worried, pard, I'm worried,
    And I'm anxious to be there.
So we ain't no more than landed
    When I lopes it for the range,

And I'm yearnin' for the bawlin'
   Of a steer--which may be strange--
But the first one I'm a hearin'
   Sounds plum human when he speaks,
So I roped him, pard, and kissed him,
   Fair and certain on the cheeks.
And this little verse I've written
   Clear explains my notions, pard,
For the mesa may be lonesome
   And the ridin' may be hard-----
      BUT----

There ain't nobody livin'
   Loves a puncher's life like me,
He's lord of all the Mesa
   And you take it, friend, from me,
That I'd rather be a zero,
   Here in Texas, than a hero
Down in Rio De Janeiro
   On a revolutionary spree.

Cyclones and Dogies.

It was snowing nice and gentle
    At the Cross-Bar-Lazy-B,
When the foreman, Wild Hoss Charley,
    Plaited a quirt and said to me:

Ever seen a cyclone pardner?
    Well, there's nicer things I know,
An' I happens to remember
    One down in Texas years ago;
It is mighty hot an' dusty,
    An' I'm headin' down a draw
Huntin' for a cussed dogie
    That had recent lost its maw,

When I hears a funny roarin',
    An' I'm lookin' up ter see--
When here comes a cyclone, pardner,
    Like a herd hell-bent for me;
An' it lifts me quick; it lifts me,
    Horse and all, and here we go,
Like the devil beatin' tan-bark,
    Up across New Mexico.

    I ain't sayin' just exactly
        What we're makin', but it's fast;
    An' I'm plumb excited pronto,
        Wonderin' if I'm gonta last.
    But I'm free to say for certian
        That I plumb enjoys it, son,
    Settin' on my bronc, Apache,
        That for onct ain't buckin' none.

So we keeps a glidin' easy
    For an hour, or mebbe two,
When we turns back into Texas--
    Which I'm glad to see us do--
An' it mebbe sounds presumpshus,
    But I kinda got the swing,
How by leanin' back an' forward,
    I could guide the pesky thing.

An' I gits it back, I'm sayin',
    To a mile or so from town;
Then the thing gets tired or somethin',
    An' it quits and lets us down;
An' I'm standin' sorta shaky--
    But I suddent has to laff--
Fer right there beside Apache
    Is the cussed dogie calf.

We had picked him up an' fetched him
    Right along from where he's hid
So you might say that the cyclone
    Sorta helped me out -- it did.
But I'm worried fer Apache
    Acts as though he's mebbe sick--
When I suddent gits back on him;
    But he satisfies me quick.

That he's plumb o.k. an' ready--
    Fer he gives a squeal an' pitch,
An' he lands me neat an' certain
    On some cactus by a ditch.
So I pats him, pard, I pats him --
    With a stroke that's good an' stanch;
Then I ropes the dogie gentle
    An' we heads back to the ranch.

    I suppose that such a cyclone
        Killed and wounded quite a lot?
    But the foreman, Wild Hoss Charley,
        Only murmured; "I've fergot."

COWBOY TAPS

I'm ridin' west on a trail alone—
    On a trail that's dim and a trail unknown,
That's leadin' on to the settin' sun
    Where camp is made and the trail is done—
And the herd's at rest from the reekin' mill—
    All bedded down, and the night is still.

Oh, I'm ridin' west,
    For a long, long rest,
Where the round up waits
    And the grass is best
And the chuck is good
    And the herdin' light,
So I'm ridin' west
    In the quiet night.

I'm ridin' west, and I shant come back,
> For the trail is closed and the sand-swept track
Is filled behind as I follow on
> The star mirage, for the sun is gone
And I'm lopin', pard, through a canyon deep
> To the camp beyond where the herd's asleep.

Oh, I'm ridin' on,
> For the sun is gone,
And the trail is dim
> Like the dew at dawn-
But the star mirage
> Leads by it's light
So I'm driftin' on
> Through the quiet night.

Oh, I'm ridin' slow
> For I'd like to know
That the trail leads straight
> Where the riders go,
(But the star mirage,
> With it's beamin' light,
Keeps callin' me
> So I must be right.)

As a dogie treads through the shiftin' loam
> To find it's way to the herd at home,
I'm on my way for the round-up waits
> The driftin' brands at the corral gates,
And the trail is closed and I shant come back,
> For I'm ridin' west on a wind-swept track.

The Herdsman

Sunset's glow in a troubled West;
    Night came down with the herd at rest.
The herdsman lighted his pipe and gazed
    At the shortened rope where his broncho grazed
The stars peeped out reluctant, dim,
    And the wind swept up from the canyon's rim
On to the North, where a darkened mass
    Marshaled its force in a sea of glass.

The lobo, true to his kin and creed
    Cried through the night to his mongrel breed
A warning note to the clan and then
    Sought safe retreat in his sheltered den,
And the she-wolves heeded their master's call,
    And fled to their whelps in the canyon wall.

And silence came--no sound was heard
    But the click of a horn when a leader stirred.
The stars were gone, and in their stead
    The blackened mass crept overhead
And cloaked the scene in a weirdly pall-
    The herd and herdsman, plain and all.

The air grew stifling--lifeless--dense--
    And quiet reigned--oppressive--tense--
When a sudden glare in the thickened gloom
    Found response in a sullen boom.
The leaders sprang from their bed of earth,
    The herdsman tightened his saddle girth
As he whispered a word in his broncho's ear
    That told of the race which he knew was near.

With a flash and a crash, the storm king spoke,
    And the muffled beat of the herd that broke
From rest to senseless, head-long flight,
    Joined with the hell of the restless night.
The work was on; and the broncho knew
    The very thing that a bronc should do,
With flattened ears he brought the race
    To the wild-eyed leaders pace by pace--

And, hanging there, the herdsman plied
    His bull whip lash on flank and side.
And thus intent he gave no mind
    To the horde that thundered close behind.
But a blunder meant the twain would meet
    Sure death from the pound of a thousand feet.

Bygone Days Of The Old West

The bronc was sure, and the rider burned
    His lash to the hide 'till the leaders turned.
To the right--to the right--he swung them still,
    And the frightened herd began to mill.
The lightning ran like melted glass
    From the clouds above o'er the heaving mass,
And broke with deafening crash of sound
    And it found its mark in the sodden ground;
While static played from horn to horn
    Of the racing herd which was tired and worn.

Around and around in a dizzy reel,
    Like the giant course of a mighty wheel,
With the broncho racing, just outside,
    And the bull lash taking its toll of hide.
Slower and slower, the circling mill
    With heaving flanks at last stood still.

The herdsman lighted his pipe and swore,
    And the broncho nibbled the grass once more;
The stars returned and the storm was done,
    And the peace and the plains and the night
        was one.
Sunrise crept towards the mighty West;
    Daybreak downed with the herd at rest.

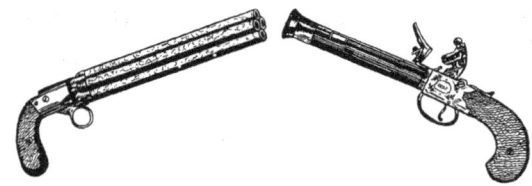

The sun hung burning in the smoke,
    A copper ball of blazing red,
The retreating Indians left behind
    Their wounded and the dead.
We left them sprawling where they fell
    Amongst the cactus and the stones,
For magpies and carrion birds
    To pick their treacherous bones.

Bygone Days Of The Old West

Near the smouldering ruins of a tepee,
    A pinto lay in the dwarf mesquite.
The plaintive wail of a papoose's cry,
    Arose from an oak-worn travios seat.
Hair as black as a starless night -
    Eyes shining like the morning dew -
A smoke finished doe-skin dress-
    And beaded moccasins trim and new.

    The Old Scout loosened the buckskin thongs
        And lifted her to his saddle seat.
    His Pard said, "Kit, nits breed lice.
        Knock her brains out agin' thet mesquite".
    But he took her to his cabin home,
        His good wife named her Running Deer.
    She soon grew to love them both
        And they thought the world of her.

Through wastes of sand and coulees long,

    A lone Chieftian made his way.

Riding far from his Commanche tribe,

    His heart was light and his song was gay.

Manitou had sent him dreams a-plenty,

    Thunder Bird had beckoned from afar.

Blood met blood in the gray mesquite,

    Love breezes whispered to the evening star.

In the wig-wam there is peace and plenty.

    A little Chieftian listens to his mother,

        Running Deer,

Telling the story of her northern tribe,

    Of the palefaces and their love for her.

The Commanche Chief sat in silence,

    Then he called his son to his side:

There will be no more war on the white man,

    So speaks the Chieftian of the Commanche tribe.

Song of the Plains

Oh, I am the song of the boundless plains—
    Of the plains as they used to be.
When the tang of the wild was in my veins
    And the men of the range rode free.
The galloping herd that I used to feed
    From the down of my billowed breast--
The light and the night and the wild stampede
    When the storm came down from the West.

The tick and the click of a million horns,
    The glare of the lightnings flash,
The race in the face of the frightened forms,
    The din of the thunders crash,
The swing and the ting of the lariat,
    The crack of the whip and gun,
The swerve and the curve when the leaders met
    And the "mill" of the herd begun.

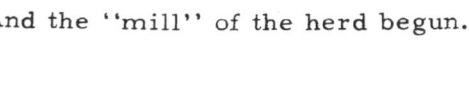

The creak and teak of the saddled mount,

    The van of the rolling crest,

The thrum and drum of the steps that count

    The life and the strife and zest,

The bold defi of the lobo's cry,

    The taunt of his mocking call,

The star specked dome of the clearing sky,

    The night--and the plains--and all.

My heart is scarred by the polished steel,

    I am bound by the fretful wire,

I miss the kiss of the booted heel--

    I chafe at the tall church spire.

For I long in my song for the boundless plains-

    For the plains as they used to be--

When the tang of the wild was in my veins

    And the men of the range rode free.

The Hunters.

The pine trees are calling you
    Where the skies know how to smile;
In the wilderness still untamed by man
    The law of the wild to survive.

    Snow-capped mountains towering high-
        Moonbeams playing on the crystal white-
    Coyotes trail along the mountain stream-
        Hoot-owls call through the silent night.

    Welcome to the old hills once more,
        Rough-hewn logs and pine-bough bed.
    Smell of pitch in the old camp stove,
        Pack-rats peering from chinks overhead.

Oaks display their bronze and scarlet
    Amongst the purple-green spruce trees.
Fresh tracks in the snow are showing
    As the old buck sniffs the morning breeze.

Up and around with a hurried meal,
    Out on the ridge with trusty gun-
Crunch of snow of moccasined feet-
    Reading sign with the hunt begun.

Its up to him to guard his herd,
    Death stalks in the cold, clear dawn.
Snap of a twig beneath the hunter's feet-
    The doe and fawn hurries on.

A rifle shot breaks the silence,
    The buck sinks slowly to the ground;
The morning sun tips the distant hill-tops,
    An old bald-eagle circles 'round.

Down on the Currumpaw

I live down there on the Currumpaw
    With the -p'tu- kids and the dawgs and Maw--
A-countin' all two dozen raw,
    An' every one a winner;
Thar ain't no place I'd rather be
    Than right down thar with my fami-lee
Whar we pound a stick on a pinon tree
    Fer to call the hawgs to dinner.

An' the wood-peckers found what the hawgs'd do,
    An' they pecked on a tree a time or two
An' the hawgs wore out a-chasin' through
    The bresh like a bunch of rummies;
I'm full of joy as a -p'tu tomb,
    Fer they got me here in a little room
With a guy called Daffy and a freak called Gloom,
    And other senseless dummies,

On Wild-cat ridge the leaves are brown,
    An' the pinon burrs will soon come down,
An' a man's a fool to stay in town
    When huntin' time aire callin';
So I'll watch my chanct fer the time to go
    Whar the wood-peck pecks and the prairie-dogs grow--
To Currumpaw, whar I - p'tu - know
    The old range cows and the hills air callin'.

They call me Buck from Currumpaw,
    An' they laff at the kids, an' the dawgs an' Maw,
An' they laff at Wild-cat ridge-- "Haw, Haw,"
    Is the stuff they're always shootin',
But let me say a thing or two,
    I'll take my old saddle-hoss - p'tu-
An' go to Currumpaw, 'n you
    Can go to H !!!!!!! a tootin'.

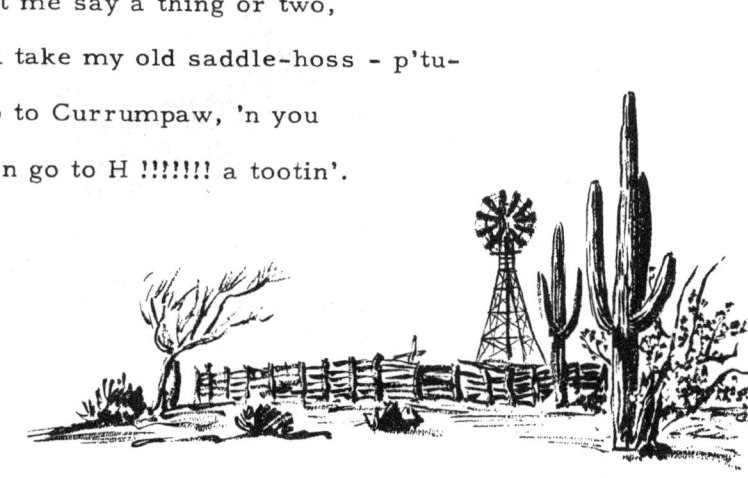

The Call

Dreamy days

Springy air

Seems to greet me everywhere;

Sorta want to drag about;

Kinder feelin' all played out;

Like to hear the buzz of bees

An' the whisper of the trees;

Want to get away an' see

All the things that are callin' me,

Callin' me to leafy ways

Dreamy days.

Trickling rills

Hidden nooks

Beckon all along the brooks.

Hungry trout are wonderin' why

They don't see me slippin' by.

There's a little spot I know

Used to rest a feller so;

Like to lie and think and dream,

Hear the gurgle of the stream;

Symphony of wooded hill

Trickling rills.

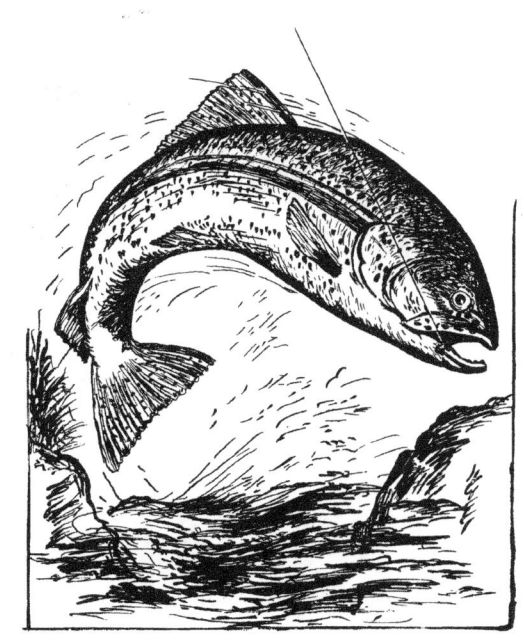

Holy hours

Want to be

Out where God seems near to me;

Like to think he is glad to know

That I love his creatures so.

Like to think that squirrel and bird

Understands me word for word.

Just to dwell in quiet thought

On the wonders he has wrought

Just to dream 'mid fragrant flowers--

Holy hours!

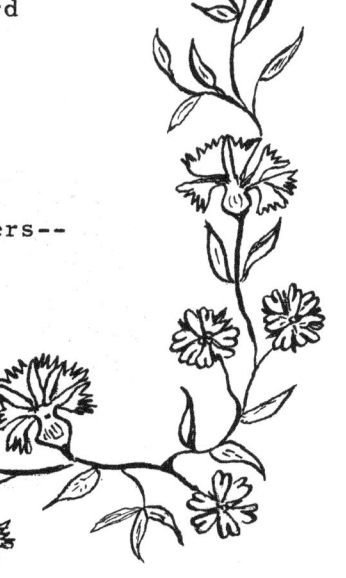

HUNTING ANTELOPE

We were cleaning our old smokies
   At the Cross-Bar Lazy-B,
When the foreman, Wild Hoss Charley,
   Rolled a cigarette and said to me.

The way to kill an Antelope
   Is easier than eatin' pie;
You lie upon the prairie
   Where the bushy grass is high.

The ramrod of your smoky
   You must hold between your knees;
And on it tie your necklash--
   To flutter in the breeze.

The Antelope will see it,
    He's as simple as a goose;
Says, he, "what's that a-wavin'-
    Like a flag of truce?"

The silly little cuss will come,
    And slowly sidle up an' near;
His thunping heart is torn--
    Twixt curiousity and fear.

He trusts too much an' comes too near,
    The blue-stem grasses part;
A searing flame, a roar o' smoke--
    A bullet through his heart.

Charley! why kill such a trusting thing,
    And what's the tarnal use?
Wild Hoss Charley only grinned and said,
    In this Old World there are no flags of truce.

CACTUS

Oh, King of the desert they say am I
    Where the sand dunes loom and the air is dry,
I live in my glory where others die
    And laugh at their mad endeavor;
I love the heat of the mighty sun
    And the glaring morn when a night is done,
The heat of a desert day begun
    Is joy to my soul forever.

CHOYAS

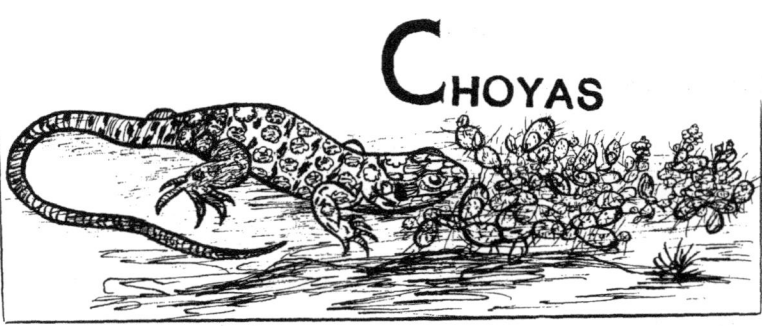

I live my life in the desert ways
    Where the lizards crawl and the Gila plays
And spread my bloom in the baking rays
    Content in the torrid weather;
So pass me by for beneath the wing
    Of my spreading leaves is a poisoned sting
Where spines from cone - shaped bunches spring
    To sink into flesh or leather.

Oh fools there be who curse my breed
    Who know me not - my code or creed;
Where water fails I fill a need
    In lands of story tragic;
Within my trunk is life concealed
    Clear water, garnered and congealed,
And fire and knife thrust make me yield
    The liquid gold like magic.

In me will be found both good and ill
    The power to cure, the power to kill,
For out of my veins do men distill
    A liquid of many uses.
As medicine my fame has grown
    And as a beverage I am known
That bring weird dreams and so I own
    To certain vile abuses.

Prickly-pear the gift I bring
    To a land where the prowling coyotes sing
And the buzzards soar on silent wing
    And the waste of sands surround me;
And many a man whose pathway led
    Where hunger conquered have I fed
My pear shaped fruit of purple red
    And glad was he then that found me.

OPUNTA

A billion insects cling to me
    That are much too small for the eye to see
But the native knows that I give them free
    And gather them in their season;
In ovens hot they bake them dry
    To powdered dust and so the dye
Of cochineal is made and I,
    As others, live on for a reason.

SAGUAROS

A giant breed of the race I stand
    A queer marked tree in a queer made land,
I wait the stroke of a sinewed hand
    And it's axe of steel to bind me
And lay me low for a people's need
    For my trunk is sought as a forage feed
So proud of my mission am I indeed,
    Though few there may be that find me.

Oh, King of the desert they say am I
    Where the sand dunes loom and the air is dry-
I live in my glory where others die
    And laugh at their mad endeavor;
I love the beat of the mighty sun
    And the glaring morn when a night is done,
The heat of a desert day begun
    Is joy to my soul forever.

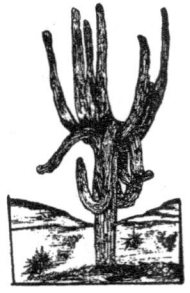

Did you ever hear of Stampede Mesa,
    Where the grass is always growing green?
Old Blanco canyon in the offing,
    With most perfect 'bed grounds' ever seen.
Headin' for the rim-rock and the chasm
    Are shadowy riders and a phantom herd,
Which is the regular ghostly round-up,
    And the cattlemen, hearts with fear are stirred.

Bygone Days Of The Old West

It was back in the early eighties
    At the close of a long weary day.
Sawyer with his herd of fifteen hundred Longhorns
    Came driftin' slowly on their way.
Passing a water hole, a squatter's cattle
    Got mixed into the herd.
Sawyer kept them movin' toward the mesa
    While the squatter cussed and reared.

He finally told the Range Boss
    If he didn't cut his cattle back,
There would be trouble on the mesa
    Sure as his name was Roy Slack.
It was a bright moonlight night,
    And the herd had bedded down.
The night guard in the distance
    With the coyotes meanderin' 'round.

The squatter on a milky-white horse
    Rode into the middle of the herd,
Followed by clickin' of horns,
    As the leaders quickly stirred.
With a yell of revenge and fury,
    He busted a cap here and there.
The stampede headed for the mesa rim
    As Old Sawyer's shriek rent the air.

With a mighty rush they cleared the rim-rock,
    A drop of two thousand feet or near.
A jumbled mass of hoofs and horns--
    A silent rider here and there.
It was the end of the fifteen hundred,
    All lying there in a sickly red.
For a head-stone, the rim-rock wall;
    The chasm, a tomb for the dead.

The Prairie Fire

From reddened dawn the wind increased
    In swelling surge that never ceased
And drove the dry, loose earth in shrouds
    Of dust, that formed in yellow clouds
And wrapped the plains in sombre light
    Of semi-darkness e're the night
Was near approached; the grass bent low
    Before the rushing gale as though
By doing thus the monster's wrath
    Might be appeased as on it's path
It swept in glee; the feeble light
    Gave way to darkness and the night

Came down with a fury in the air
    While plainsmen, scattered here and there,
Scanned anxiously the south and west
    Nor for a moment dreamed of rest
But watched -- all fearful of the thing
    The angry, tortued night might bring.

Then -- came upon the air a taint

    Of smoke - at first uncertain, faint,

But growing stronger; through the air

    Came bits of cindered grass; a glare

Now showed and lighted up the south

    On toward the west as though the mouth

Of hell had opened; women prayed

    And men courageous were afraid

And chilled; now bright and brighter glowed

    The heavens as the red line showed.

Far flung for miles - a wall of fire

    Fast driven by the mad winds ire

At racing speed and in it's van

    The varmints of the plain now ran

In headlong, terror stricken flight

    Like spectres through the troubled night

They fled for life; the rumbling sound

    Of herds stampeding jarred the ground

While whimpering wolf and bawling steer

    Joined the symphony of fear

As men, near sick, and women pale

    Sought furrowed field or pond or swale

Wherever shelter could be found

    To shield their broods and now the sound

Of roaring flame became supreme-

While heat, smoke laden, like a stream
Poured down upon them as the wall
In leaps fantastic smothered all
From earth it seemed; the moments passed
As hours until the fiend at last
Swept on as quickly as it came
But left each habitude a-flame
To burn to ash as on and on
It raced to the northward--and was gone.

Then died the wind; the monsters will
Was broken and the plains were still
And silent once again except
Where here and there a family crept
With broken cries back to the spot
Where home had been -- and found it not.

Then came the dawn - calm, quiet dawn
And threw the light of day upon
A sea of black; the billowed roll
Lay tranquil as a painted scroll
And only lazy, drifting smoke
Rose languidly from tufts and broke
The dreary scene where silent lay
The carcasses that had to pay
The fire God's toll and once again
Man's work was blotted from the plain
Mute witness of the mighty foe
That conquers when wild winds blow--
And grass is brown.

OLDEN DAYS of the GOLDEN WEST.

Weird and deserted is Dobe Town,
    With its shacks of mud that have tumbled down.
The only signs of its old-time thrill
    Are the half sunk mounds on the sage-strewn hill.

The Gila plays in the streets that teemed
    With the men who rode, and the men who dreamed,
In the days a-gone when the West was young
    And the song of the plains was yet unsung,
When Dobe town on the mesa shone
    With a glamour recked its very own.

And the men who rode, the men who vied,

    The men who dared and the men who died,

And the game of life in the desert whiled

    The play, with the joker running wild.

If dobe dust could speak to tell

    The deeds of good, and the deeds of hell,

The story would eclipse the dream

    Of fiction wove from the strangest theme.

For conquest, love, and deadly hate

    All played their lead from the deck of fate.

And the flash and crash of a ready gun

    Were the might and right when the game was done.

Now there's naught but the purple sage,

    The sunken mounds of a bygone age

To tell the tales we must guess in part

    Of a town that breathed with a beating heart,

Where men and women, bad and good,

    Played out their hands as sportsmen should

Until the deal that is made to all

    Was run, and the players, forced to 'call',

Laid down their cards -- and the dobe town,

    Like the hands that built it, tumbled down.

Oh, God-forsaken is old Dobe Town

    With its shacks of mud that have tumbled down,

The sage grown street that is weird and still,

    And the guard asleep on the half-mile hill.

Black Bart.

We were talking about hold-ups
    At Cross-Bar-Lazy-B,
When Foreman, Wild Hoss Charley
    Told of an outlaw that used to be:

"He wasn't a grizzled bandit
    No hardened bandit's poise,
But a youngster kinda driftin'
    From his home in Il-linois.
He took to the plains and mountains,
    The brakes and coulee vales,
And felt the spell of sunset,
    The thrill of the rim-rock trails.

He loved the lure and silence,
    He rode the unbeaten track
With the only pal he wanted -
    A hoss that was shiny black.
It could've been hot adventure
    That lurked in his blood, then
The devil himself might a caused it
    (It's hard to explain some men).

"On down in Blanco canyon
    Is where his career begun
Robbin' the stage lone-handed,
    So easy he called it fun.
And just for the brag he whittled
    A "Swastika" on the door
While holdin' the stage-coach patrons
    At bay with his old forty-four.

"It got to be sort of a habit,
   His robbin' the Fargo Line,
And always he'd cut the symbol,
   The swastika cryptic sign.
He skillfully dodged pursuers,
   And rode like a bandit king
'Till they shot his hoss, and caught him
   One evenin' at Ancho Spring.

"The walls of the prison claimed him,
   As many a bad man before;
And the spirit within him shattered
   With clang of the old iron door.
At last, when his term had ended,
   Exulting in freedom's breath,
He went to the mountain fastness
   Where he found both gold and death.

"He wasn't a grizzled bandit
   With a hardened bandit's poise,
That day he came a-ridin'
   From his home up in Il-linois.
And if you should get to tracin'
   You'd find that the family name
Was Bowles, right highly honored,
   (Fate deals such a funny game).

"Asleep in his lonely cabin:
    The sun on a hot summer day
Shone full on a glass that reflected
    The heat of its dancing ray
Full on a cap of a rifle
    That fate had decreed a part
That hung with its muzzle pointing
    Direct at the sleeper's heart.

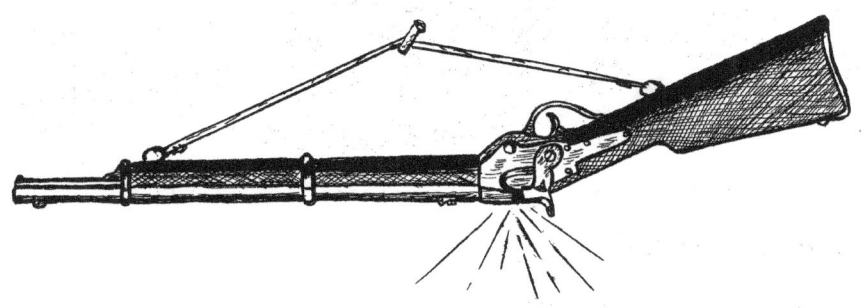

"And the ray, with increasing fervor,
    Kept on 'till the work was done-
The life of the youngster ended
    With the crack of the heated gun.

"Carved on the board above him
    A "Swastika" has its part,
Only the name of his canyon days
    Is penciled thereon 'BLACK BART".

MY OLD HORSE & I

How I love to be in the mountains
    When the summer day is almost done
My old horse and I on the mountain trail
    At the setting of the golden sun
But our round-up days are almost over
    Our hard riding days are done
My old horse and I just dreaming on
    At the setting of the golden sun.

    I surely love these old mountains
        Many secrets in their hearts they hold
    Indians and hunters after the wild-life
        And miners seeking the yellow gold.
    Columbines and daisies in all their sweetness
        Smiling among the boulders here and there
    Cattle grazing on the distant hillside
        Coyotes yelping from their hidden lair.

There are many rough trails a-winding
    To the far places that I know
Which I love to ride in the moonlight
    And watch the shadows come and go
The old spruce and pines so friendly
    With the little streamlet talking low
Calls from a hoot-owl on the nearby rimrocks
    Friendly looks from an old buck or doe.

When the sunshine is gone from the valley
    The high peaks are still tipped with gold
As God uses his many paints and brushes
    As the shades of night slowly unfold
A myriad of colors dancing on the rimrocks
    Of which no artist can construe
Such is our Western mountain sunsets
    Underneath a sky of turquoise blue.

How I love to be in the mountains
    When the summer day is almost done
My old horse and I on the mountain trail
    At the setting of the golden sun
Then there's real joy in the silence
    Which is broken only now and then
By ringing steel striking on the malpi
    And the soft murmuring of the wind.

Old Cayuse

Old cayuse of mine, we have traveled together
The mesa, the plains, and the deep rugged hills;
Through sunshine and rain we have battled the weather
O'er alkali wastes and by clear trickling rills.

When the stars shed their beams through the nights, and their glory
Was 'round and about us, the breeze blowing free—
The calm, silent plain and its unwritten story—
Just God, and the night, and my cayuse, and me.

And you're old

Very old

For a horse -- but the hold

You have on my heart strings can never be told;

The years have been kind,

And there comes to my mind

The wide sweeping space where the tangled trails
    wind;

And my dreams take me back where the far places be-

To God, and the night, and my cayuse, and me.

Old cayuse of mine, the day of our parting

Is nearing; and soon, in a country unknown-

Each one will go forth on his journey starting

Down trails that we must travel -- but travel

    alone;

It seems' if I knew I could ride you forever,

The stars shining down and the breeze blowing free;

We'd go on and on, and the end would be -- never--

Just God, and the night, and my cayuse, and me.

And I pray -

How I pray -

That somehow there may

Be a trail we can follow together some way.

Though the tangled trails wind,

I would know in my mind

That secure you would follow, and sure you would find

The end and the camp where the range opens free;

And -- God, and the morning, old cayuse, for me.

DRIFTIN' ALONG WITH THE CATTLE.

I'm driftin' along with the cattle
    From the force of the wind and snow
No livin' thing could face it
    Only the one direction to go.

I'm driftin' along with the cattle
    My horse's head is hangin' low
Shadowy forms are all around me
    Their backs covered with ice and snow.

I'm driftin' along with the cattle
    Calves givin' forth their plaintive bawl
Coyotes yelpin' along the mesa crest
    In answer to the winter's call.

I'm driftin' along with the cattle
    With the dark of the night comin' on
My old horse has grown leg weary
    But the fury of the blizzard is gone.

I'm driftin' along with the cattle
    They are beddin' down and peaceful lie
The moon shines forth in all her glory
    As the silver clouds go driftin' by.

I'm driftin' along with the cattle
    Sun is shinin' nice and warm
Soon we'll reach the home range
    And forget all about the storm.

I'm driftin' along with the cattle

    Singin' an old trail herd song

Happy again as the blue-jays and magpies

    Knowin' that winter will soon be gone.

I'm driftin' along with the cattle

    Smell of pine-smoke comin' o'er the breeze

There's the old rancho and the bunk-house

    Nestlin' among the dark spruce trees.

I'm driftin along with the cattle

    Boss standin' down by the corral gate

My ol' hoss and I hungry as two coyotes

    With the breakfast hour growin' late.

Such are the cold wintery blizzards

    Cattle driftin' along with th' wind and snow

Such is the life led by the brave cowboys

    That only those in range-land know.

The Lament of the Navajo.

We were talking about Hopi and Navajo
    At Cross-Bar Lazy-B,
When Foreman, Wild Hoss Charley
    Told of an Indian Chief being treed:

"A CHIEFTAIN of the Navajoes,
    Brave warrior, Eagle Claw,
Set forth to the Hopi Tribe
    To seek a comely squaw.
It is not well that I should take
    A Navajo, he said,
For they, I think, are not too quick
    At earning meat and bread."

"Among the Hopis' he pursued
   The search until he found
A squaw who used a workin' hoe
   And kept the doughmeal ground.
She swung an axe with skillful stroke;
   She garnered chuck and wood.
Spoke Eagle Claw, with her my squaw
   I'd say this life is good.

"Her tawny cheeks were full o' fire,
   Her lips as yet unkist,
He bought her with an otter skin
   And two big hunks of twist,
Then took her to his native heath
   And showed her many rows
Of husky weeds, some garden seed,
   And two left-handed hoes.

"Heap much-um dig, heap much-um plant,
   Heap much-um grow, he said.
She looked surprised, then grabbed a club
   And whacked him on the head.
Where do you get that dig-um, Chief,
   That 'plant-and-grow-um' stuff?
I hope I am the Hopi squaw
   To call your ancient bluff.

"So Eagle Claw laid down the law
    With high and lordly mien,
But Mrs Claw, his legal squaw,
    Would tear it up again.
You may be big, you may be brave,
    Ugly, mean and stout,
But I'm your Squaw, Eagle Claw!
    I'll make you step right out!

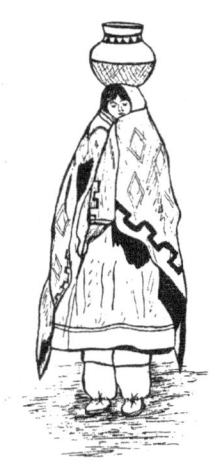

"He journeyed to the Hopi tribe
    His haughty head bent low,
A sorry, most dejected and
    Repentant Navajo.
The Hopi grinned a friendly grin,
    Then boldly laughed, Haw, haw!
Too much-um light, to much-um fight,
    Too much-um Hopi squaw?

"Two Injun steeds, ten strings of beads,
    A bear robe, tanned and black,
A dozen mink, two otter skins,
    If you will take her back.
Ten arrows and a bow--
    I give-um these, you take her, p-l-e-a-s-e?
Proclaimed the Navajo.

"When in the breast of Eagle Claw
    Springs deep desire to wed,
His hands caress the lingering bump
    Upon his dusky head.
Too much-um fight, he meditates,
    Too much-um pow-wow 'round.
I hope I miss that Hopi Squaw
    In the Happy Hunting Ground."

PARDNER, I'M A-LEAVIN'

Can't you hear the call, Pard,
    Drown the city's roar;
Don't you feel the lure, Pard,
    Callin' you once more,
Out upon the long trails
    Where the eagles soar?

Dim trails, long trails,
    'Trails we rode together;
Home ranch in the distance,
    And the night a-comin' on;
Always in the saddle, Pard,
    Facin' wind and weather,
Can you bear to think, Pard,
    All them days are gone?

Gone ne'er to return, Pard,
    We are left behind -
Can't you hear the herd, Pard,
    Bawlin' down the wind?
Was it jest a fancy,
    Passin' through my mind?

Storm a-comin' on, Pard,
    Watch the critters mill!
Say, why don't you sing, Pard,
    Sing a puncher's trill;
Shoot the leaders down, Pard;
    Shoot, and shoot to kill!

Easy, Pard; go easy;
    The herd is millin' roun'!
Now we've got 'em headed,
    And they'll soon be beddin' down,
Soon as we corral 'em,
    The bunch'll hit the town!

Dim trails, long trails;
    Trails we rode together;
Pardner, I'm a-leavin',
    I can hear the Foreman call;
Hand me down my slicker,
    May be cloudy weather;
I'm a-goin' ridin'--
    Biggest ranch of all.

THE BLIZZARD.

The sun, slowly rising in a haze of red,
    Cast feeble rays of luster o'er the plain
Where sported, here and there, light gusts that shed
    A film of dust that settled back again.

    The sky dimmed o'er by hazy, purple gray,
        Hung low, and seemed to wrap the earth about
    As some great mantle spread, and when the day
        Drew on gusts, increasing, sent the dust to rout;

But not to rest again, for, growing strong
  And stronger as their forces multiplied,
They swept the light and loosened earth along
  To join the static force, electrified.
And, as the wind increased, the dust cloud grew
  Until the air was dense, and one could see
But dimly through the mist of earth that flew,
  Driv'n by the giant force unceasingly,
Until the sun was hid, the mad winds raced
  Wild as they swept, the obstructed main
In screaming triumph, boasting as they paced.
  The tortued plain.

  The plainsmen, knowing well the desert ways,
    Rode eager in their quest for wandering strays,
  And turned them down the coulees and the brakes
    That led to the canyon wall, whose shelter makes
  A rendezvous from storm; their mustangs strode
    In short, uneasy canters as they rode

The wind that seemed to beat them back,
>Or swing them from the narrow, beaten track
Or twisted trail; the herds, uncertain, broke
>In scattered bunches, lowing as they spoke
Their vague unrest; The Lobo sought retreat
>While the slinking coyote whimpered to complete
The symphony of beasts whose cries combined
>With herdsmen's yips to drown the roaring wind.

>And then, where bedlam reigned--as though agreed
>>By tempest, man and beast and plunging steed--
>The din was stilled
>>Like some great silencer the thing was done;
>>>The elements and all obeyed the One
>>>>Who willed.

All sensed the change

    From northward, rushing down across the range,

Came winds of ice;

    Came winds of ice, and in their teeth they bore

The stinging sleet hard frozen snow -- and more

    And more the winds increased and landscape fled

From sight before the onslaught that they led,

    While herd and herdsmen lost their sense of form

And, helpless, drifted southward with the storm.

    The darkness came while yet the sun was high

    And man and beast again put forth their cry,

        Well knowing that tomorrow, on the plain,

    Stilled forms would lie to never rise again.

        On through the night

    The women of the plains kept fire and light

        For storm-worn men.

    For storm-worn men that rode and knew it not;

        For tired, dazed men, half frozen, as they fought

To keep awake, for well they knew to sleep

    Meant death and so their senses needs must keep

Them on their guard as drifting through the night,

    Their eyes, ice-glazed, searched for light---

A light to guide them, but the strongest light must fail

    To pierce the wall of sleet, driv'n by the gale

Of fury such as none may feel or know

    Except the lonely riders of the range who go

Into the night when winds bite sharp and deep

    And seek to lull brave men to sleep.

At last came dawn,
  Cold, cruel, stinging dawn;
The storm, as though ashamed, passed on
  And left a wind, subdued, but with a sting
That seemed to crisp the flesh and everything.
  The cattle, hump-backed, pleaded in their way
For food, while here and there about them lay
  The fallen, in drifts all around,
The storm king's toll in carcasses is found.

  And here a tired-eyed watcher of the night,
    Sad-hearted, waits beside the beacon light
  That failed, as from the plain
    The stragglers of the storm seek home again.
  But one comes not--it is the price that's paid
    By the sturdy plainsmen, gallant, unafraid,
  When blizzard reigns
    Supreme and mighty in their quest
  Of the plain.

THE PASSING OF FARO DAN.

"Cactus Nell" in a gaudy gown
    Of a dance hall vamp in a border town,
Had tried her wiles on a man who seemed
    To read her smiles as he stood and dreamed
And paid no heed to the tell-tale leer
    Of the brothel queen as she lingered near,
But turned and walked to another place
    Removed from the glare of her painted face.

The she-thing paled with a tang of hate
    At the slight implied by his measured gait;
Each step seemed telling as words might say
    He despised her breed and the tinseled way;
And she raged within as the dance hall clan
    Observed the move of the silent man;
And she made a vow that the man should pay
    For the public slight in the brothel way.

A whispered word -- and a hurried plan

    Was told in the ears of "Faro Dan",

Who hitched the guns in the belt he wore

    And wandered out on the dance hall floor,

Then stopped a bit as an idler would--

    Quite close to the place where the stranger stood;

And Nell--With the hate of her creed and race--

    Stepped close and spat in the stranger's face.

Then silence fell and the place was still--

    Like a stage scene set where the actors kill--

As the stranger stood and calmly viewed

    The taunting face of the woman lewd.

Then her eyes were turned till they rested on

    Her consort near with pistol drawn,

And he slowly grinned, then turned his head

    To the brothel queen when he calmly said;

"I reckon, gal, there has been a day
    When a Mother loved in a mother's way
And prayed--I guess--as her baby grew,
    She never would be a thing like you;
And so for her and the child she bore
    I've pity, gal , and I've nothin' more,
But (turning again to "Faro Dan"),
    "I'm callin' you, hombree--man to man."
The call was quick as a lightning flash,
    And the shots rang out in a single crash
As the stranger stood with a smoking gun
    And viewed the work that his skill had won.

Then walking slow to the dance hall door,
He turned to the awe-struck crowd once more;
"I just dropped in from the alkali,
And now I reckon I'll say--good-by."

The Last Shall Be First

We were fishing down a canyon
   On the Cross-Bar Laxy-B,
When the foreman, wild hoss Charley
   Cut a pole and said to me:

"Did I ever tell you, Bozo,
   Of the race at San Marshell,
When I beats a game of bunco
   An' I wins a job, as well?
Yeah, I sorta was a loafin'
   In that burg in early fall,
For there wasn't any ridin'
   On the Mesa, pard, a-tall;
So I'm jest a restin' easy,
   Doin' nothin', when I see
Quite a bunch of hombres, pardner,
   That is interestin' me.

"They was takin' turns at faro,
    Lettin' on they're strangers, Bo,
But they're all plumb well acquainted,
    As it happens that I know;
An' I knows the game they're fixin',
    For I'm ca'm and free to own
That I seen 'em pull it, Bucko,
    In the spring down in San Antone.
It was that old bunco, pardner,
    In a foot race where they fix
So the fast one loses, pronto,
    An' they trims a bunch of hicks.

"So I watches while they're layin'
    Out the 'come-ons', for a week,
But I'm silent, Bo, I'm silent,
    For it ain't my time to speak.
An' I'd never whispered, no, sir,
    If they hadn't sneaked a bet
With a fellow that I'm likin';
    But I ain't a-talkin'--yet.
He had bet 'em mighty heavy,
    An' he didn't have a chance
But to lose ten thousand cattle
    An' a twenty-section ranch.

"Yeah--I done some mighty thinkin'
  Till I gets it figured out,
Then I tells him how it's standin'
  An' he's crazy, Bo, about.
But I tells him what I'm plannin',
  An' to show I know my place,
Why I'm bettin' every bucko
  That I had upon the race.
Then I saunters, sorta cas'al
  Where the bunch of them can see,
An' I does some fancy shootin'
  From the hip and fannin' free.

"There's a swallow comes a dartin'
  Through th' azoor overhead,
An' they hollers, 'Git-'m, cow-boy!'
  So I drops him cold and dead.
Then before the race is startin'
  I'm talkin' ca'm and low
To the gink that aims to lose it,
  But there's things he doesn't know
So I whispers, easy, Judas,
  When you start to run this race,
I'll be standin, firm and certain
  In a most conspicious place;

"An' I'm jest remarkin', Judas--
    Lis'en, friend, an' get it all--
If you don't come in a winner
    You ain't comin' in a-tall.
For the minit you're a fallin'
    From your place, (which is ahead),
Why, I reckon I'll be shootin',
    So remember what I've said.
'Course it might be that I'm missin',
    But it ain't an even bet,
For I've shot a lot of varmints
    An' I've never missed one yet."

"Yeah--he won it. Won it easy;
    An' I don't mind sayin', Bo,
That I've never seen a human
    Throwin' dust an' gravel so;
An' I don't mind sayin', either,
    It was mighty good for me--
Fer the man that bet the cattle
    Owns the Cross-Bar-Lazy-B,
An' he brings me here as foreman
    When he heads from San Marshell,
So I wins some buckos, pardner,
    An' a darn good job as well.

"Did they ever try to get you,
    After beating them that way?"
But the foreman, Wild Hoss Charley,
    Got a bite--and didn't say.

RIDIN' the TRAIL

Ridin' the trail in the driftin' sand
    From Yuma down to the Rio Grande,
Where gilas play and the canyon wall
    Gives back the cry of the lobo's call
And the tracks dim down 'till the trail is lost.

And the white dust lays like an autumn frost,
    And the bright mirage with its waters' gleam
Before the eyes like a happy dream;
    Where cactus, sage and a thousand things
With a thousand fangs and a thousand stings
    Await the chance they have learned so well
On a desert trail in the heat of hell.

Ridin' the trail when lightnings glare
    Their stream of fire in desert air,
The wind and sand bite down to the bone
    As you and your Bronc fight it out alone;
And you curse the day when you chose to ride
    Where the trails grow dim, and the plains are wide,
And the coulees dip and the sand dunes stand
    Like souls forgot in a wind-swept land,
And the nights are deep, and the days are long,
    The trail is steep or the trail is wrong,
And the dangers lurk on the weary way
    Where the lobos call and the gilas play.

Ridin' the trail...Well, who can quit
    When he's felt the call and tang of it
With a tarp, and a rope, and a bronc that knows?
    Who cares for the wind, the sand that blows,
When billowed plain for a thousand mile,
    With its lyin' beck, and its lyin' smile,
And its open space that grips your heart
    Till you seem to be of the plains a part,
Keeps callin', callin', all the while,
    Till you answer back with a gleamin' smile
And head the bronc for the settin' sun
    And ride the trail 'til the trail is done.

We were ridin' on the Black Mesa
    South of the Cross-Bar Lazy-B,
When the foreman, Wild Hoss Charley,
    Reined his bronc and said to me:

"See those deep ruts down in the vale
    Markers dim of the Santa Fe Trail.
I had Kate, the kids an' a yoke of steers,
    A little furniture, implements and gears.
We came West across these old plains
    With ploddin' oxen and clankin' chains.
We sang aloud the Pioneer's refrain
    Driftin' along in the WAGON TRAIN.

"As the sun sank low in th' west,
   We camped down on the rocky crest
By a spring in the brown mescal,
   With schooners drawn in a circle corral.
With th' oxen grazin' in the coulee below.
   All gathered around in the firelight's glow,
We sang aloud the Pioneer's refrain
   Driftin' along in the WAGON TRAIN.

"As the silver moon dropped from sight,
   Apache war yells split the night!
Ponies circled the vale to left and right
   Eagle head-dresses showin' in th' comin' light.
With our thinnin' belts and hot carbines,
   Coyote howls blended with deathly screams,
We sang aloud the Pioneer's Refrain
   Driftin' along in the WAGON TRAIN.

"This land of promise and sure retreat,
   With crystal streams and grasses sweet,
We built our home on the mesa near,
   Where the oxen mingle with the deer.
We enjoy the freedom of th' God-given West,
   Love of all nature at its very best.
We often sang the Pioneer's Refrain
   Driftin' along in the WAGON TRAIN.

THE OLD STAGE COACH.

Travelin' along the canyon rim
    With all six horses on the run
Road curving like a rattlesnake
    Buckskin poppin' like a gun.

Soapy Smith handlin' the ribbons
    An ol' puncher up by his side
Chain claterin' against the single-trees
    On a wild and reckless ride.

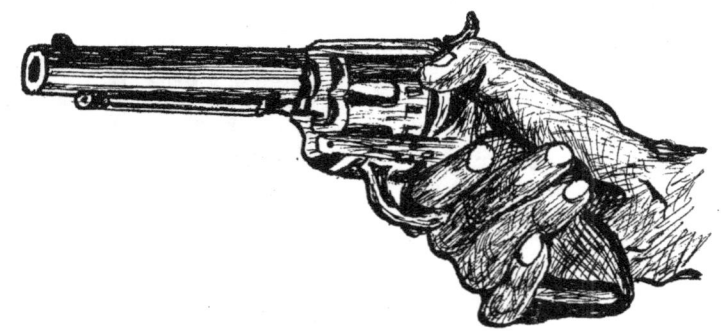

Suddenly comes a call to halt!
  Brake goes on with a bang
Soapy Smith reaches for his rifle
  Another hold-up by Black Jack's gang.

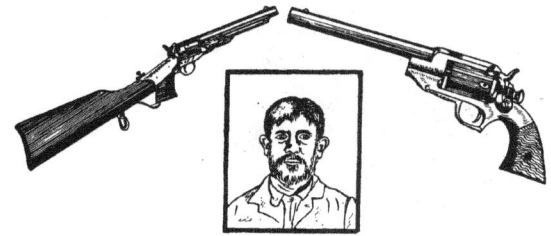

You fellows - drop those smokies
  Reach right up for the blue
Boys, drop the bullion-box against that boulder
  Shoot the locks through and through.

Now, all of you in the 'old herse'
  Step out - Line up on the road
Where are you goin' Mabel Henderson
  How's your 'Old Dad' and Uncle Lode?

  My 'Old Dad' is in Cimarron and very ill
    I have medcine here from Dr. Cline
  He said it would save my Dad's life
    If I could get it there in time.

  You don't know me young lady
    But it has not been too many years ago
  That your 'Old Dad' saved my life
    In a shootin' down at San Angelo.

  Hurry up driver, grab those ribbons
    Set those horses on the run
  Get this old herse down to Cimarron
    Before the settin' of the sun.

It is written down in western history
  How Soapy Smith made the drive
How Mabel Henderson reached the bedside
  And her 'Old Dad' is still alive.

Tumbling, tumbling - tumble weeds,
    Soon you'll go bouncing on your way
In and out amongst the coulees
    O'er the prairie green and gay.

Tumbling up, tumbling down,
    Tumbling over, tumbling 'round,
Tumbling here, tumbling there,
    Tumbling, tumble weeds
without a care.

Playing hide and seek in the cactus,
    Gently caressing the yucca blade -
Rolling along the foot-hill crest -
    A moment's stop in the pinon shade.

Tumbling up, tumbling down,
    Tumbling over, tumbling 'round,
Tumbling here, tumbling there
    Tumbling, tumble weeds
        without a care.

Bouncing along on the cattle trails -
    Across the alkali and sand -
A sudden drop from the rim-rock wall
    To the malpi breaks in 'No-Man's Land'.

Tumbling up, tumbling down,
    Tumbling over, tumbling 'round,
Tumbling here, tumbling there
    Tumbling, tumble weeds
        without a care.

Answering roll-call at the drift fence,
  Coming in like soldiers on the run -
Piling up in countless thousands,
  Sleeping in silence in the summer sun.

Tumbling up, tumbling down,
  Tumbling over, tumbling 'round,
Tumbling here, tumbling there
  Tumbling, tumble weeds
    without a care.

I've caught up my old pack hoss,

    I've got my bed-roll tied on tight;

Trailin' down through the Sangre del Cristo

    I'm off for old Cimarron town tonight

Where the Sou'west cowmen always gather,

    From the ranges for miles and miles around;

I'm due to greet all the frontier ladies,

    Down there in that old Western town.

    There'll be violin and guitar music aplenty,

        There'll be ranch outfits by the score;

    It'll be a regular "Old Timers" gatherin',

        How could any cow-puncher wish for more.

    There'll be hands I rode trail-herd with,

        In the days of long, long ago--

    When all the range was wide and open

        An' the punchers and cattlemen had a show.

Catch up your Sunday Hoss ol' timer,
    Just let the remuda and cattle stray;
An' meet down in that tough Cimarron town--
    We will 'liker-up' and pass th' time away.
Throw your feet in an old frontier dance,
    An' mill the ladies so and so:
"Balance all!" Alaman left - lift the leather
    Swing 'em all--Dow-se-doe."

"Rope that dogie an' throw the calf,
    Swing your pardner once an' a half!
Ladies to the center, gents outside!
    Step out peelers! Get your stride.
Swing the next one roun' and roun'
    Rear back, waddies, kick a hole in th' ground!
Watch 'em steppin'...Watch 'em prance....
    Shirt-tails a-floppin' when cowmen dance.

Waddies, rope out your top hosses,
    Cinch your saddles on good and tight;
An' brush off your old gray Stetsons,
    An' hit that sage-brush trail tonight.
Let's put off all that range ridin ,
    Let the little dogies browse aroun
For you are sure to get a Western welcome
    When we ~~hit gool~~ old Cimarron Town.

GOLDEN HOURS.

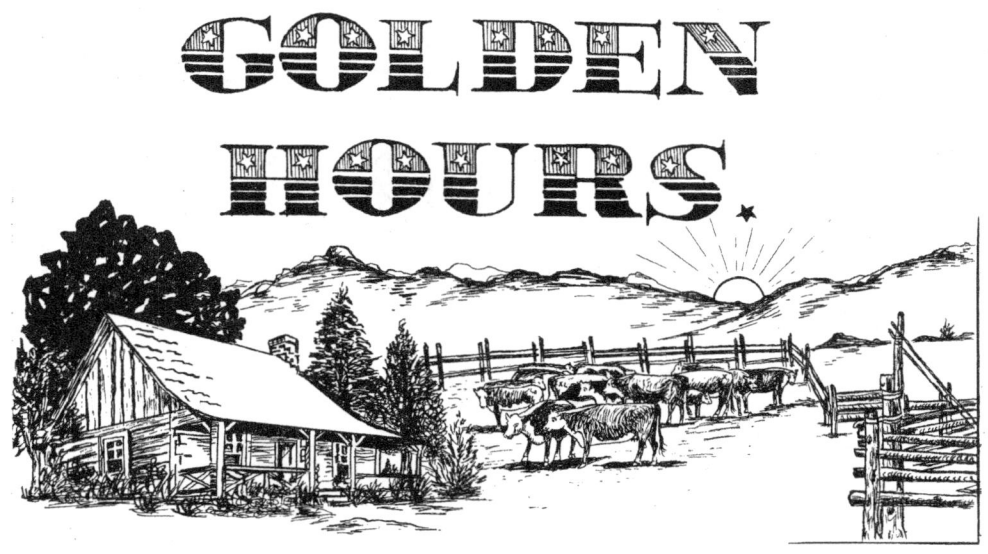

Out where the open prairies
    Roll on to the mountain crest,
Where the pine trees are soughing
    And the eagles seek their nest.

Out where the trail is winding
    Across the mesa to the old corral,
Where the evening shadows are falling
    Coyotes slink through the brown mescal.

Out where the hours are golden
  Crystal air and cactus bloom,
Where fields of scented, purple blossoms
  And the alfalfa's sweet perfume.

Out where the cattle are browsing
  Neath the star-kissed sky of blue,
Where moonbeams glisten on yucca blades
  And sweet silence comes to you.

Out where the little, spotted dogies
  Are nodding in the Western sun,
Where the mountain streamlets are flowing
  And the cowboys' work is done.

ROUND-UP TIME

When the meadow-larks commence singin'
    And the prairie-dogs start to bark
The range is gettin' green and grassy
    Rain clouds showin' up quick and dark,
All the old cow-waddies are really busy
    Seein' their string are shod and in prime
Sunnin' out their clothes and bed-rolls
    Hur-ra! Once again it's ROUND-UP TIME.

"Nevady" is checkin' up the brandin' irons
    Lookin' fer the extra ropes and morrals,
The "Old Cook" is cleanin' out the chuck-box
    Sortin' up the tools, pots and pans.
The chuck-wagon is gettin' an overhaulin'
    "Smithy" is tightenin' up the felloes and bolts
Puttin' on some new brake-blocks
    Oilin' the spring-seat to eliminate the jolts.

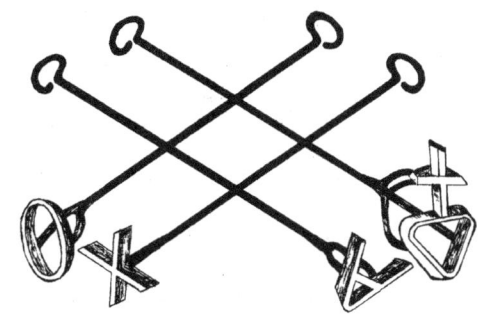

Tucson and Mason are sure enough busy
    Fastenin' a fresh cooney to the hounds
Bill has emptied and cleanin' out th' jockey-box
    With tools and horse-shoes scattered 'round.
The Boss is givin' orders - Listen to him now -
    "Get out those new wagon-bows and sheet,
Tighten up the hoops on the water-keg,
    Pack the spuds and sow-belly under the seat."

Bygone Days Of The Old West

"Rafael', put a new popper on the blacksnake
    Roundup a good shovel, axe and pick
'Tex', rustle up the dutch-ovens and pot-rack
    And enough pot-hooks to turn the trick.
I'll find some extra ropes and hobbles,
    'Jim', put the flour in that new tarp
Tell the cook to put in his prunes and coffee.
    See that his knives are good and sharp."

Out all you waddies - tie up your bed-rolls
    Daylight is breakin', the remuda is comin'
Robins and meadow-larks singin'
    Breakfast is cookin', dogies are sunnin'
Our first camp will be in Palo Duro canyon
    Get your chuck-wagon there rain or shine
Everyone is surely feelin' fit and happy
    Hur-ra! Once again it's ROUND-UP TIME.

Smoke Signals.

Back in sixty-nine and a wagon train
    Slowly driftin' across the Western plain,
Weary oxen, creekin' wheels and clankin' chain,
    Cloudless sky with no chance of rain.
Stretches of yucca and dwarf mesquite
    Water holes dry and the copper heat.

The trail leads on through malpi brakes
    Where sun, the lizards, gilas and rattlesnakes
With sand and cactus and the bitter alkali
    And buzzards waiting for those that die,
Through smoky haze and heat-waves long
    With lying mirages beckoning on and on.

Smoke signals rolling toward the sky,
    Apache messages for watchful eyes
On the sand dunes far, far away
    The return smoke signals plainly say:
Many prairie schooners and paleface men
    Are headin' for Raton Pass again.

Kit Carson the old trail scout
    Senses danger as he circles out,
Knowing well Apaches are sulking there
    Like wild animals in their hidden lair
Kit discovers Pintos in the rough terrain
    So he hurries back to the wagon train.

Schooners quickly swung into a circle wide
  With the pioneers all safely inside,
War-whoops comin' from far and near
  As Pintos and war-bonnets quickly appear.
With singin' arrows and hot carbines,
  Thinnin' cartridge belts and dry canteens.

   Dead and dyin' scattered here and there
     As buzzards circle in the sultry air.
   Faintly from a-far comes a bugle call
     Heard by Apaches, pioneers and all,
   A ringin' cheer as the Indians retreat
     To sand dunes far in the gray mesquite.

   Into Raton Pass drifts the wagon train
     As the sun dips low 'oer the Western plain,
   Campfires gleam where dark shadows meet
     While the oxen graze in a safe retreat.
   The pioneers give thanks to God and those
     That saved the wagon train from the dusky foes.

The New Foreman.

There's a brand new foreman joined the outfit
    Up and ridin' with the wind and sun
Piggin-string and rawhide rope on his saddle
    Make a darn good cowman before he's done.

    Bat wing chaps and Justin's fancy box-toe kicks,
        Crockett spurs with lock-rowels and danglers,
    It's a double rig Frazier with a heavy swell
        Taps that are used by the Montana wranglers.

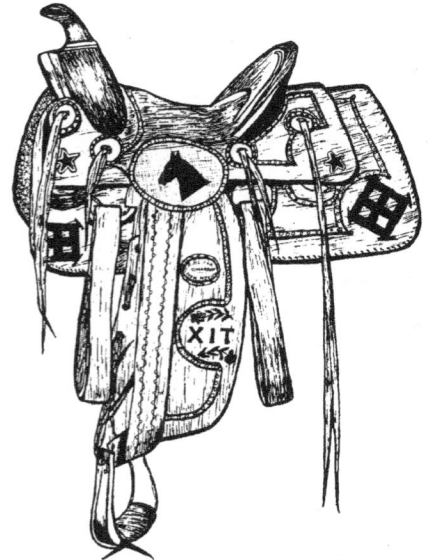

    An oregon shirt with a purple necklash
        Shadin' under a new bonnet-string Stetson,
    No Sunday or shadow ridin' for this 'hombre'
        Even though his outfit is new and fetchin'

His face looks like tan and wrinkled leather
  And his lips have a darn determined dip,
Yes, I'll bet his trigger finger is handy
  With that old hawg-leg on his hip.

  Guess he's just about as bow-legged
    As most any ol' puncher I ever seen,
  His hair is surely black and curley
    And his eyes are blue and keen.

  See how easy he handles that palomina filly
    With that braided hackamore and rawhide bosal
  Bet you a silver dollar he's a "dally man"
    And can fore-foot any bronc in this old corral.

Alkali, look in my chaps and get the makins
  You've sized up this hombre pretty well
But you never told me his handle...Did he
  Drift up here from San Ann-tone or San Mar-shel?

Las Velas de Dios! Candles of the Lord!

Foliage green, flowers cream and white
    Beckon on and on, day and night,
No matter where I go or ride
    You're always smiling at my side.
Yuccas, yuccas -- How I love you
    Kissed by moonbeams and the dew
In your prairie rendezvous
    Underneath the skies of blue.

Fragrance far, far beyond the rose,
    Or any prairie flower that grows,
As far, far West as I can see
    They're callin' to my horse and me.
Yuccas, yuccas -- How I love you
    Your charms no other can subdue
Your colors no artist can construe
    Underneath the skies of blue.

Now you're noddin' in the laggard sun
    Knowing the day will soon be done
Then comes the twilight's Holy Hour
    Bowing in grace to the Evening Star.
Yuccas, yuccas -- How I love you
    Your smiles that are always true
In sweet memory you pass in review
    Underneath the skies of blue.

When the end comes bye and bye
    Let no tear bedim your eye
I'll sleep beneath the skies of blue
    Where God always seems nearer you.
Yuccas, yuccas -- How I love you,
    Each settin' sun I bid you adieu
Each morning hour I see you a-new
    Underneath the skies of blue.

A Navajo Blanket

Weave, weave, weave, nimble fingers sending to and fro
   Threads that tell their story in the blankets of the Navajo,
Sombre the expressions as the truant shadows come and go
   Dark fantastic legends that the dusky weavers know.

Telling tales of journeys long beset with storm and danger
   Eagle feathers, dreary camps and wallow holes gone dry-
Warriors painted - heat of hell - the passing of a stranger-
   Flints aplenty, bow strings taut and Thunder Bird on high.

Signal fires in paleface camps and wigwams drear and lonely

    Winters harsh and venison grown wary of the chase

Council meets of grave portent for tribal chieftians only

    The sighing of a wee papoose and famines ghoulish face.

Now brighter colors change the trend of cryptic story

    Softened is the features of the stolid weaver-squaw

Nearing to a smile - sometimes - in telling of the story

    When the warriors filled their scalp-locks and upheld

        the tribal law.

Dangers past and famine gone - no evil foe transgressing-

    Dance around the Totem pole - the night birds plaintive call,

Tom-toms beat their gladsome tale - The Rain Gods send their

        blessing-

    And Manitou— Great Manitou— is watching over all.

Bygone Days Of The Old West 432

Thus the threads and colors tell their story in the weaving
    And the Paleface sees but understands no part or sign
Carelessly he glances at the symbols ne'er believing
    It is aught but multi-color done in semi-crude design.

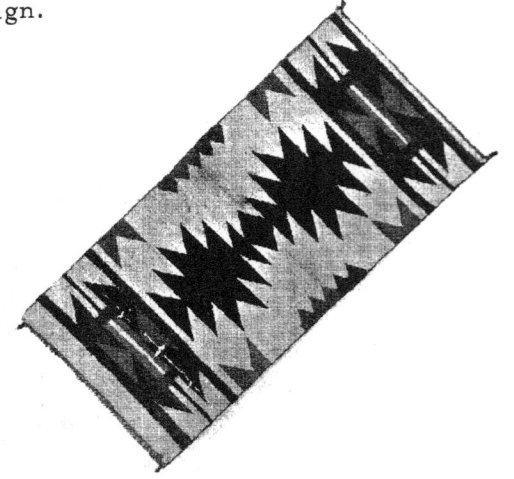

    Weave, weave, weave, tired fingers sending to and fro—
        Threads that leave their message in the blankets of the Navajo.
    Telling tales of romance, love and tragedy an age ago—
        History and legend that the dusky weavers know.

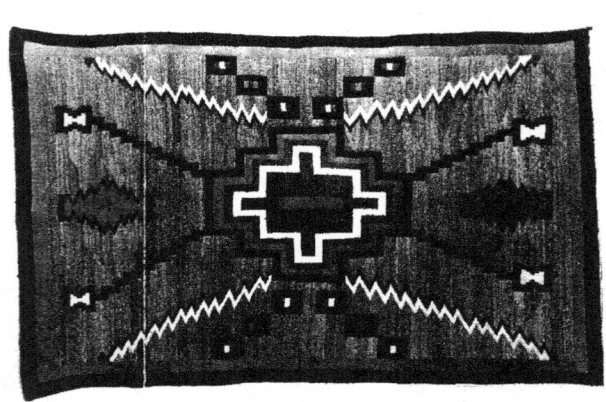

They Have Me Fenced In

I may be a knocker, but here's what I think,
    Cow country in the West is on the blink;
Conditions are such, or I'm loco, that's all,
    T'drive an old puncher t'timber that's tall.
Now I can remember - an' look am I grey? -
    When the West was the place for a puncher to stay,
When a man had to ride, if he hankered t' live,
    An' know how t' shoot, an' to' take an' t' give;
He had t' be able, cold weather or warm,
    To sleep on the prairie, not mindin' th' storm.

Bygone Days Of The Old West

Th' boys in them days were kings of th' range,
    For hundreds of miles - an'it didn't seem strange
Sets you to guessin' what th' endin' will be —
    The country was open, and now what do you see?
Corn, fences an' chickens an' windmills an' plows,
    An' people who really go milkin' th' cows.
Th' ranchos have women as thick as th' men —
    If th' boys start cussin', "Don't do it again".
Yes, that's what they hear, an' never sass back —
    A female in petticoats bosses the shack.

An' what do they eat? nough t'giv you th' itch;
    No sow-belly now, fer their blood is too rich;
They sugars their coffee, and butters their bread,
    Puts cream on their oats, have a tablecloth spread.
T' Lord only knows how th' jim-cracks they eat,
    Kin giv' them th' strength t' stand on their feet;
Jest peep at th' Home Ranch, lace curtains an' rugs,
    There's sheets on th' beds an' no sign of th' bugs.
A parlor built on, an' a pianer's in there —
    With cushions an' pickures, an' glitter an' glare.

Say, Old Timer, will you giv' me a good whack —
    Not easy but heavy, right square on my back —
Much 'obliged ! I feel better — I kind o' get weak,
    When I think of th' subjects you're hearin' me speak.
A thump on the back sort of stiffens my spine,
    Brings ol' memories back, when livin' was fine.

Now ranchos hev telephones, 'lectrics an' style,
  Steam heat an' hot water, an' bath rooms o'tile;
Th' rural delivery brings mail most every day —
  An' off in th' fields they bales up th' hay,
I mought be all wrong — or mebbe I'm right,
  Ol' punchers like me hed better giv' up th' fight.
Jest mind what I say, for twont be long now —
  Till a noisy machine will be a-herdin' th' cows;
They'll round up by auto and ship by balloon —
  Brand claves by wireless to radio tune.

Th'ol' cow-hoss will vamos — they'll hev in his place,
  Planes an' Autos that will keep up th' pace;
Th' saddles and spurs — Tra-la-la to th' Eden Museme
  Along with sech statues o' relics lik' me.
Jest look at my finish — I see it, don't you?
  A-loomin' up black an' a-readin' "Skiddo"!
Shal' I learn a new trade an' slave for a trust —
  Or tak' t' th' highway an' rustle for dust.
Say, what's th' answer, I'd like you t' tell,
  They've got me fenced in —
        BUT DON'T IT BEAT H——?

The Trail Herd.

Stories of cattle drives often told
   That followed the trails in days of old
Across alkali flats and through dwarf mesquite,
   Waterless springs and the copper heat.
Bull whips crackin' and flappin' chaps
   Dust clouds rolling across coulee gaps,
The cowboys singin' an old cattle song
   With mirages beckonin' on and on.

Not a rain-cloud in the heavens,
    Grama and buffalo grass short and dry,
Rattlers curl in the yucca shade,
    Sunflowers droop their heads and die.
A lonely mound beside the trail
    Where some cowboy lies at rest.
Prairie dogs sunnin' on their mounds
    Coyotes slinking along the malpi crest.

The leaders circlin' and doublin' back
    Through the blades of the brown mescal,
Where bleachin' bones the desert's toll
    Lie half buried in the shiftin' sand.
The chuck-wagon driftin' on in silence
    As turkey buzzards cut the blue,
Tail-riders and broncs grown weary,
    Tumble-weeds and dunes build on a-new.

Now the scene is suddenly changin'
    With the herd almost on the run
With the smell and sight of water,
    Mountains showin' in the evenin' sun.
Cowboys kickin' up a dust cloud
    The remuda bringin' up the rear
Trail-boss ridin' a-long a-grinnin'
    Yuccas noddin' a welcome here and there.

A pitch-pine camp-fire brightly burnin',
    Chuck wagon on a carpet of green,
A coulee dip for the remuda herd
    Most perfect bed-ground ever seen.
Shadows dip to the call of night
    Moon comes up in all its glory,
The cowboys around the camp-fire sit
    Smoke and spin a trail herd story.

Herd is bedded down and peaceful lie,
    The remuda bell is softly tinklin',
The old cook and cowboys fast asleep,
    Overhead a million stars a-twinklin'
The night guard is softly singin',
    Hoot howls answer with their lonely call,
Such is life out on the trail herd
    In the springtime and in the fall.

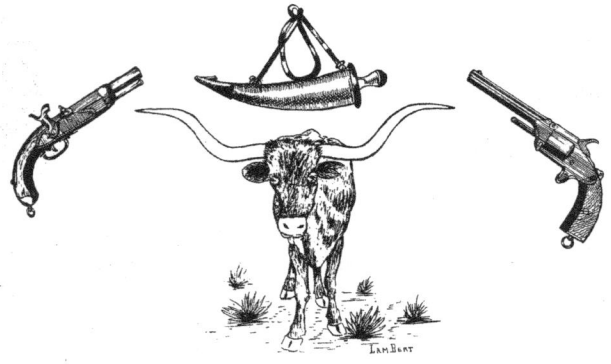

The Range Foreman's Daughter.

The new range boss has a daughter
    Just as purty as she can be
She rides a silver-mounted saddle
    A bronc branded Cross-Bar Lazy-B.
Purty ringlets of bright burnished gold
    Dreamy eyes of a turquoise blue
Little poutin' lips red as a cherry
    A smile fresh as the mornin' dew.

A nifty little pearl-handled smoky
    Swung to her belt at her side,
Conchos shinin' on her leather skirt
    A brown sombrero dipped and wide.
Silver inlaid spurs on shapely boots
    Buckskin jacket with beads and fringe,
Gauntlet gloves trimmed with porky quills,
    A necklash bright with an orange tinge.

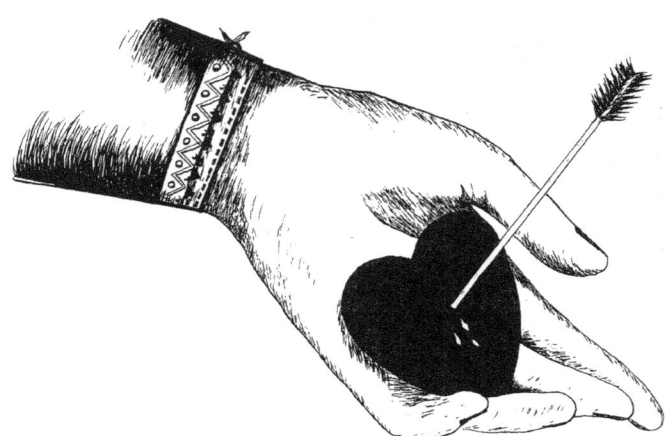

She can throw a loop quick as lightnin'
    And forefoot or heel 'em on the run,
Tie down a yearling with a piggin'-string,
    Ride the trail until the day is done.
I'm tellin' all you young waddies
    She's got a helper, he's mighty smart,
His weapons are a bow and arrow
    And his brand is the double hearts.

He'll singe you, sure as shootin'

    And leave a scar on your heart,

Smilin' sweetly she will leave you

    These words to you she will impart:

"Dad says there will be no love makin'

    When I happen out among you boys

I've got to be sedate and lady-like

    As my old Aunt who lives in Illinois".

She's got all the cowboys millin'

    Just as loco as they can be,

Even I have a bug in my bonnet

    And I'm nigh on to fifty-three.

Her Pard is partial to the moonlight

    But he's 'alwus' on the job

He's surely desp'rit after mavericks

    And is mighty fond of raisin' hob.

- - - - - - - - - - - -

Don't know what will be the finish

    Just TO WHO will she her love impart

And leave it to her little partner

    To brand him with - The Double Hearts.

MEMORIES OF MOTHER

THERE'S something keeps calling, calling to me —
    Like a silver bell in its melody —
One long, clear call from a memory —
    Mother, mother of mine —
    Mother, mother of mine —
I hear your voice when the shadows fall
    Like the vesper song of a night-bird's call —
"Down came rock-a-bye baby and all —"
    Mother, mother of mine.

And my heart awakes to the eager thrill

    Of childhood days as the old time trill

Comes from the yesterdays over the hill —

    Mother, mother of mine —

    Mother, mother of mine —

Oh, what a balm to a heart and its woes —

    Down through the years as its symphony flows —

"Ten little fingers and ten little toes —"

    Mother, mother of mine.

Could I but know in the stampede ride,

    When the storm is high and the herd is wide,

That I could creep to your waiting side —

    Mother, mother of mine —

    Mother, mother of mine —

I'd have no fear of the canyons' deep

    With thee, secure from the lightning sweep —

"Now I lay me down to sleep —"

    Mother, mother of mine —

    Mother, oh, mother of mine.

Go to sleep you old Longhorns
    It's the last night out on the trail
Tomorrow we'll drive you to the stock-yards
    You'll be loaded and hittin' the rails.
Stop pawin' up snake-weeds and alkali dust
    Shakin' your horns and switchin' your tails
Your old bellerin' is mighty poor music
    Only echoes drift back along the old trails.

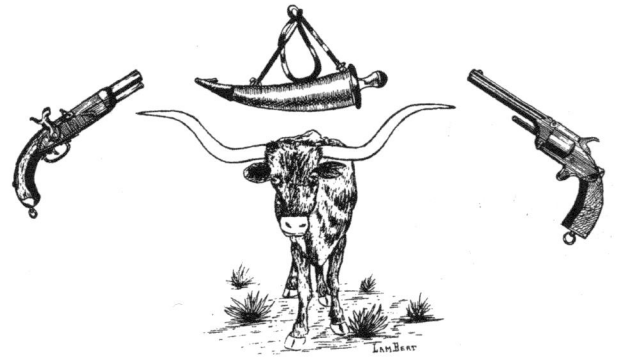

Maybe you realize this is th' last roundup
    Your eyes are red as the wind-swept sun
You're millin' when you oughta be sleepin;
    Moon is now risin' and darkness is done.
It breaks my poor old heart with pity
    To know just how scattered you'll be
Butcher will cut you in steaks and roasts
    And a few hamburgers for the likes of me.

Your horns will be used for combs and ash trays
    Tough old hide into harness, saddles and shoes,
Your hair into paddin' mattresses and plaster
    Hoofs into the best of Le Pages glue.
The bushy end of your tail for a duster
    Will be used by some batchelor buckaroo,
Your liver will go to some old 'lunger'
    And 'ox-tail soup' will be on the menu.

Your fat will be made up into fancy soap
    Used by a beautiful blonde on her hair,
Your bones ground up into chicken feed
    Your "HOLLER" will go up in thin air.
So adios to all you old Texas Longhorns
    No more trailin' through sage-brush and sand
Or wild stampede in the darkness of night
    And lookin' for you in "No-man's Land".

Wild Hoss Charlie

Wild Hoss Charlie's my name, a vaquero I am,
    I'm keepin' old batch on an elegant plan.
You'll find me out West on the New Mexico plains,
    Quit cow-punchin' and have a six-forty claim.
My house is built of good old adobe soil,
    The walls are erected according to oyle;
A split-roof, covered with grass from the plain,
    I'm sure to get wet if ever it rains.

Hurrah for Colfax County the land of the free,
    Home of grass-hopper, bed-bug and flea;
I'll sing of its praises and tell of it's fame,
    While starvin' to death on my six-forty claim

Hurrah for Colfax County! Hurrah for the West

    Where the sheepherders and cattlemen are ever at rest;

They've nothin' to do but sweetly remain,

    And see us starve to death on our six-forty claim.

I have a good time, I sure live at my ease,

    On sour-dough biscuits, corn-syrup and grease;

Come to Colfax County, there's room for you all,

    Where the wind never ceases, and the rain never falls.

Where the sun never sets but sweetly remains

    Till it burns up your crops on your six-forty claim;

My clothes are all ragged, my language gettin' rough,

    My tortilla is case hardened and awful tough;

My traps and junk are scattered all over the room,

    And the floor gets scared at the sight of a broom.

How happy I feel when I crawl into bed,
  The pack-rats rattle a tune at my head;
And the gay little tic devoid of all fear,
  Crawls up my back and into my ear.
Then the old bed-bug so cherry and bright,
  Keeps me scratchin' and lookin' most of th' night;
At daybreak the old blue-bottles buzz in,
  Light on my neck and tickle my chin.

I have nothin' to eat, and nothin' to wear,
  So nothin' from nothin' is honest and fair;
Oh it's here I am settled and here I will stay,
  My money's all gone so I can't get away.
Nothin' left, but a puncher hardened and profane,
  Just starvin' to death on my six-forty claim.

Hurrah for Colfax County where the jack-rabbit abides,
  Where the alkali never ceases and the burros never die;
Come join in the chours and tell of its fame,
  You poor, hungry sucker on a six-forty claim.

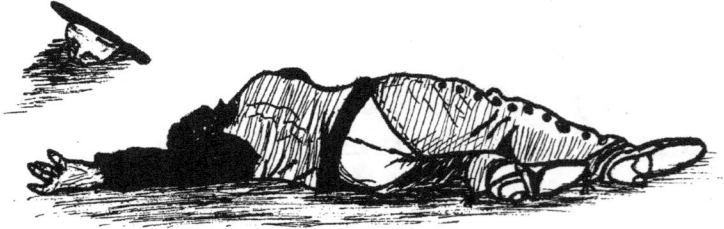

Just Waitin'

Lazy days along the old Cimarron
    All my time is my very own
A fishin' rod and plenty of bait
    Nothin' to do but watch and wait
With not a single worry, toil or care,
    Watchin' smoke rings in the air.
A deer the only livin' thing in sight
    Just waitin' for the trout to bite.

With my camp beneath a spruce tree
    Just as lazy as I ever dared be,
Watchin' th' clouds in the turquoise sky,
    Seein' some wild turkey go slippin' by.
Shadows sinkin' lower on the rimrock wall,
    A catamount's cry and answerin' call;
See that old bobber go out of sight,
    Sure have got another dandy bite.

Shadows gather at the call of night
    The campfire burnin' nice and bright,
Bacon and eggs sizzlin' in the pan,
    Coffee boilin' in the old black can,
Makes a fellow hungry as can be
    Eatin' by firelight under the old tree.
Moon's now up and a-shinin' bright-
    Just wonder if the trout would bite.

Guess I better wait until another day
    Wash my tools and pan, put my chuck away
Stake out my old horse "Pinto" to graze
    Toss on more pitch for a brighter blaze,
Get out my old tarp and make down by bed
    With a million stars twinklin' overhead.
In my dreams all through the night,
    Just waitin' for the trout to bite.

Pines are sighin', daylight is breakin'
  'Robins chirpin' it's time to awaken,
Indian Paints smiling, sweet columbines too
  Like shinin' diamonds is the mornin' dew.
Smoke curlin' upward - sun shinin' down
  Breakfast over, chipmunks scamperin' aroun',
I'll sneak along - keep out of sight
  Am sure that soon the trout will bite.

- - - - - - - - - - - -

Lazy days along the old Cimarron
  All my time is my very own,
A fishin' rod and plenty of bait
  Nothin' to do but watch and wait.
I'm just as happy as I can be
  A millionaire has nothin' on me.
Here I lounge in the bright sunlight,
  Just waitin' for the trout to bite.

It is twilight on the prairie,
    Silently I ride the Yucca trail,
The coyotes are singin' a lullaby
    As the night-hawks sweep the vale.
'Tis the Christ born (Christmas) night
    A story that was taught to me
When I was just a little waddie
    Sittin' on my mother's knee.

Yes, He was born in a stable manger
    Among the animals and the hay
Just the same as any little dogie
    Is born at the rancho today.
She told as how the Wise Men
    Came ridin' across the sandy waste
With that same star up yonder shinin'
    To guide them in their haste.

How the shepherds on the prairie
    Looked up in wonder and surprise
As an Angel dipped down among them
    Like a golden eagle from the sky.
How the people in their gladness
    Gathered in from far and near
Singin' out the glad tidings
    So all the world might hear.

The Eastern star shinin' up yonder
    Has oft times guided me
While ridin' trail or night herd
    In stormy weather or wild stampede.
Oft time in the darkest moment,
    A picture of Mother Dear I could see
Fear and heartaches were forgotten,
    Just God, the night, old cayuse and me.

On this beautiful Christmas evenin',
    As I ride down the yucca trail
I offer up a thankful prayer,
    As moonbeams kiss the grassy vale.
I seem to hear someone singin'
    Yes, a song I love to hear
Is it only the prairie breeze a-sighin'?
    To me it sounds sweet and clear:
    Silent night, Holy night
        All is calm, All is bright.

THE CLOUDBURST

Dark clouds gather with marvelous rapidity
    As darkness flashes across the blue sky,
Wild winds thresh the malpi and sage brush
    Frightened antelope madly go dashin' by.
Prairie chickens searchin' for a thicket cover
    The bob-white's plaintive call to its mate,
Wild horses lookin' for a more secure retreat
    As the old Storm King vents his hate.

There comes a stampede of Texas cattle
    With static jumpin' from horn-to-horn
With cowboys racin' along beside them
    In the wake and fury of the storm.
Look! There's an old Mexican freighter
    Down in that large arroyo bed
With a heavy load and a balky team
    And a long sandy pull out ahead.

He knows the peril of the 'Cloud-burst'
    And senses the danger he's in
The horses are pullin' at the heavy load
    Flashing lightnin' and a thunderous din.
Hear the dull crack of the bull-whip
    With curses he urges the horses on and on
Through the drivin' rain and stingin' hail
    Hope of savin' his outfit is gone.

So he quickly cuts the leaders loose
    Astride one he makes a furious ride,
To beat the dark angry rollin' water
    That fills the arroyo from side to side.
Look! The wall of water has reached them
    They are making a gallant fight
Now they are caught in a whirlin' eddy
    Both horse and rider sink from sight.

The cloud-burst and storm is over
    Sun shines brightly once more,
The prairie-dogs sit on their mounds,
    Large hail stones cover the coulee o'er
Dark waters in the arroyo rollin' onward
    Dead wild-life scattered here and there,
Old Storm King rumbles off in the distance
    With a soft good-bye on th' evenin' air.

END OF THE TRAIL.

I'm crossing the Big Divide,
    Slowly ridin' the Milky Way.
The Eastern star is shinin'
    Brighter than a new-born day.
Over the trail dust legions blow,
    Haunted by mirage, visions untrue.
Scenes stranger than fiction,
    Unravelin' them-selves to view.

I'm checkin' the Trail Herd,
    Silently they go driftin' by.
There's dogies, stray yearlings,
    And mavericks unbranded on high.
Some run the race of black despair,
    A challenge to the Great Unknown.
Other souls in ecstasy go forth,
    While quietly I drift on alone.

Christ flies his signal code,
    Radiant beyond all compare,
The sky is tinged with gold,
    Angels' harp music on the air.
Gone are the cares of life
    Threading the cryptic vale.
My day is set. My day is done.
    This is the END OF THE TRAIL.

A Prisoner For Life.

Adios to the old adobe cantina

    Where at Monte I lost all my dough

The beautiful Senorita that smiled at me

    Her gay Caballero dark looks did bestow.

Augardente and vino flowin' freely

    A dreamy waltz floatin' on the air

I, a lonely Gringo cowpuncher smilin'

    The dark-eyed Senorita taking the dare.

Adios to all sense of reason or fear

    Not a care of what the endin' would be

The Caballero in anger with stiletto awaitin'

    The end of the waltz, Senorita and me.

The three greasers that came to his biddin'

    They thinkin' for safety I would run

Though the endin' was quite different—

    Up came my hand with a smokin' gun.

Adios and a quick run for the hitch-rack
    But my horse and saddle were gone
I quickly reloaded my trusty old smokie
    In the dark shadows hurried along.
Sheriff and his deputies closed in on me
    I knew it was the end of the trail
The angry Mexicans wanted to hang me
    But the sheriff landed me safely in jail.

Adios to the judge and the jury
    A condemned prisoner for life
Just a poor, lonely dogie cowpuncher
    No love from sister, mother or wife.
Here all alone they have put me
    In this dark, dismal stone cell,
Bars of steel on the window small
    A jailer as onery as Satan in Hell.

Bygone Days Of The Old West

Adios to all you old waddies
    Ramblin' along without a thought or care
Oh! What I gladly would give
    Such freedom to have and to share.
Nevermore to see the beauty of sunshine
    Or look up at the moon and the stars,
Or sit with the boys in the ol' bunkhouse
    Singin' songs and pickin' th guitar.

Adios to all the green hills and the valleys-
    To the old oak corral and the rancho adieu.
Pines and the snow-capped mountains
    Sad and lonely, I'm leavin' you.
Nevermore shall my tear-dimmed eyes
    By your freshness and beauty be blest
Or the golden rays from the western sunset
    Soothe my tired soul to a haven of rest.

Adios to all my old horses and cattle,
    To the eagles that soar in the blue sky,
To the yuccas bloomin' on the hillside
    And the mountain flowers that wither and die.
Life without liberty is nothin'
    A broken heart with only pain and strife
God have mercy, pity and pardon
    A poor, lonely prisoner in for life.

New Mexico Rattle-Box.

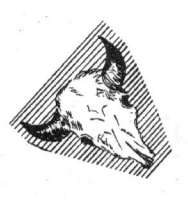 

What if I do crawl under a yucca or cactus,
    Lay around basking in the morning sun
Just letting the rest of the world go by,
    Really - I have no work to be done?

    Sometimes I get out in the early morning
        Meander down through the sage and mesquite,
    Visit with the prairie-dogs and little brown owls,
        For my breakfast have a rabbit or quail to eat.

    I'm not like the sneakin', dusky redskin
        Silently waitin' in ambush behind a sandy mound
    I always rattle and give you a warning
        Whenever you trespass on my 'stompin' ground'.

They say that God put us all here for a purpose
But it seems I'm condemned at every turn,
Even the jack rabbits and the coyotes abhor me
And the Road Runner's eyes with hatred burn.

The Hopi Indians catch me for their "snake dance"
Or they'll burn me then and there.
The white man will shoot and kill me
Seemingly no living thing wants to treat me fair.

Love and Hate

In October when the sand and malpi grow cold
And I see a cowboy's campfire burning bright
I watch until his supper hour is over
Then I crawl under his tarp for the night.

When I see blue-jays and swallows a-driftin'
    Pack-rats getting in their winter's store,
At nights the wolves and coyotes dismal howlin'
    And the cold 'north-winds' blow once more;

It is then I find an old prairie-dog mound,
    Adieu to the dark of night and light of day
I crawl many feet down in old Mother Earth
    Bear-like I dream the winter months away.

When I hear the little prairie-dogs barkin'
    I know springtime is here once more
I crawl to the world above with a sky of blue
    And watch the Golden-eagles soar.

ALL YOU OLD WADDIES.

Come on - all you old Waddies
    Out of your bed-rolls, up with the sun,
Grab your tools chuck is about ready
    Remuda is comin' there's work to be done.
The onery coyotes have quit howlin'
    There's a sweet blowin' breeze from the west,
Hawks are soaring high in the blue heaven
    Ye Gods, get up old waddies - get dressed.

The herd is up and feedin'
    Yuccas smilin' a sweet welcome to you,
Sow-belly, sour-doughs and Java is ready
    Dam your old souls - what will I do?
The flies and sand lizards are comin',
    Brandin' irons still cold and blue
If hot water wasn't so darn scarce -
    Old Waddies, I'd be scaldin' all of you.

Bygone Days Of The Old West

The leaders are millin' and restless
    There comes the boss ridin' like mad,
WATCH 'EM - shake chaps and throw leather
    I orta feel sorry, but Gee I'm glad.
Maybe in time you all will be learnin'
    When I beat the pan an' give th' call
It's time to be up, washed and ready
    Old Waddies, a hot breakfast or nothin' at all.

While you are wranglin' up your horses,
    Cuttin' out strays and lookin' for brands
I'm busy roundin' up wood and water
    Wranglin' the greasy old pots and pans.
The boss is givin' you a good work-out
    You deserve it, full well that I know
While you are punchin' the cattle
    Old Waddies - I'm punchin' the dough.

Adios to the round-up and chuck-wagon
    Even to the chuck-house, rancho and all,
I'm drifting with the blue-jays and robins
    Old Waddies - I'll see you again in the fall.

TALE OF THE GOLD TRAIL

Nigh on to forty years of prospectin'
    From the Ute Creek on up the Rio Grande
With my camp outfit and two old burros,
    A season's grub-stake, tools and pan.
I've got the summer months ahead of me
    With miles of sage, arroyos and flats,
I know every wash and good place to camp
    Prospect holes made by the old desert rats.

    The desert demons often come and mock me
        With thirst, burning heat and sand
    But I jus' go ahead pickin' and pannin'
        Lookin' for gold in No-man's Land.
    There's rain clouds in the near distance
        I'll make a good camp near that rocky bluff
    With plenty of grass, water and wood
        And a vein of color showin' in the rough.

What's the matter with you old burros
    But perk up and hurry right along
For there's thunder in those flashes
    And the wind is comin' strong.
See the coyotes and antelope a-runnin'
    We just reached this bluff in time
See those big hail-stones a-comin'
    How that old storm does twist and whine.

Did you see that flash of lightnin'
    Hit this old bluff right over there?
Gosh! Are my old eyes deceivin' me —
    Look, just look, gold nuggets everywhere,
Old burros, we have hit the Jack-pot
    We are now a bunch of millionaires,
I've got enough yellow boys in this old bag
    To buy a grub-stake for another twenty years.

ADIOS

Old West -- good-bye;
    The night is falling.
Go to your own where sunsets lie;
    From butte and plain sound voices
        calling
Their last farewell--
    Old West -- good-bye!

All things have changed;
    The range seems lonely,
The coulee strange, the lobo's cry
    From canyon breaks the stillness only
In sad refrain--
    Good-bye --good-bye!

Romance is dead;

   The herd, stampeding,

Had bedded down and peaceful lies.

   O'er the divide the bronchos feeding

Roam riderless--

   Again -- good-bye.

Great were your days;

   No other ever

Shall be as you; your henchmen lie

   Beneath your sod to leave you never--

Inseparable--

   In the good-bye.

Rest ye in peace;

   The rough trail wending

Leads but to rest; and in its ending

   From canyon's depths to sunset's sky

Find ye your own--

   Old West -- good-bye.

RANGE DICTIONARY

LOCALISMS OF THE SOUTHWEST.

Many of the geographical names of the Southwest are Indian, or Indian corruptions.

There is no definite authority upon pronounciation, and no attempt has been made to give them. On the other hand many of the Mexican names are mis-spelled, often to the extent that it is not possible to trace their original significance. Some of them are abbreviations by ear. The pronounciation is the chief thing of value.

A COLD MEAT PARTY....Sitting up at night with a dead person.

ADIOS...........Good-bye (A Spanish word).

ADOBE....Unburnt dirt brick dried in sun.

ALKALI.........A substance which combines with an acid and neutralizes it, forming a salt.

ALFORJAS..................Pack-saddle bags.

AMBLE....To walk along with an easy, careless gait.

APACHES......A group of North American Indians, natives of New Mexico and Arizona.

ARIZONA.............................Arid zone.

APAREJO..........................Pack-saddle.

ARMED TO THE TEETH.....To carry six-guns, a winchester and a belt of cartridges.

BACK FALL....A horse while bucking rears up on hind feet, loses balance and falls backwards.

BACK THROW.....When a horse is bucking with a rapid movement hurls itself backward and falls to the ground.

BALLY.........A bald-face horse or cow.

BASTOS....Back part of the saddle behind the cantle.

BATCHING......When a man does cooking, washing and housekeeping.

BAYO COYOTE....A dun colored horse with a black stripe down his back.

BED GROUND......A spot selected for the trail herd to be held over night.

BEEF-STAKED....To make a saddle sore on horse's back.

BEEVES....(Corn-fed)-Cattle that have two or three months rations of generous grain or cake feed.

BEEVES.........(Prime finished)-Cattle that have been made strictly fat, generally from 6 to 12 months liberal feed of grain, cake or other rations.

BEEVES........(Fancy)-Cattle that have the prime or ripe finish and in addition carry a full quantity due to being high grade or pure bred stock.

BELL MARES...........Generally old mares (wearing a bell), used as leaders in pack trains or put in a remuda to locate where horses are grazing at night.

BITCH LIGHT... A light made by filling a

BITING THE DUST........Mortally wounded.

BLAB........A thin board or piece of tin 6x8 inches, fastened by one edge in calf's nose. When a range cow gets poor this is oft times done to wean calf although he can graze with blab on.

BLACK SNAKE....A short, heavy whip made of leather or rawhide, plaited tightly and the handle filled with lead, shot or piece of iron.

BLANKET STIFF.. A Western tramp who carries a blanket.

BLAZED TRAIL... A trail indicated by the blazing or chipping of trees.

BLIND.....A broad piece of leather or a folded neck-lash which is used as a blindfold on a broncho's bridle...Is removed after horse is saddled and mounted.

BLOCKER........A large loop made with a saddle rope.

BODY SNATCHER.................Undertaker.

BOLOGNA BULLS....Are bulls not carrying much flesh, just enough to be classed as beef type.

BONNET STRINGS....A long buckskin string run half way round crown of sombrero then through a hole on each side and ends knotted, placed under chin or around back of head which keeps hat in place in windy weather or when riding a bucking broncho.

BOSAL......A leather, metal or rawhide ring fastened around horse's nose above the mouth; the bosal is held in place being fastened to the bridle, pulling up on the reins shut off horse's breathing.

BOODLE..........A bribe or stolen money.

BOOMER........A man that earns a few dollars, goes to town and puts on a big splurge for a short time then drifts on to a new location.

BOX CANYON.....A canyon completely enclosed on both sides and one end with a high rim-rock. (CANON)

BRAKES.....Rough and brushy hills leading out from water courses or small foothills at base of mountain range.

BRAND ARTIST.....A person that burns over a brand creating an entirely new design which is identical with some registered brand.

BRAND (Blanket)....Is made by interposing a wet sack or saddle blanket between animal's hide and branding iron which causes brand to look as though it had been on animal a long time.

BRAND (Box)....Where a brand's design bears framing lines it is called a box brand.

BRAND (Broken-bow)....When a calf is two or three months old notches are sawed in underneath part of horns at base causing horns to grow in a downward position. This brand originated in Texas.

BRAND (Dewlap).....Is a brand made by cutting a 1x3 piece of skin loose on brisket of an animal leaving it to dangle, and which laps the dew when grazing.

BRAND (Jingle-bob)......Is a brand made by cutting a 1x3 piece of skin loose on jaw of an animal leaving it to dangle.

BRAND (Jug-handle).....A brand made by cutting a small slit in the hide on brisket of animal, then tying a small piece of rope or wire in slit causing same to heal leaving a round hole in brisket hide.

BRAND (Twattle-brand)...Is a brand made slitting each ear deeply on an animal, so that the top of the ears drop or dangle over.

BROOM-TAILS.....A class of range stock (horses or mares) that are not worth a thin dime.

BRONCO....An animal that has never been broken to saddle or harness use. Also spelled BRONCHO, BRONK, BRONC.

BUCK......................A silver dollar.

BUCKAROO..................A sporty cowboy.

BUCK-BOARD.......Four wheel vehicle, having long elastic boards resting on the axletrees, no springs.

BUCKSKIN......A soft leather made from the skin of deer, elk or antelope.

BUCKSKIN HORSE. A yellow colored horse.

BUCKING STRAIGHT AWAY...When a bronc is bucking and makes long jumps straight ahead without any twisting or rearing.

BUFFALO CHIPS....Old and dry buffalo or cow dung, used in the prairie country as fuel. Also called Boise de Vache.

BUFFALO SOLDIERS.....Negro soldiers.

BULL........................Male of the ox kind.

BULL BOATS......A small round boat made by stretching a well oiled buffalo hide over a frame of oaks or willows.

BULL DOGGING......The knack of throwing a steer without the use of a rope. By riding horse up on left side of steer, throwing your body quickly from saddle to the right side- landing in such a position as to catch steer around the neck and left horn, using your weight to twist animal's neck until he loses his balance and falls.

BULL RIGGING.....A broad strap or cinch equipped with leather hand-holds, used in wild steer riding.

BULL WHACKERS....Drivers of ox-teams with the old time freight wagons and prairie schooners.

BULL WHIP....Is made with a short handle and plaited rawhide or leather, extra long with a buckskin lash.

BUM LAMP.......................A bad eye.

BUM MITT............A sore or crippled hand.

BUM SHAFT............A sore or crippled leg.

BUM STEER.................False information.

BUCK HOOK......A blunt-nosed, up-curved piece of steel fastened to frame of spur a- bove the shank iron - In riding a bronco the "Buck-hook" fastens or locks in the cinch giving the rider a good foot hold.

BUCK STRAP....A strap that is fastened to base of saddle horn, forming a loop which offers a hand-hold when rider is riding a bronc.

BUCK TIE........Lashing the wrists together, passing the hands and arms over knees, then inserting winchester or stick between the joints of the knees and elbows.

BUNCO....................To rob or cheat.

BUNK-HOUSE......A house on a ranch that is used by the cowboys as a lounging place and dormitory.

BURNING OVER A BRAND...Where an addi- tional mark, letter or figure added to an old brand entirely changes the looks and reading of it. For instance take a V brand and by connecting another V you have the flying W brand.

BUST A CAP........................Fire a shot.

BUTTE....A detached ridge rising from the surrounding plain.

CABODDLE........................Entire amount.

CABRESTO..................A horse-hair rope.

CACHE.........A secret place for concealing gold, water, or provisions.

CACIQUE.......An Indian chief. Also spelled "Cacia".

CACKLE-BERRIES..........................Eggs.

CALICO..................................A woman.

CALIFORNIA JACK......A game of cards re- sembling seven up, or all fours.

CAMISA....................Shirt a Spanish word.

CANTINA................................Saloon.

CANNED.....................To get discharged.

CANYON DRAW.....Where a canyon heads.

CARPA.....................................Tent.

CATTLE (Beef).......Are the heavier, older, thick-fleshed type of steers, heifers and bulls bought by the packing houses.

CATTLE (Butcher)..Are usually trim weight stock, either cows, steers or heifers, carry- ing good flesh, weight from 550 to 1100 pounds.

CATTLE (Cutters)....Cattle one grade better than canners, though not carrying enough flesh to be classed as beef type.

CATTLE (Drifting).....In a blizzard or sleety weather cattle out in open country will start drifting seeking food and shelter.

CATTLE (Feeders).....Cattle with sufficient growth and flesh to make them suitable to place in feed lots.

CATTLE (Grass).....Cattle fed on range or pasture grass only.

CATTLE (Heavy Yearlings)..Cattle weighing from 250 to around 500#.

CATTLE (Heretic)....Inbred Southern cattle between the veal and yearling type, weighing from 150 to 350 #.

CATTLE (Light Yearlings)..Cattle weighing from 150 to 250#.

CATTLE (Short fed)...Cattle that have had from two to three months of generous rations.

CATTLE-SPREAD.....A cattle ranch. This word used little in the Southwest as a ranch is often called by their brand such as the XIT outfit, or the Cross L outfit, or the Rancho Grande, or the Crow-foot Ranch.

CATTLE (Stockers)...Cattle that are suited to go back to the country for further growth before being ready or classed as feeders.

CATTLE (Warmed up)....Are cattle that have been fed from three to six weeks on grain.

CATTLE (Yearlings)....Are cattle beyond the calf and under the two-year-old class.

CAVVA-YARD.....The extra saddle horses used on round-ups and trail herds. From Spanish word "Cavallada" also called Cavvy.

CAYUSE...................A range-bred horse.

CENTER-FIRE SADDLE.....Saddle with but one cinch which is fastened to center of saddle tree. Generally used by the California 'sloper' (cowboy). Often used in breaking bronks.

CHAPS.....The leather or hairy leggins worn by cowboys as protection against the brush and weather..Shortened from the Spanish word "Chaparejos". Sometimes called "Skeleton Overalls".

CHAPS.(Shotgun)....Fringed chaps used in Nevada and California. Pulled on as trousers have no snaps and rings.

CHAPS (Batwing)...With big extra flaps of leather, rings and snaps.

CHAPS (Angora).....Finished with long Angora hair used up in Wyoming and Montana and open prairie country.

CHAPARRAL.......A dense-tangled brushwood that grows in the Southwest and Old Mexico.

CHEW THE RAG...............To visit and talk.

CHICKEN FEED..U.S. silver coins of small denominations.

CHILI PICKER......An Old Mexico Mexican.

CHIPMUNK...A small western animal of the squirrel family.

CHOUSE..................................To chase.

CHOCOLATE DROP....Western for a negro.

CHUCK..............Food stuff or provisions.

CHUCK-HOUSE.......Where the cowboys eat their meals-In Mexican is called a CUISINE.

CIMARRON..........A Spanish word meaning "Wild and Unruly".

CHUCK WAGON.........A range or round-up wagon which carries the chuck, bed rolls, water-kegs, branding iron,Etc., also called the "Hoodlum Wagon".

CINCH.........A band five or six inches wide made of small cordage or horse-hair with iron rings fastened at both ends-used to hold saddle on horse.

CIRCLE RIDERS.......Cowboys starting at a designated point, widely separated as soldiers in a skirmish line gather the cattle and driving them to the round-up grounds for branding and tallying for ownership.

CLOSE SEAT.....Keeping a steady and firm seat in saddle when horse is bucking

COFFIN NAILS......................Cigarettes.

COFFIN VARNISH.............Poor whiskey.

COLD DECK.......A marked deck of playing cards.

COLD FEET.........Lost courage, no nerve.

COLORADO......Spanish adjective meaning "Red".

Bygone Days Of The Old West

COMMUNITY LOOP.....A slang expression to convey the idea that the roper threw an extra large loop.

COME AND GET IT..Dinner is now served.

CONCHAS....Round, flat metal plates made of nickel or silver-used as ornaments on bridles, saddles, chaps and spur straps.

CONTENTED COWS............Canned milk.

COONEY.......Underneath the chuck-wagon bed a green cowhide is tied behind the front hounds and back of the brake blocks, allowed to bag in middle and used as a carrier for cow chips for fuel out in the prairie country.

CORRAL......An enclosed space or pen for livestock.

COULEE....A deep draw with enclined dirt sides.

COWBOY BOOTS......... Are made with high heels to keep them from slipping through stirrups and as a brace in roping, and easy riding. Honest-to-God cowboys have their boots hand-made, while the Drugstore cowboys wear store boots.

COUNTY BRAND...A small figure or letter branded on neck of animal in addition to the owner's recorded brand- The neck design is used as an extra precaution against rustlers.

COWS.......In range parlance all cattle are "Cows".

COW HORSE...A horse that trained to roping, cutting, working out a cow-herd.

COWMAN.......A ranch owner that makes a living raising cattle.

COW-PUNCHER......Also called Cow Poke, Waddie, Cowboy, in Spanish a Vaquero.

COW SENSE...A horse that has been broken to the use of roping, cutting and general cow work.

COYOTE...................A predatory animal.

COYOTE (Meztizos).......A person of mixed Indian and Mexican blood.

COYOTE (Zambos).......A person of mixed Indian and Negro blood.

COYOTE.......A person of mixed American and Mexican blood.

CREASING..........Shooting a horse through the cartilage of the neck, which completely stuns the animal though causing no serious injury-Creasing is an easy method of catching wild horses.

CRITTER.......Often in speaking of cows or horses a cowman calls them a "Critter".

CROAKED................................Killed.

CROSSED THE BIG DIVIDE.............Died.

CROW BAITS....Very poor horses, decrepit animals.

CROW-HOPS.....When a horse is loping along and suddenly puts only one foot down at a time in little, short quick steps.

CUT....A bunch of cattle that are cut from the main herd.

CUT FOR SIGN......To examine the ground for tracks and fresh droppings.

CUTTING GROUNDS......On a round-up the range boss rides to a designated place called the 'cutting grounds'. All cattle rounded-up are driven to this point where they are cut out, branded, earmarked and tallied for ownership.

CUTTING HORSE.......Certain cow-horses used at a round-up in cutting out cattle for ownership and brand.

CUT THE MUSTARD......When a person or animal pulls off some unusual stunt.

DALLIES........Half-hitches or turns taken around saddle horn to hold animal after roping it. Taken from the Mexican word "Dally-welta". (Spelt as sounds).

DANGLERS.......An inch long, metal pear-shaped pendants hanging from end of rowel axel on spur, causing a jingling noise when walking-also called Jingle bobs.

DAY HERD......Cattle that are cut out from round-up herd and held apart for shipment to market-Or on a trail herd the cattle are held over for a few days rest and grazing.

DAY WRANGLER....Cowboy that takes care of the remuda in the daytime.

DEAD SOLDIER....An empty whiskey bottle.

DEARBORNS........Light carriages used for easy riding.

DEATH RATTLE...When a cowboy snores in his sleep.

DESERT RATS..Old prospectors and miners.

DIVIDE..The main ridge of a mountain range.

DOBES......Calves classed as scrubby stock from lack of food and shelter in the cold winter months. Also called 'Leppies'.

DOCILE...............Gentle, easily managed.

DOFUNNY......................Useless object.

DOGIE..An orphan calf. A calf whose mother has died and his daddy has run off with another cow.

DOG TENT....A small circular tent that can be pitched without the use of a pole.

DOUBLE CROSSED.....For a man to go back on his word or betray a friend's confidence.

DOUBLED-UP
GOT HITCHED.....................Got married.

DOUBLE RIG SADDLE.........A riding saddle with two cinches.

DOPE................................Information.

DOUGH GODS......................Hot biscuits.

DOUGH...Money.

DOUSE THE GLIM............Put out the light.

DRAG IT.......................Be on your way.

DRIFT BACK TO THE STICKS........Leaving town, going back to the ranch or brush country.

DRIFT FENCE.......A cross fence made for the purpose of keeping cattle from drifting or leaving home range during stormy weather.

DROP OF THE HAT............To act quickly.

DUDS...............................Old clothes.

DUFFER...........................Old codger.

DUG-OUT.....A one-room house built in the ground or on hillside.

DUMP................................A low resort.

DUSKY MAIDEN......A good looking Mexican or Indian girl.

DUTCH OVEN......A flat bottom iron kettle with heavy iron lid. sets on 3-iron legs, used in camps for making sour-dough biscuits - hot coals are placed underneath and on top making it a hot oven.

EAR-MARKED....In range parlance ear is cut so that it reads overslope, undercrop, underslit, swallow fork slash, Etc., used to help identify ownership of cattle.

EASY DOUGH...Money made without physical effort.

EATING DIRT.....To get thrown by a bronc.

EGG-SHELL LID....................A plug hat.

EL DIABLO...........................The Devil.

ENCHILADAS......A Spanish dish consisting of corn-cakes, eggs and chili.

EYE OPENER........Or, morning's morning First drink of liquor at the early morning hour.

FAIR TO MIDDLIN'......Feeling fairly good.

FAN 'IM............When a cowboy is riding bronk and fans him with his hat.

FANDANGO..................A Mexican dance.

FANNING IT..........The art of firing a 6-gun by holding it in left hand and lightly hitting the hammer with the outer side of right hand.

FEADOR.......A looped cord made of buckskin, leather or braided horse-hair, fastened on front of bosal then upward and over horse's head -- This cord is used to hold bosal in place.

FENCE RIDING.....A cowboy that rides the fence lines that surround the ranch, pastures and grazing land - seeing that fence is kept in repair and gates closed.

FINER THAN FROG HAIR.....Feeling extra good.

FIRST RATTLE OUT OF
THE BOX..........Results at the very start.

FIRE FIGHTING TOOLS..Wet gunny-sacks and green cow hides.

FLANKING A CALF..The art of throwing a calf by grabbing a flank, over the bakc and under and throwing him off balance.

Bygone Days Of The Old West

FLANK RIDERS.........Are the cowboys that ride on each side of a herd to keep the cattle from wandering off of the trail, also to keep outside cattle from mixing in with the herd.

FLAP-BOARD....Lid on the chuck box, used as a table.

FLAPJACK........Made of thicker dough and larger than a pancake - Is turned over by a quick flip of frying pan.

FLOATER.....A man that has no means of livelihood and drifts from place to place.

FONDA......................Spanish for hotel.

FOUR POINT.....A mackinaw having 4-color lines woven into edge of material, denoting extra quality.

FOX TROT....A horse making extra steps between a fast walk and a trot..A good easy saddle gait.

FRIJOLES...............Dried Mexican beans.

FRISK......................,To search.

FROM HELL TO BREAKFAST........Doing a thing from start to finish.

FROG STICKER..........A cheap pocket knife.

FUZZIES OR FUZZ-TAILS.......Wild range horses.

GABOON................................Cuspidor.

GALORE..Plenty.

GARBAGE JOINT.........A cheap restaurant.

GAT................................A revolver.

GELDING....It is a range custom to let male colt run at large until he becomes a 2-year old, he is then castrated and becomes a gelding.

GET DOWN AND
SHOW YOUR SADDLE...An invitation to dismount and eat or stay all night.

GHOST CORD...A small string tied over a horse's tongue, passing under lower jaw and on up to rider's hand..This is an instrument of cruelty, often used on outlaw horses.

GLAD HAND.........................Welcomed.

GLIMS...................................Spectacles.

GO HEELED.........To carry a six-shooter.

GOT WIND...............Received information.

GRAZING BIT.....A small bit with a curb in the mouth-piece so animal can graze without removing the bridle. This class of bit is generally used in Arizona.

GREASER....Cowboy's insulting name for a Mexican.

GOLD DIGGER.......Women that hang around gambling dens in mining camps or cow-country...Waiting a chance to fleece a miner or cow-puncher out of their money.

GOLD FISH....................Canned salmon.

GONE TO THE TOOLIES....A person that is a physical wreck.

GONE TO THE HAY...............Gone to bed.

GONE UP SALT CREEK...................Died.

GRINGO......Mexican's insulting word for an American.

GRULLA..............A mouse colored horse.

GRUB...................................Groceries.

GRUB STAKE..A supply of groceries given to a person, the recipient to pay its donor an agreed share of whatever profit he may derive from the interprise he is undertaking.

GUNNIN'.....When a man arms himself with a gun and goes out looking for someone he holds a grudge against.

HACKAMORE.................A rope or bridle head-stall without the bit...The buckskin or hair cord which goes around the nose is called a "Bosal".

HAIR TRIGGER.Is made by filing the notches on a six-shooter's hammer in such a way as to cause the six-shooter to be discharged by a very light touch of the finger.

HAMSTRING.....An easy way to cripple an animal is by cutting the large sinew on the hind leg just above the hock.

HAND OUT........................Begged food.

HANG OUT.A rendezvous for cattle thieves and rustlers.

HASH SLINGER......A waitress.

HAWG'S LEG....An old long barrel Remington or Colt's six-gun.

HAY SHOVELERS.....Cowboys who run the feed wagons in the winter months and scatter the alfalfa or hay to the cattle.

HAZER....A bull-dogger's assistant. After a bull-dogger has leaped from his pony to steer, the hazer mounted, catches bull-dogger's horse and protects him from being gored when he releases steer.

HE SPIELS THE LINGO..He speaks Spanish fluently.

HEAR THE OWL HOOT....To have exciting experiences.

HEIFER BRANDED....Oft times at western ranch dances there is a shortage of female partners for square dance. Some of the cowboys take the ladies places and are marked by having their necklash tied around their left arm.

HELL-A-POPPIN'.....When something goes decidely wrong.

HEP..........Being wise to certain knowledge.

HIGH LONESOME...On a big drunk all alone.

HIGH, WIDE & HANDSOME...A thing neatly done.

HITTING THE GRIT......Traveling.

HOBBLES.......A piece of rawhide, rope or straps used for fastening horse's front legs from straying away.

HOCK SHOP......A loan office.

HOGBACK....Top of small hills that lead back into the main mountain divide.

HOG-TIED.....After cattle are thrown their two hind feet and one front foot are securely tied together with a short rope called a 'Hoggin-hitch'.

HOLDING SPOT.......A certain place agreed upon by a round-up crew to bring the herd to-gether for branding, ownership and cut for shipment.

HOLE UP.....When rustlers take refuge in a hidehout, cave or cabin.

HOLLOW-HORN.....A myth disease...In extreme cold weather cows horns and hoofs sometimes freeze and on thawing out fall off...A newcomer starting in the cattle business thinks this is some kind of a dreaded disease.

HONDO......A small ring made of metal or rawhide and fastened in end of saddle rope.

HOODLUM WAGON....A wagon that carries the wood, feed and water kegs on freighting trips or on round-ups.

HOOF IT......To walk.

HORN IN.....To interfere in someone elses business.

HORNY TOAD....A small, short, dirt-colored lizard with a large mouth and body covered with small horns. Found in the Southwest and Old Mexico.

HORSE MAULER.....A cowboy who handles his string with deliberate cruelty.

HOSPITAL CATTLE......Poor, weak cattle.

HOSS-WRANGLER......A cowboy that cares for the remuda or saddle horses on a round-up.

HOT AIR....Senseless talk - In Indian "Whahoo".

HOULIHANING...Running your horse alongside a running steer and leaping to the right side and forward alighting on the neck of the steer, as in bulldogging, taking hold of horns and twisting the animal's head until he falls to the ground. This is barred at practically all contests.

HUNCH......A presentiment.

HUNKERS....Often in visiting a cowboy will decline a chair and squat and rest his body on the calves of his legs-on his hunkers.

HUNKY-DORY......Everything is all O.K.

WOULDN'T THAT
JAR YOUR KNUCKLES
FROM HELL TO BREAKFAST.....The very idea, I'm surprised.

IDAHO......Gem of the mountains.

I'M CALLIN' YOU....In a gun fight where a man wants to give his opponent a chance to pull his six-gun he says - I'm callin' you".

Bygone Days Of The Old West

JACK-KNIFED......When riding a bronc or driving an animal in harness to have it suddenly turn backward at an acute angle.

JAMBOREE..................A drunken debauch.

JAVA......................................Coffee.

JENNETTES....Offsprings from a Jack burro, and a small mare.

JERKED BUFFALO.....Small pieces of flesh pulled off as a sheath with covering left around each muscle - dried on willow poles.

JERKY.....Meat cut into small strips and dried on a line in the sun - Spanish name "Tassejo".

JERK-LINE.......A single rein fastened to the brake-handle, down through hand of driver (who is astride of right wheel horse, the line continuing along the file of horses backs up to the leaders.

JERK NECK. In cart-trains when one driver has two or more carts and mules to care for, each trail mule is tied to the cart ahead so that driver can handle them all.

JOCKEY-BOX. All freight and chuck-wagons has a 'jockey-box' used for carrying a horse shoeing outfit and axle grease.

JOINT....................A board-front saloon.

JUICE THE OLD
SISTER...................To milk a cow.

KICKS..Shoes.

KIDNEY PAD......A flat Eastern saddle without a horn.

LA LUNA...............................The moon.

LARIAT ROPE.....A rope carried on saddle used for roping.

LASH ROPE.....A rope some thirty feet long with a special made cinch, used to tie packs on pack animals.

LASSO.........A saddle rope made of rawhide some forty feet long without a single splice in it. In Spanish it is called "La Reata".

LATIGO......A strap 2-inches wide and four feet long, fastened on left side of saddle, connects with cinch ring to hold saddle on horse.

LAY-UPS....When freighters or trail herds stop over for rest, feed or bad weather longer than their usual stop.

LEAD RIDERS......Two cowboys that ride on each side of the 'lead steers' in a trail herd. They swing the steers in the general direction they wish to follow.

LECHE.....................Milk, a Spanish word.

LEERY...Cautious.

L'ENVOI.....Closing lines of a poem - farewell. last message.

LID..Hat.

LIKE THE DEVIL
BEATING TANBARK..........Fast and furious.

LIKER UP..........................To get drunk.

LIMBO...In jail.

LINE CAMP......On large ranches they have the headquarters and line camps at convenient places near water and shelter.

LINE RIDING.........When a cowboy ride an imaginary line on the open range to turn cattle back to their own grazing ground.

LITTLE JAG......................Small amount.

LO.....A cowboy's name for any breed of Indian.

LOBO..............................A 'loafer' wolf.

LOCKED SPURS......To wire or fasten spur rowels so as to prevent their revolving.

LOCO WEED....A poisonous weed that grows in the Southwest, is the first thing that turns green in the spring. Three different species, purple, pink and white.

LOCOED..........Horses and cattle become addicted to the eating of Loco weed, thereby causing the victim to become thin, injury to eyesight, muscular control and brain; causes an abnormal growth of hair on the mane and tail of horses - on cattle an extra increase of hair on flanks.

LONG YEARLING.....A cow-critter over one year old and up to eighteen months.

LONGHORNS.......A breed of Texas cattle which are of big bone and extra long horns.

LONG-ROPE COWBOY.....A cattle rustler that ropes and burns over brands.

LOONEY STEER......A steer in a herd which keeps the rest incessantly nervous and on the prod.

LOOSE HERD.....Allowing horses or cattle to graze freely over large acreage.

LOSING A STIRRUP.....In compliance with contest riding rules a bronk rider keeps his feet moving in a kicking motion, if foot slips out of stirrup this disqualifies the rider - saying is, 'He lost his stirrup'.

LUMP JAW......The forming of a tumor on the lower jaw under the ear, or between the lower jaw, caused by hay fungus or fodder, infecting a scratch on the jaw, gums or tongue of a critter.

LUNGER.......One affected with tuberculosis.

MAIL ORDER COWBOY.....An Easterner (Shorthorn) that wants to become a real cowboy - also called A Monkey Ward Cowboy.

MAIN GUY............The owner of the Rancho.

MAKE A DRIVE....To move a large herd of cattle from range to range.

MAKINGS......Smoking tobacco and papers.

MALPIAS.....Rough, broken-up or extremely rocky country, sometimes spoken of as the Malpi Country.

MANADA.........A Spanish name used in the Southwest when refering to a bunch of horses.

MANANA.....That's 'Mex' for to-morrow - reckon that's their word for hell, too. Whenever it comes time to work a Mexican with roll a cigarette and mutter somethin' 'bout Manana.

MARAHUANA....A Spanish weed, which dried and smoked acts upon the nervous system in a manner similar to opium.

MARBLE ORCHARD.....A graveyard and the tombstones.

MATACHINES....A Mexican dance performed by grotesque figures.

MAVERICK.....An unbranded stray that is found running-at-large on the open range, he becomes the property of the cowboy who puts his brand and ear-mark on him. Frequent controversies arise, leading to trouble and even to killings over the ownership of unbranded cattle.

MEADOW LARKS ARE COMING....In range parlance this means 'Roundup Time'.

MEANDER......To wander along in an aimless fashion.

MECATE.....................A Horse-hair rope.

MESA.....High, flat tableland with cliffs descending to the surrounding plain.

MESS......A wagon crew is divided into parties of ten to twelve persons - called the mess. Each mess is furnished with a complete camp outfit for cooking purposes.

MESQUITE....A small shrub or bean tree of the Southwest and Old Mexico.

MILLING......As soon as a stampede starts the cowboys make an attempt to catch up with the lead steers, swerve them slowly in a circle to the right until they get the entire herd to milling, down to a walk, peace and quiet.

MIRAGE....Heat waves on the prairie causing an optical illusion by which distant objects appear inverted, distorted, or fantastic propo rtions- They disappear as suddenly as they come.

MOCCASIN TELEGRAPH...........News or messages carried by a runner on foot.

MOOLEY....Milk cows without horns - a saddle without a horn.

MORRAL.....A canvass receptable for holding grain - Is hung on horse's head by a strap fastened much as a hackamore.'

MOUTH PIECE.....................A lawyer.

MULE SKINNERS.........Drivers of mule teams on the old time freight wagons.

MULLIGAN......Most any king of a camp stew - everything in it but the dish-rag.

MUSTANG................A wild range horse.

MUSTANGERS......Men who trap, catch and break wild range horses.

NAVAJO TWIST....................Stick Candy.

NEARSIDE........Is the left side of a horse.

NECK-LASHES..Large handkerchiefs which the cowboys use knotted around their necks- used as mask against the dust and cold weather. Generally of balck color, knotted no "Do-dads".

NECKTIE PARTY....................A hanging.

Bygone Days Of The Old West

NEW MEXICO....Named after Old Mexico- This name originally from 'Mextil' thd War God.

NESTERS........Homesteaders and Squatters who locate on range land.

NIGHT HERDERS....Cowboys that constantly ride around the herd at night, holding the cattle under a spell by singing to them until they bed down for the night-keeping a close watch in fear of a stampede.

NIGHT HORSE.......A horse staked out near camp and most of the time kept saddled in case of stampede, also used to bring in extra horses used on the night herd.

NIGHT WRANGLER.....A cowboy that herds and cares for the saddle horses during the night.

NOTCHES ON SMOKY......A notch filed or made on a six-gun handle for each man killed by owner of said weapon.

OFF SIDE........Is the right side of a horse.

ON THE PROD..................Fighting mad.

OPEN BRAND.........When a brand bears no framing lines it is called an 'open brand'.

OPEN RANGE....Grazing ground that is not under fence or private ownership - free grazing - free water -open range.

OUTLAW BRONCHO.........A bucking horse whose spirit is unconquerable.

OUT RIDER......A cowboy commissioned by the range boss to roam the open range or holdings to give watchful care to all livestock.

PACK SADDLE...........A cross-buck' pack saddle is made of two pieces of oak 1x5x16 inches. The four ends of these boards are bolted at the base of two wooden cross-trees then finished with a 'riggin' or set of cinches.

PACK SADDLE "APAREJO". A Aparejo pack saddle is made of a large, stuffed leather pad which covers as much as possible of animal's back and sides - Used by Mexicans as a riding saddle on mules and burros.

PRAIRIE SCHOONER..........Is a heavy built wagon constructed with a storage and carrying capacity of 7000-pounds, wooden bows and canvass cover...Conestoga Wagon.

PALO FLEACHADO....Arrow wood. (Paloflecha)

PALOMINA.....A buckskin colored horse with a contrasting colored mane and tail.

PANNIERS..............................Pack bags.

PARFLECHE....A buffalo hide with the hair removed, used for making shields, saddles and soles for moccasins.

PASS A WORD....On the open range when a man comes within speaking distance he should 'pass a word' before changing his course - a violation of this is regarded as an insult or a confession of some sort of guilt, such as trespassing or rustling.

PEELERS......Drivers of teams on Grading outfits.

PENCIL PUSHERS.....................Clerks.

PENITENTE.......Mexicans that whip themselves, suffering pain and sorrow for the remission of sins.

PIEBALD......A streak of white on a horse's forehead extending to the nostril like the letter T inverted.

PIGGIN' STRING....When a steer is roped and thrown he is tied down with a short rope called a piggin' string.

PILOT.....A cowboy that pilots the chuckwagon across a roadless plain and through the brakes to different camp sites.

PINTO.......A paint or spotted pony. A Mexican (Frijolle) bean.

PINWHEEL....When a bucking horse jumps forward, upward and then turns feet while in air and lands on its back.

PIROOTING.....................Fooling around.

PLEW..............................A beaver pelt.

PRAIRIE........An extensive tract of land, level or rolling, without trees, covered with grass and scrub vegetation.

PRAIRIE DOG POISON.....A cheap brand of corn syrup.

PAISANO.......'Road-runner' also called a 'Chaparral Cock', the New Mexico state bird.

PRICKLY PEARS......A small, eatable fruit which grows on the cactus plant.

PROD-POLE......About a 6-foot pole with an iron prod on one end, used in loading cattle onto railroad cars...also used to keep cattle stirred up and on their feet during transit.

PUTTO....A wooden stake which is driven in the ground to which a stake rope is fastened.

PULLING LEATHER....A term applied to a bronk rider in grabbing any part of the saddle in riding a bucking horse in order to steady himself, this disqualifies the rider- "Choking the horn", "Squeezing Lizzie," "Shaking hands with grandma," means pulling leather.

PUNK.................................Bread.

QUIRT......Thongs of leather, rawhide or buckskin braided into a short riding quirt- with lead-shot or an iron bar braided in as a handle.

QUININE STEER..Is a poor, inferior animal having every appearance of disease, extremely inbred

QUIPU.....A cowboy's calendar is a long string in which he ties a single knot for each week day, and a double knot for Sunday.

RANCH....A large tract of land under fence, used for raising cattle, horses or sheep.

RANCHERO........Is the owner of a ranch, spread, or an 'outfit'.

RANGE BOSS....Manager of a cow outfit out on the range.

RANGE SIGNAL OF DISTRESS...The firing of three shots evenly spaced as to time is a range signal of distress and need of help.

RANNIES...........Cowpunchers that feel the pinch of fences, neighbors, settlements, and commence figuring where to go next.

RARIN' TO GO................In a great hurry.

REMUDA.....All saddle horses on a roundup are thrown together and are called a 'remuda' The remuda is in charge of a cowboy whose duty is to herd and bunch them when the cowboys want a fresh mount. Sometimes called a 'caviada' or 'Cavva-yard'.

RIDE 'EM SLICK COWBOY.......Rider must rake the shoulders and rump of his broncho with his spurs, and fan the animal at every jump by swinging his hat with a full arm sweep, and MUST NOT pull leather or touch the saddle with either hand.

RIDING SAFE....Sitting tight in the saddle, legs tightly clinched against the horses sides and suprs set firmly in the cinch.

RIDING STRAIGHT UP...Consists of a bronc rider sitting straight up in saddle, holding reins free of saddle horn and raking animal's sides with spurs while in motion.

RIDIN' THE CHUCK-LINE....When a cowboy is out of work and rides from ranch to ranch seeking employment, is not charged for food and lodging.

RIMFIRE SADDLE......The old-style double cinch saddle of the southwest, has extra large horn.

RIM-ROCK......Walls of solid rock that line sides of a canon.

RING BITS.......A riding bit that is made by fastening a large ring to summit of spade or mouth iron, fitting up close under jaw of animal.

ROAD BRAND....A trail herd might include cattle of several different brands and ownership....A small road brand is used. Then if outside cattle become mixed with the main herd they can easily cut out.

ROCKY MOUNTAIN CANARY.....A burro, sometimes called a Colorado Mocking bird.

RODEO.....Has come to signify a cowboy contest, but it is Spanish for roundup.

ROMAL.....When reins on bridle are fastened together continuing into a braided quirt... the headstall made of hair or fancy leather, trimmed with silver conchas...mostly used by Mexican vaqueros.

ROUGH NECK.................A western bully.

ROUND-UP.....The spring and fall gathering of cattle on the ranges in order to brand and ear-mark the calves, cut out for ownership and those wanted for shipment to amrket.

ROUGH STRING....Saddle horses that buck every time they are saddled, some never become real gentle.

Bygone Days Of The Old West 482

ROUND-UP BOSS....Manager of a cow-outfit when out on a round-up.

RUN FIRE GUARDS....To plow two parallel set of furrows about 50-feet apart...grass between furrows is then fired...done as a prevention against prairie fires.

RUNNING BRAND...Brand made with a cinch ring or a wagon end-gate rod.

RUNNING IRON...A straight shank iron, end-gate rod or ring used for branding horses and cattle.

RUNNING MOUNT....Taking grip on saddle horn and by suddenly leaping from ground to saddle...without using stirrup to mount.

RUNNING WALK....Saddle gait between a walk and trot...Sometimes called a jiggle-gait.

RUSTLER.............A horse or cattle thief.

SABINE......Bark of the Cottonwood tree.

SAVVY.........................To understand.

SCALAWAG HOSS........A horse that is no longer fit for punchin' cattle.

SCATTER GUN.........................Shotgun.

SHADOW RIDING....A cowboy that rides along while admiring his shadow.

SHAG.....To follow or drive along a bunch of cattle or horses.

SHAKE-TOO....A temporary house with roof only.

SHEEPHERDER'S DELIGHT...Cheap mixed candy.

SHIN-DIG.......................A ranch dance.

SCRATCH 'EM...The act of keeping feet moving in a kicking motion while riding a bucking bronco or raking from shoulders, one of the acts, with spurs, sometimes necessary in a bronk riding contest.

SEEING DAYLIGHT...A term applied when a rider leaves the seat of his saddle with each jump of the bronk, so that bystanders can see daylight between rider and saddle.

SET BRAND...Is a brand made by a branding iron which has the whole design made together.

SIDE-LINING....Is the act of hobbling a horse by connecting a front and a hind foot, also called cross hobbling.

SIESTA.........................Afternoon nap.

SINEW.....A tendon out of a deer, elk or antelope and used by the Indians as thread.

SIGN CAMP....Camps that are scattered about an entire range...The cowboys stationed at these camps herd back all cattle that might drift off of the range.

SINKERS.........................Poor biscuits.

SETTIN' HER....When a cowpuncher gets to keeping steady company with a young lady.

SKY PILOT....A minister of the gospel.

SLEEPERS...Cattle that are earmarked but not branded.

SLICK EAR......Yearling calves or colts found running on the open range who have escaped being earmarked in the round-ups of the season before.

SLICK TREE....Fork of a saddle that has no swell-later made saddles have a swell fork which makes a big difference in riding a bronc.

SLOPPY RIDING......Sitting loosely in the saddle, allowing the body to flop about in response to the pitching of a bronk.

SLOPERS..................California cowboys.

SLUNK...............A prematurely born calf.

SNOW PAINT...A mixture of soot and grease daubed on cheeks and under eyes as a preventative of snow blindness.

SNUBBING POST....A post set in the middle of a corral and used for branding, saddling bronks Etc.,

SOOGANS.....Old comforts used in camp beds sometimes spelled 'suggans' or 'Sougans'.

SON-OF-A-GUN..An iron frame set over a camp fire which answers the purpose of a stove, sometimes used instead of a potrack and hooks.

SOPAPILLAS........An unsweetened bread. cooked like a doughnut.

SOURDOUGH....An old, experienced ranch' hand or miner or Batchelor.

SOW-BELLY............Old, white salt pork.

SPADE BITS....A bit that is made with a flat piece of steel about 1x3-inches long, bent backward at one end and fastened to center of mouth bar...Oft times called a 'stomach pump'.

SPLIT-EAR BRIDLE...A heavy, plain headstall with leather slitted on one side only so that ear of animal can go through same doing away with the use of a throat-latch. Used mostly in the North country.

SPOOKY BRONK....A horse that is always shying.

SPREAD...Is a number of acres of grazing land, also called a ranch or rancho.

STACK, SLICK & GREASE.......Pan cakes, syrup and butter.

STAG..........A bull that is allowed to run two or three years then castrated.

SNAKED...In a camp or at a round-up where the cowboys with their ropes and saddle horses 'snake' up fire wood.

SNAKEY................ .Wild and deceiving.

SNAPPING BRONKS....Breaking horses to ride.

SNEEZE WAGON...............An automobile.

STAKE ROPE... A long saddle rope that is used for grazing purposes.

STAKING OUT.....A mode of range punishment meted out to an individual that has violated the range code in regard to a lone woman...The culprit is laid on an ant hill with legs and arms tied to stakes driven in ground, eye-lids stuck back with pitch........ soon to go crazy from the heat of the sun and ants...finally to lose all vestage of flesh....a cruel, cruel death.

STAMPEDE......The range boss and cowboys on a round-up exercise the greatest of care on a round-up, especially of a night to prevent a stampede...a sudden fright will start the cattle running at full speed, in one general direction, with a roar and rumble like thunder, sweeping all to destruction in their pathway. Cowboys, horses and cattle are often trampled to death...shooting of the leaders sometimes stops the herd...Or, by gradually turning the leaders until the herd commences to mill.

STAMPIN' GROUND..An area where horses or cattle loiter around, watering place or near the home corrals...They 'stamp' their feet to free their legs of flies. A certain location used by a cow-outfit or cowboys.

STETSON.......A cowboy's hat, generally a sand color, sometimes having an extra high crown and a four to six-inch brim...Acts as an umbrella in stormy weather, a shade for the eyes in hot weather, the brim when grasped between the thumb and fingers and bent into a trough makes a good drinking cup...It is also used to fan into activity camp fires.

STEER......................A castrated animal.

STICKERS......................Postage stamps.

STIRRUP.....A circular piece of wood or iron used on a saddle for supporting a horseman's foot: 5 styles: Ox-box, Moran, Contest, Visalia, Hagelstein.

STOCK HORSES....Brood mares and colts.

STOCK SADDLE.............A western saddle.

STRAY....An animal found strayed away from owner or from the range where it belongs.

STRAW BOSS....Next in authority to the foreman on a cow ranch.

STRING....Each cowboy is alloted from four to eight horses to use in his work...they are called his 'string'.

STRING-HALTERED HORSE...Oft times by a sudden twist a horse's hind leg becomes effected at the knee so that when he walks it is with a movement as if he had a broken hip.

STOGY............................A cheap cigar.

SQUATTER.....A person that locates on a tract of land, holds undisputed possession for a number of years he then becomes rightful owner of same.

SQUAW HITCH....A certain way of tying a rope in fastening a pack on a saddle.

SQUAW-MAN.....A white man that takes to himself an Indian squaw, lives with her and in time calls her his common law wife.

SUN FISHER....When a bronk bucks and twists his body into a cresent, and throws head alternately to right and left...looks as though he is trying to sun both side of his body.

SUNDAY HOSS....A good looking horse with a good gait...Used to go to town or to go 'gallin'.

SWALLOW FORK....A ear mark commonly used on sheep and cattle.

SWAMPER......Freight wagon outfits have a man of all work called a 'swamper' who feed and water the oxen or mules and sit on the brake handle going down hill and blocks the wheels with rocks going up hill.

SWAPPING ENDS...When a bronk is bucking and goes up facing one direction but lands facing the opposite direction.

SWING RIDER......Are the cowboys that keep the main body of the trail herd together and keep them moving.

SQUAW-MAN.....A white man that takes to himself an Indian squaw, lives with her and in time calls her his common law wife.

TAIL RIDERS......Cowboys that follow the trail herd and keep the cows and young calves a-movin'... Especially those that are tired and draggy.

TAILOR MADES..Manufactured cigarettes.

TAILING UP........Oft times on account of hard winters and shortage of feed, cattle become very poor, get down and cannot regain their feet without the help of a cowboy. They are raised up by getting hold of their tails and twisting until the agony forces them to rise.

TAILING....Riding up alongside of a rapidly moving animal, seizing it's tail, quickly giving the latter a pull to one side, throwing the animal off of it's balance causing it to fall...Sometimes called 'changing ends'.

TALLY-MAN....A cowboy that stands beside the branding-fire at a round-up and makes a tally mark for each animal branded and ear-marked showing to whom it belongs.

TAOS....Large Spanish town in New Mexico. Taos meaning; Great, imposing.

TAPS.....Shortened from the Mexican word "Tapadera" a leather cover for the saddle stirrup to protect rider's feet from brush and cold weather.

TAPADERAS......Toe guards fastened onto the stirrups of a saddle.

TARP......A piece of 16 to 20 ounce canvas about 6x18 feet used as an outside covering for bed roll.

TEQUAS...MOCCASINS......A foot covering made of buckskin worn by the Southwest Indians.

TEXAS......Tribe or confederacy of Indians.

TEXAS TOOTHPICK........Large, one-blade pocket knife also called a 'Rib-tickler'.

THEY GOT HITCHED.....They got married.

THIRTY BUCKS AND BEANS....Generally a cowboy's salary for a month's work.

TINHORNS.........A cheap class of gamblers that risk only small amounts in games of chance.

TRIMMING THE HERD....In a cattle drive a herd is oft times halted and the animals bearing a certain brand are cut out and delivered to owner.

THREE-QUARTER SADDLE..A stock saddle with only one cinch that sets further ahead than a cinch on a center-fire saddle.

THUMBING IT........The art of firing a six-shooter by thumbing the hammer and not using the trigger....The trigger is sometimes tied back or the hammer notches filed.

TIE-MAN....A cowboy roper that ties end of rope to saddle horn while roping horses or cattle.

TOAD SKINS....................U. S. currency.

TOGGED UP.....When a cowboy dolls up in his Sunday clothes.

TOPPING HIM OFF....When a cowboy rides a bronco.

TOP HORSE....Every cowboy has his pick of the horses in his string...this horse is only used as a cutting or roping horse.

TORTILLA.....A Mexican bread made with flour, water but no shortening - cooked on top of stove.

TRAIL CUTTER....Is a cowman that causes a herd to be stopped so that he can make an inspection to see if any of his cattle are mixed in the herd.

TRAVIOS.....A stretcher made of two long poles one fastened to either side of a cayuse the other ends draggin' on the ground...near the ground-end a framework of oaks or willows are woven together..Within this framework or basket an invalid, papoose, meats, camp outfits are carried....used mostly by Indians.

TWISTER...A small loop of rawhide or cordage with both ends fastened to a small stick ...Is placed vertically around animal's upper lip then tightened by twisting stick...used to bring unruly horse under submission.

TWO-GUN MAN.........A man that carries a smoky on each hip and knows how to use them both at the same time.

UNDER COVER......................Hiding out.

UPTRAIL......Hiring out for a long trail drive.

U.S. DIAMOND HITCH....A certain tie used in fastening a pack on a pack animal.

VENT BRAND....When a ranchman sells his neighbor an animal which bears his recorded brand..the animal is rebranded with an additional small brand called a 'vent brand .

VAMOS THE RANCHO..................Get out.

WAGON BOSS....The man that has charge of a wagon train...sometimes called the 'bull'.

WAGON WHEELS....U.S. Silver dollars, (Iron Men).

WAGON TRAIN...Generally consists of 25-schooners, ox teams, a wagon boss, a straw boss, cook, night herder, cavallard driver, and 25 bull whackers.

WAGON TRAIN COCINEROS....In a wagon train..The cook or cooks are selected from amongst the teamsters, they receive extra pay, and are relieved from guard duty and other work that falls on the drivers while in camp.

WALLOW STONE.....A smooth stone about the size of a large pea...stone is put in mouth under tongue and wallowed around, acts same as chewing gum in keeping the mouth and throat moist.

WAR PAINT.....A dark red Indian paint put on the cheeks and under the eyes as a medium in deadening the sun's rays when traveling in hot weather, also a decided help in looking at objects in the same direction from which sun is shining.

WET PONIES.....Stolen ponies which have been smuggled across the Rio Grandee from Old Mexico.

WET BACKS....Mexicans that swim the Rio Grande to get past the line riders into the U.S.A.

WHEELERS..........First team attached to a freight wagon.

WHELPS....The young of the wolf or coyote.

WICKY-UP...A small framework of poles covered with tree limbs or brush and grass.

WIND RIVER BIBLE...A mail order catalogue.

WINTER RANGE...In the winter months the cattle are kept in the lowlands or the prairie country....or in the brakes near the home ranch..When severe storms come they are fed from feed wagon or ricks.

WISDOM BRINGER..........A school teacher.

WOODEN OVERCOAT.................A coffin.

YELLOW BOYS.................U.S. Gold coins.

YELLOW HAMMERS...A class of large bone longhorn steers, hammer-headed and which originated in Old Mexico. Some are a dirty yellow color, while others are blue and roans.

YOKE....A heavy, solid wooden timber used as a collar and harness, necking two oxen together for work purpose.

Contents

A Bunk-House Tale	322
Adios	468
Adios To All You Old Longhorns	444
A Grizzly Bear	77
Alkali Phipps	124
All You Old Waddies	464
A Nature Soliloquy	88
A Navajo Blanket	430
Annie Lowery On The Guard	170
A New Mexico Rattle Box	461
A Preacher Of Cimarron	180
A Prisoner For Life	458
A Ranchero Of Mexico	252
A Tale Of The Gold Trail	466
A Tenderfoot Cowboy	249
Black Bart	376
Black Wolf	266
Branding Irons	19
Broken Trail Of Life	260
Buffalo Skulls	49
Cactus	364
Calling	204
Casino Sam	111
Christmas Night	452
Cowboy Taps	346
Coyote's Lonely Call	135
Cupid And Cactus	82
Cyclones And Dogies	343
Desert Ships	314
Dogies	54
Down On The Currumpaw	358
Driftin' Along In The Wagon Train	408
Driftin' Along With The Cattle	385
Driftin' Jest A-Driftin'	132
Echoes From Yokel Row	107
End Of The Trail	456
Fool Around And Fish	190
Frijole Pal	25
Gallo Day	289
Ghosts Of Cimarron Town	100
Horse Sense	174
Hunting Antelope	362
I Love The Lure Of The Open Way	230
In Santa Fe	332
In The Long Ago	62
In The Land Of Manana	282
In The Name Of The Law	119
Jog On Jehoshaphat	136
Jaun Espinosa	192
Just Waitin'	449
Lariat Joe	187
Little Bally	236
Little Papoose	313
Liquid Gold	43
Lonesome Land	228
Love, Honor And Away	106
Memories Of Mother	442
"Mex" From Over The Border	155
Mistah Buzzard Explanes	130
Mother Of Mine	234
My Old Horse And I	380
Old Cayuse	382
Olden Days Of The Golden West	373
Old Fort Union	317
Old New Mexico	218
Old Pal Betsy	232
Old Pal Of Mine	330
Old Santa Fe	263

Pardner I'm A-Leavin'	392
Prairie Dogs	68
Range Revolutions	338
Ridin' The Trail	406
Rocky Mountain Canary	144
Round-Up Time	420
Ruminations Of A Buster	292
Running Deer	351
Sage Tang	56
Sand Dunes	212
Sculduggery	257
Silver Plume	146
Smoke Signals	423
Song Of The Plains	354
Stampede Mesa	367
Sun Of The West Goodnight	45
Sunset	105
Sunshine Nell	22
Swan Song Of The West	328
Tale Of The Gold Trail	446
That Dadburned Little Pea	160
That Dodgasted Saxophone	40
That Old Western Town	416
The Blizzard	394
The Buffalo Hunt	201
The Cabin Of Logs On The Hill	71
The Call	360
The Cimarron Canyon	143
The Cloud-Burst	454
The Coyote	164
The Cowboy's Return	65
The Cross-Bar Lazy-B	278
The Desert	58
The Cruise Of The Espinosa	114
The Guard Of El Diablo	214
The Herdsman	348
The Hunters	356
The Indian Love Song	335
The Last Shall Be First	402
The Lament Of The Navajo	388
The Land Of The Setting Sun	298
The Legend Of Abo Crag	96
The Legend Of Angelo	16
The Life Line	168
The Long, Long Trail	300
The Lure	325
The Mexican Sheep Herder	278
The Mirage	91
The Mountains	244
The Maid From Durango	220
The New Foreman	426
The Night Rider	80
The Old Camp Cook	296
The Old Stage Coach	410
The Old Water Hole	46
The Pack Rat	178
The Pack Train	320
The Passing Of Brimstone	28
The Passing Of Faro Dan	399
The Penitentes	224
The Pines	158
The Pioneer's Thanksgiving	246
The Plow-Handle Ruminations Of Hiram	241
The Prairie Fire	370
The Range Foreman's Daughter	437
The Ranger's Old Six-Gun	140
The Rattlesnake	138
The Relay	128
The Return Of Juan De La Padilla	31
The Rustler's Last Retreat	173
The Santa Fe Trail	13
The Trail Herd	436
Tenderfoot Blues	86
Texas Lou The Law Wants Yu	276
Thunder Bird	206
Tumble Weeds	413
Uncle Tom Curtis On A Calico Trail	308
Vacation Days	280
Water Bound	273
When Billy The Kid Went Out	302
When The West Calls	52
Wild Hoss Charley	446
Yuccas	428

www.ingramcontent.com/pod-product-compliance
Lightning Source LLC
Chambersburg PA
CBHW080752300426
44114CB00020B/2710